Creative Criticism

Creative Criticism
An Anthology and Guide

Edited by Stephen Benson and Clare Connors

EDINBURGH
University Press

Edinburgh University Press Ltd
The Tun – Holyrood Road
12 (2f) Jackson's Entry
Edinburgh EH8 8PJ
www.euppublishing.com

Typeset in 11.5/14 Monotype Ehrhardt by
Servis Filmsetting Ltd, Stockport, Cheshire,
and printed and bound in Great Britain by
CPI Group (UK) Ltd, Croydon CR0 4YY

A CIP record for this book is available from the British Library

ISBN 978 0 7486 7432 9 (hardback)
ISBN 978 0 7486 7433 6 (paperback)

Contents

Illustrations

Acknowledgements

The editors and publishers would like to thank the following for permission to use copyrighted material.

Excerpts from 'Comprendre', 'Contacts', 'Dedicace', 'Identification', 'Mutisme' and 'Tel', from *A Lover's Discourse: Fragments* by Roland Barthes. Copyright © 1977 by Editions du Seuil. English translation copyright © 1979 by Farrar, Straus and Giroux, Inc. Reprinted by permission of Hill & Wang, a division of Farrar, Straus and Giroux, LLC.

Excerpts from *A Lover's Discourse: Fragments* by Roland Barthes. Published by Jonathan Cape. Reprinted by permission of The Random House Group Limited.

'Where Are We Going? And What Are We Doing?' from *Silence: Lectures and Writings* © 1961 by John Cage. Reprinted by permission of Wesleyan University Press.

'Every Exit Is an Entrance (A Praise of Sleep)' from *Decreation* by Anne Carson. Published by Jonathan Cape. Reprinted by permission of The Random House Group Limited.

'Every Exit Is an Entrance' from DECREATION: POETRY, ESSAYS, OPERA by Anne Carson, copyright © 2005 by Anne Carson. Used by permission of Alfred A. Knopf, an imprint of the Knopf Doubleday Publishing Group, a division of Random House LLC. All rights reserved.

'Insomnia' and an excerpt from 'The Man-Moth' from *The Complete Poems: 1927–1979* by Elizabeth Bishop. Copyright © 1979, 1983 by Alice Helen Methfessel. Reprinted by permission of Farrar, Straus and Giroux, LLC.

'Without end, no, State of drawingness, no, rather: The Executioner's taking off', translated by Catherine A. F. MacGillivray, from *Stigmata: Escaping Texts* by Hélène Cixous. Published by Routledge. Reprinted by kind permission of the author.

'Aphorism Countertime' by Jacques Derrida, translated by Nicholas Royle, from *Acts of Literature*, edited by Derek Attridge. Copyright © 2013. Published by Routledge. Reproduced by permission of Taylor & Francis Books UK.

Excerpts from *Out of Sheer Rage: Wrestling with D. H. Lawrence* by Geoff Dyer. Copyright © 1997, 2009 by Geoff Dyer. Reprinted by permission of Picador.

Excerpt from *Out of Sheer Rage: In the Shadow of D. H. Lawrence* by Geoff Dyer. Reprinted by permission of Canongate.

'Gertrude Stein: A Retrospective Criticism' from *Experiments in Criticism* by Benjamin Friedlander. Reprinted by permission of The University of Alabama Press.

Excerpts from *Stanzas in Meditation* by Gertrude Stein. Published by Sun & Moon Press. Reprinted by permission of David Higham on behalf of the Estate of Gertrude Stein.

Excerpts from 'Before the Flowers of Friendship Faded Friendship Faded' by Gertrude Stein. From *Look at Me Now and Here I Am: Writings and Lectures 1909–45*, edited by Patricia Meyerowitz. Published by Penguin. Reprinted by permission of David Higham on behalf of the Estate of Gertrude Stein.

'Correspondences of the Book' by Peter Gizzi. Reprinted by kind permission of the author.

'Music Lessons' from *Beethoven's Kiss: Pianism, Perversion, and the Mastery of Desire* by Kevin Kopelson. Copyright © 1996 by the Board of Trustees of the Leland Stanford Junior University. All rights reserved. Used with the permission of Stanford University Press, <www.sup.org>.

Excerpt from 'Piano Life' by Wayne Koestenbaum. Reprinted by kind permission of the author.

'Lyric Selves' from *The Words of Selves: Identification, Solidarity, Irony* by Denise Riley. Copyright © 2000 by the Board of Trustees of the Leland Stanford Junior University. All rights reserved. Used with the permission of Stanford University Press, <www.sup.org>.

'The Castalian Spring, a first draught' and 'Affections of the Ear' by Denise Riley. Reprinted by kind permission of the author.

'Jane Austen and the Masturbating Girl' by Eve Kosofsky Sedgwick. Reprinted by permission of the University of Chicago Press.

'Green' by Ali Smith. Copyright © 2010, Ali Smith, used by permission of The Wylie Agency (UK) Limited.

'Imperfect Pitch' by John Wilkinson. Reprinted by kind permission of the author.

'Anew Again' by Sarah Wood. Reprinted by kind permission of the author.

A Note on the Texts

As far as possible, we have retained the original formatting and referencing of each of the anthologised texts. These formal features are not incidental to creative-critical writing.

Introduction

Here is your final assignment:

Write an essay on any two of the set texts you have read for this course. (You will need to agree your title in conversation with your tutor.) Your argument should be supported by quotations from your texts and by a close analysis of these. It should be clear in its theoretical methodology, and demonstrate knowledge of critical debates in the field. You will want to consult the department style sheet for information on how to present and reference your essay, and the general marking criteria document for further advice on what is expected of you at this level. Please make sure you are also aware of the university's plagiarism policy.
Word count: between 2,000 and 2,500 words
Deadline: 3pm, 1 May 2014

If you are a student, or a teacher, on most higher education literature and arts courses, a version of this rubric will be – predictably, or heart-sinkingly, or gut-wrenchingly – familiar to you. Such instructions, with their toll of admonishing imperatives – 'write', 'you will', 'make sure' – are in part bound by the protocols of the institution whence they are issued. They have an important function in ensuring the clarity and fairness of assessment procedures, and in guaranteeing that students know what is expected of them. But they are also underpinned by more general notions of good scholarly practice. They rely on and invoke agreed conventions as to what constitutes an accomplished piece of critical writing. Such conventions are at work, too, in academic and literary journals, and indeed haunt writing about literature and culture beyond the academy. There is nothing

– necessarily – *wrong* with them. Indeed they are on the side of much one might want to celebrate: lucidity, close attention, rigour, wide reading. But oh, how achingly distant they seem, in their language and their assumptions, from the very 'texts you have read' and about which you are being asked to 'write'. Where, here, is the recognition of the passion and lostness and wonderment of reading, or of the mutable matter of reading as event or encounter or happening? Where is any intimation that *what* 'you have read' might make a quite different claim on you, enjoining you to respond to it – to write, and to live – in ways the 'general marking criteria' will not and perhaps cannot register? Where is the sense that any of this *matters*, beyond its capacity to get you a degree or make you a career? It is as though, in being asked to give an account of what you have read, you are required to pretend that nothing *happened* in the course of your reading. No wonder that many critical essays sound dry, robotic and somewhat ventriloquised. And no wonder, either, that literature and arts students and academics often feel alienated by the language of the very subject that they chose – out of love, interest or at least aptitude – to pursue.

Gathered in this *Anthology* is a small crowd of critical writings, each member of which, in its own singular way, dares to imagine that things might be different. We are calling these writings, collectively, 'creative criticism'. Others have named such writing, or at least aspects or versions of it, otherwise: post-criticism, deformative criticism, anarcho-scholasticism, ficto-criticism, visionary criticism, Other criticism, philosophic criticism.[1] This very roll call is testament to the sense that something is amiss on the main drag of critical writing, and to the fact that there are moves afoot to do something about this. Creative criticism is, to be sure, nothing new: quite the opposite, as we shall see. But it is true to say that it has emerged most visibly over the last four or so decades, and it is to its most recent and visible manifestations that our gathering is devoted.

As this introduction unfolds we will describe more precisely what we take creative criticism to be, and explore its various instantiations, innovations, qualities and effects. If this book is an *Anthology* it is also a *Guide*, by which we mean, in part, a sort of 'field guide' to the different kinds of creative criticism you might find out there. *What are the signs? How will you know for sure when you're there, when you're in it or with it? Or perhaps you're in it already. We've arrived. This is it! Really: is this it? Have we been here all along?* But since creative criticism is also an *intervention*, we want to suggest as well how, why and where it intervenes. In what follows, then, we are going to take our cues from the fabricated (but by no means fantastical) rubric with which we began. Picking out a number of its key terms, and identifying also its underlying assumptions, we will explore the model of critical writing implicit in its stern injunctions, and its leaden bureaucratese. And we will use these explorations as a way of showing how and why it is that creative criticism exploits, distorts, works over, hyperbolises, erases or plays with the conventions of academic critical prose.

To sound our own note of admonishment before we begin: creative criticism is no holiday; it offers no mandate to relax, no licence for an easy ride. Creative criticism does not get you off the hook, and nor is it irresponsible. While creative criticism can be playful – and while we, too, play a little in our introduction – the stakes are high. The game has commenced. Let's begin.

READING AND WRITING

'*Write* an essay on any two of the set texts you have *read*,' urges our rubric. This is surely at the heart of all criticism: the marking in writing of our reading or looking or listening; the making of a relation between a work and an act of writing. Reading and writing, attending and responding. It sounds so simple. Reading is that cultured but primitive-feeling habit we acquire as children. For many of us it is a skill that quickly comes to feel indigenous, as natural and necessary as breathing. Remember Scout in *To Kill a Mocking Bird*? 'Until I feared I would lose it, I never loved to read. One does not love breathing,' she writes.[2] But when we learn – in establishments of further and higher education, say – to read *critically*, and to respond *critically* in our own writing, it can often feel as though, even as we acquire new skills, we are losing something. What Proust calls 'that enchanting childhood reading' becomes disenchanted, grown-up and jaded.[3] It's as if, in disciplining our reading, and subduing it to learned protocols, we leach the life out of it. Threaded through the pages that follow is an animating desire, variously marked and variously performed, to stick with and attend to what is vital in our reading, and so to acknowledge aspects of reading that critical writing can at times simply repress, or dismiss, or neglect.

Too often, in the course of our critical apprenticeship, we are cowed into submission, and so into silence, by a presiding feeling of illegitimacy and belatedness that comes from our confrontation with the expectations of what we learn to acknowledge as tradition. T. S. Eliot talks confidently, in this regard, of 'the proper critical reaction', even, outrageously, of 'the right liking'.[4] It's hard not to feel panicked. What *is* the proper critical reaction? Are we sure we are or will be right in our likings? And is it right to cultivate rightness? Such anxieties have consequences for our own critical writing. Either we are rendered speechless at the thought of speaking out of turn, of lacking the right and proper knowledge; or a workaday deference to the right and the proper leads to that all-too-familiar end, a piece of writing devoid of any signs of the life, including the life of reading, out of which it must perforce arise. Too much criticism has the stale air of something learned by rote, the air of a nothing new for which apparently there is no alternative.

In university literature departments the conventions for *writing* about what you have *read* are inherited in part from the notions of 'close reading' or 'practical criticism'. The history of the installation of close reading at the heart and origin of the discipline of literary criticism is an oft-told tale, and not one we need to recount here – which is not at all to suggest that creative critics simply eschew this form of reading.[5] It's just that they refuse to be shackled by its pieties or strait-jacketed by its underlying assumptions.

So-called close reading worries away at the details of a text's meanings and form. It focuses on areas of nuance, ambiguity, tension, difficulty or felicity. But its governing aim is, as one of its chief proponents W. K. Wimsatt puts it, 'to give a valid account of the relation between poetic form and poetic meaning'.[6] Note that 'valid': like Eliot's notion of a 'right liking' it is another one of those appeals to some ratifying measure. Wimsatt's compatriot Cleanth Brooks writes that: 'The structure of a poem resembles that of a ballet or musical composition. It is a pattern of resolutions and balances and harmonizations, developed through a temporal scheme.'[7] While Brooks registers the dynamic and temporal aspects of reading (in his case, as with many 'New Critics', reading a poem), the emphasis is on the total effect of an artwork. Well-behaved criticism, good close reading, relates part to whole and meaning to form. It homes in on details, but in order to show how they nuance the total pattern. But when you're really close to something, you don't see it whole. You love it to bits, or become fixated on a particular bit *of* it. You look at it from odd angles, or see how it relates to other things. Or else you internalise it, learn it, or aspects of it, by heart. Sometimes it becomes part of you, its idiom weaving itself into the fabric of your own response to it, or to other things you read, look at or hear, so that it's not always clear where *it* stops and *you* start. It changes you, so that the 'you' who 'gives an account' of it is not the same as the you who first came to it.

Each of the pieces gathered in this *Anthology* has been impassioned in different ways by its encounter with what it has read or seen. We might say that such impassionment leads to a loss of perspective, to things – texts, words, subjects, objects – getting blown out of all proportion. Geoff Dyer, for instance, has read D. H. Lawrence so faithfully, so closely, that arm's-length, closed, 'close reading' is anathema to him. Lawrence's own writing of 'life' is felt to demand – and indeed produces, in Dyer's written response – something in which the question of distance is in flux, still mobile. Anne Carson's deep knowledge of the literature of sleep fosters a kind of writing that – like the dreaming mind, for Freud – makes sidelong connections across great distances, all from the intimate space of a bed. And Eve Kosofsky Sedgwick, in her reading of Austen's *Sense and Sensibility*, unsettles received wisdom on correct critical distance in being at once provokingly, even immodestly, intimate with her materials and also, in terms of readerly perspective, resolutely distant. Each piece knows its stuff, and has clearly dwelled long and attentively on it, read around it, mulled it over. But none claims to offer a totalising account of a whole. The ratifying measure of Eliot and Wimsatt yearns to verify, to establish and promote a norm from which to mark near and far, greater and lesser. The measured, the graded, the determined, the relatively positioned – all the verifications of the assessed and the tested. Creative criticism is a frustration of such scales. Not for those pieces here gathered the comfort of appropriate distance, rather the revelation or disorientation that comes from an opening of the possibilities of critical and writerly perspective.

Creative criticism, in short, is writing which seeks to do justice to what can happen – does happen; will happen; might or might not happen – when we are with an artwork. We can call that being-with an encounter, and say that an encounter is something, or some part of something, that has not already been set in place, which is to say something that has not already happened. To encounter is to be turned, whether for a moment or for life; to encounter is always in part not to know, to be a little or to be very lost; to encounter is to surrender something of oneself, willingly or otherwise, even to lose a sense of what one's self is or to be faced with other forms of such sensing; to be provoked or unsettled into losing one's place. And to have an encounter is to make a thing encountered. Creative criticism is the writing out of this event, writing which endeavours in its own wordful stuff variously to register, and so to acknowledge, the event as a matter of language. It does not ignore tradition, or pretend that its encounter happens outside the world, or outside history. Our critics are no Caspar David Friedrich wanderers, lonely on a cliff top above the mist. They work with what's there, what's already happened, and, in their different ways, acknowledge these things. And yet they refuse simply to be cowed by or to kowtow to tradition or convention. Singular by nature (and therein lies the rub), this is criticism identifiable as a mode by its divergence from the levelling norms of professionalised academic writing, norms acknowledged as valuable but which cannot but be called into question here. For there has to be a cost. Creative criticism is a response in writing to the encounter, writing which bears out Robert Duncan's summons: 'Responsibility is to keep / the ability to respond'.[8] To *keep* that ability is no mean feat. Indeed, it may well require us to risk irresponsibility, even to risk acknowledging that we do not know what we are doing. Because without such an acknowledgement nothing will be possible; and possibility is everything.

ESSAY

Write an *essay*.

Oh dread imperative! It comes with a whiff of chalk or the whiteboard, of homework and exams, red-inked marginal notations and tick-box assessment objectives. But the essay as a genre – and it's worth pointing out that it *is* a genre, one form of writing amongst others – was initially a wayward form. In the work of Montaigne, who gave it its name in the sixteenth century, it emerges as a series of personal, venturesome forays, and acts of tentative reading and thinking. Montaigne explicitly resisted dogmatic, received pieties and the top-down authority of medieval scholasticism. His three-volume, multiply and palimpsestically re-edited *Essais* addresses a whole range of subjects – there are essays on thumbs and on friendship, on vanity and on smells, on cannibals and on clothing, on sadness and on happiness, on life, death and, finally, climactically, on experience.[9] And the personal, anti-dogmatic and idiosyncratic qualities we find in Montaigne's essays live on today in essays written outside, or on the margins of, the academy, in literary periodicals and journals of art criticism, such as the *London Review of Books*, *Cabinet* or *n+1*, and in the occasional writings of poets and novelists who also produce critical prose. Quite which or how many of the pieces collected in our volume would best be described as 'essays' is a difficult question. In fact, we might take it *as* our 'essay question' in this section of the introduction. To answer it will entail an exploration of just what an essay *is* – and what it might be.

Where to start, then? That's another essay question, of course: what to put in the introduction? But it's also a question quite deeply bound up with what an essay is – with the 'essence' of the essay, supposing it has one. Virginia Woolf, for example, writes at the start of her essay 'The Modern Essay' that it is 'unnecessary to go deeply into the history and origins of the essay . . . like all living things its present is more important than its past'.[10] For her the essay is something vital, organic, always up for reinvention. And for that reason, there's no need to begin an account of it by narrating its history, tracing its trajectory through the philosophical excursions of Bacon and Locke, the journalistic jewels of Addison and Steele, Charles Lamb's conversational *Essays of Elia*, the cultural criticism of Arnold, the ground-breaking reflections of Emerson, and on into the musings of Woolf, Yeats, Eliot and Pound.

Perhaps we should start instead with the *word* essay? According to Brian Dillon, one of a number of twenty-first-century critics who write fervently in favour of the continuing relevance of the essay's reinventive powers, 'it's customary to inaugurate an essay on essays with a spot of amateur etymology'.[11] This seems a convention that is hard to avoid. Dillon, while aware that mindlessly beginning in this way goes against the idea that an essay precisely isn't hide-bound by tradition, proceeds to make the very etymological excursion he alludes to, and to remind us of the connection between the word 'essay' and the French 'essayer', to venture or to try. This sense is borne out in the tentatively exploratory nature of many essays, starting with Montaigne's: 'I pronounce my sentences in disconnected clauses, as something which cannot be said at once all in one piece'.[12] But this meaning of 'essay' is, as Dillon makes clear, only half the etymological story. Erich Auerbach has pointed out that the implication of Montaigne's title, *Essais*, is something more like 'Tests upon One's Self' or 'Self-Try-Outs'.[13] The word has a bolder sense, then, than that of an abashed attempt; a sense to do with toughing it out or running a gauntlet, seeing how far you can go, like a test-your-strength machine at the fairground. This is the kind of valence it has at the opening of Montaigne's 'experience' essay, for example, where he writes that 'we assay all the means that can lead us' to knowledge.[14] A more explicitly and thoroughly etymological account of 'essay' is offered by Starobinski in his essay 'Can One Define the Essay?'. Starobinski takes us back to the word's Latin roots, and points out its connections to an examen – the needle or point/tongue on a scale – and also, oddly, to a swarm of bees; and the joint origin of *these* words in the verb exigo, 'to push out, chase, demand'. Taking off from this range of senses, he engages in a little flight of thought:

> How enticing if the nuclear meaning of today's words had to result
> from their meanings in a distant past! The *essay* might as well be the
> *demanding weighting*, the *thoughtful examination* but also the *verbal
> swarm* from which one liberates development.[15]

Starobinski is pointing out here that etymologies do not give us fixed or
eternal truths. The meaning words have today *doesn't* always have much to
do with their 'meanings in a distant past'. But at the same time, as he well
knows, what he arrives at by dreaming that they do *is* no bad definition of
the essay. And his verbal daydream itself *performs* the dynamic and specula-
tive qualities that, as he also suggests, we connect with the essay form.

Not all essays, of course, need to begin with etymologies; and that old
stand-by opening 'according to the dictionary' is certainly a cliché ripe for
reinvention. But the fact that essays upon 'the essay' itself seem compelled
to reach back to the roots of the genre's name has something to tell us about
that form's properties. Essays, that is to say, precisely aren't philosophy.
They don't have to clear the decks, and start from first principles or prime-
movers. They are fascinated, rather, by what is given: by things, ideas,
emotions, conventions, phenomena already there in the world. They put
a new spin on these things, treating them as found objects, rather than
creating *ex nihilo* or starting – like Descartes, say – with the indubitable.
Etymology is one such set of historically determined givens. It represents
the twists and turns and adventures of words and thoughts over time, the
material and conceptual adventures of language itself, its slippages and
nonsenses and half-senses and rhymes, and these are the track and the
ether, both of history and of thought.

Theodor Adorno, in one of the richest and most stimulating, not to say
essayistic, accounts of the subject, celebrates the essay as a form of writing
and thinking resistant to the very idea of a total or totalising knowledge of
its object. It acknowledges its own contingency, its own dynamic involvement in the world from which it ventures out in its acts of evaluation
and description and analysis. Adorno suggests that the essay 'does not
begin with Adam and Eve but with what it wants to discuss', and that
its writing 'reflects a childlike freedom that catches fire, without scruple,
on what others have already done'.[16] This is not lazy empiricism, but an
acknowledgement that – to quote a closely related point made by Jacques
Derrida – 'it is impossible to justify a point of departure absolutely'.[17] We
can't simply wipe the slate clean, in order to start some knowledge project
absolutely neutrally. Like hoovering the floor, there's always going to

be the bit left that we're standing on, and muckying up. Best to learn to accept a bit of dirt; best celebrate the fact that we're already here, living in this space.

Adorno loves, too, the way the essay doesn't attempt to repress or efface its own form. This is, again, because it doesn't believe in some kind of transcendental neutrality, or hygienic conceptual vocabulary. It acknowledges that it must meet and respond to its object, shape itself around that object a little in order to know it from its various angles and aspects. Adorno recognises the risks of this: the chief danger of the essay is that it will drift into 'skillful superficiality', revelling in its own graceful moves and twists, narcissistically besotted, forgetting its purpose.[18] But on the other hand the stakes are high here. At issue in Adorno's cherishing of the essay *as form* is nothing less than the future itself, a point he works out towards the end of his own essay in a tussle with Kantian philosophy. He argues that the ultimate goal of Kant's thought – utopia – is precluded by the very form of that thought – the theory of knowledge, which won't tolerate anything that doesn't already exist, isn't already knowable. His ringing, paradoxical, conclusion – his turn on the notion of the essay – is this: 'the law of the innermost form of the essay is heresy. By transgressing the orthodoxy of thought, something becomes visible in the object which it is orthodoxy's secret purpose to keep invisible.'[19] Adorno's essay on the essay does what he says the essay should do: it makes visible in *it* something that has been kept invisible. It keeps in play, keeps mobile and vivid, something that has been shut down by objectification and commodity culture. He unmakes the essay, to show what *it* can make, and can be: a form that participates in the making-unmaking of so-called 'objects' themselves.

This sounds like no bad definition of many of the works brought together in the present volume. Their innovations weave and unweave texts – *Sense and Sensibility*, the *Odyssey*, *To the Lighthouse*, *Romeo and Juliet*, 'The Man with the Blue Guitar', D. H. Lawrence's letters – and also concepts, ideas, figures or 'things': love, sleep, piano teachers, quotation, guitars, masturbation. They put these things to the test, in singular ways, venturing out from the place where they find themselves and making a virtue of this contingency, in order to open up new futures. 'Facing me is a photograph of what I cannot see,' begins Sarah Wood, starting with what's in front of her. 'I want to make a praise of sleep,' kicks off Carson, beginning with the promptings of her own desire. 'There aren't many women in this book,' says Kevin Kopelson conversationally, pausing to reflect on the content of the other essays in his book *Beethoven's Kiss*, and making of that reflection the motive for a new excursion. None of these beginnings is artless of course. In fact each opening is so beguilingly disingenuous that we imagine considerable thought and rewriting has gone into its making, as it has into the writing which unfolds from it. What's remarkable here is not the 'naturalness' or otherwise of these introductions, but rather their frankly occasional nature. No God nor law nor convention decrees their point of origin, and nor is any absolute justification sought for it. And no law governs what proceeds from this origin either; these writings seem rather to take their bearings from their own object, letting themselves be governed by its urgings and their own responses to these.

For all these reasons, the essay – uncowed, inventive and attentive – has much to do with what we are calling creative criticism. But for all that, it's by no means certain that all the pieces gathered here are essays. Derrida, for example, offers a series of aphorisms. Peter Gizzi, with the finest of threads, stitches together a revelation of quotations. John Cage's four-voiced performance piece is a silent lecture. Now, we could say that this formal variety is in keeping with the very heretical logic of the essay form itself. This is the argument made by Rachel Blau DuPlessis in her 'f-Words: An Essay on the Essay'. Blau DuPlessis's essis gathers under the broad roof of the term essay all sorts of 'intransigent wilful writing' of the kind sometimes called 'creative nonfiction' – 'a singularly unlovely and antiseptic term, particularly the word "creative",' she says.[20] (We've more to say about the word 'creative' later, in the 'Title' section of this introduction.) For the moment, let's just say that perhaps fixing on *any* single name as the final and best moniker for critical writing risks closing off some new angle, insight, experience or nuance. The essay, various and promiscuous as it is, might even on occasion have to cede its own name. Critical prose might sometimes need *not* to be recognised or recognisable as an essay to answer its own truest calling, to respond to the work that it meets and the thinking it needs to do about that work. Sometimes? Is now the time? Are we ready for a break from all this essaying, a break that will be perhaps the truest mark of affiliation with the form at hand? But then should the break be made smoothly, as if the time of the writing – this, here, now – has been ever ticking towards what we will come to acknowledge as the appropriate moment in which to have made a move? Or should the break be an untimely intrusion, a cut? Should it hurt?

To cut to the chase, it is a question of whether or not to accede to the workings of and institutionalised demand for

CONTINUOUS PROSE

prose, that is, rather more fluently continuous than that currently in train. Admittedly, the play with the transition here is a little obvious, perhaps gratuitous. And why not? Creative criticism admits the possibility that words will do things, rather than merely recount what they have done or what they might or should do. Is our interruption a momentary lapse of taste or a strategic shunt in the writing? It should at the very least have caught your attention, and served also to draw attention to the mechanics of writerly movement, hence to the matter of continuity. And this is just as well, for one key mark of the kind of writing for which we are your guides – one feature by which it may be identified – is the break: an interruption or series of interruptions in the prose, or more generally, in the text in question. Charged with irresponsibly taking a break from the discipline of critique, creative criticism replies with a critique-in-practice of the discipline of the break. The features of such practice can be easy to identify: the jumps from prose to poetry in Denise Riley and John Wilkinson (little surprise to find poets working the break), or between the different voices in John Cage; but also more subterranean, as in Hélène Cixous and Sarah Wood, where we feel at times something slipping as we pass between paragraphs, as if the conventions of writerly continuity are being undone in the interests of an unfamiliar logic of unfolding. We feel the break at the same time as we sense it may not be a break after all, and that we're learning to read differently.

Having identified a distinguishing feature we should add a caveat and say that the idea of the break is best treated with caution. As with all guidebooks, the tell-tale signs are rarely as unequivocally telling as one might hope. We have used the idea of the break because compared to the stately uniformity of conventional critical writing, with its regular motions and rhythms, creative criticism can appear broken up, jittery, as if marching to a different beat; or as if not following a beat of any kind but rather a mazy motion of another order. Creative criticism is indeed marked by the break – we're not entirely unreliable guides – but this should not necessarily be taken to mean that some whole is being broken into (although that may on occasion be so). It is more a matter of part writing, of writing in bits each of which, while ostensibly whole, is allied with other bits such that our sense of and desire for wholeness are unsettled. Something is happening in the relation of the parts. The writing is intermittent, variously interrupting itself; there is a marked rhythm of continuity but also of discontinuity, hence of continuity *in* discontinuity. We find it in Barthes's non-serial series, in Kopelson's wild leaps of tone and in Gizzi's juxtapositions. The breaks and the resulting rhythm of the relation between parts are a part of what the writing is doing.

Kevin Kopelson wonders whether his performance will be a 'fragmentary *tour de force*' or a 'miniature fiasco', offering thereby a clue not only to the staged cheekiness of what's to come but also to how we might account for prose such as his. Fragments are what we are supposed to overcome as we write, to join together in the interests of consistency, continuity and, in the end, completion. Fragments are what we have when we're yet to finish.[21] The achieved consistency of critical writing tends to be in the service of an ideal of closure, of what is often called with good reason the sense of an ending: that strong sense in which faith in the belief that an end is coming, that it will and should happen, figures instrumentally in the writing as a structuring principle, and is felt to do so.[22] What a strange thought: that writing will allow us to be done with reading, even that writing will be the record of our having answered the questions and put reading to bed. By this measure a fragmentary *tour de force* is an oxymoron, something like a strong failure; because in being within itself broken off it is necessarily incomplete, perhaps even something of a fiasco. And so it is. If the notion of creative criticism has the air, or at least the form, of an oxymoron, it is in the continuity-in-discontinuity of much of the writing in question – in the overtly composite pieces as much as in the night logic of those ostensibly more conventional in form – that we find evidence of why that might be so. Rather than the sense of an ending the aspiration here is towards the possibility of an opening. As Wayne Koestenbaum puts it, 'To break up a piece of writing is . . . to extend the threshold'.[23] Let's say that we're concerned with identifying the marks of a writing of openings in which there is room to move and air to breathe; writing which makes and maintains space for the possible. As such, the current volume is in part a guide to what is not present – not because it is absent, but because it is in the making. You'll know it not when you see it but when you feel it, for it is the contentful forms and rhythms of the writing that hold a significant part of its sense.

A loftier account, one concerned with parallels and precursors, would reach back to the idea of the fragment as imagined and practised by late-eighteenth-century German writers such as Novalis and, in particular, Friedrich Schlegel. Like the essay, a form to which it is closely related, it is an idea with its own precursors, not to say a number of weighty inheritors;

and it is an idea much glossed.[24] For our purposes we can say that the fragment, here in the fertile years of early German Romanticism, is a form of promise, hence a form concerned for the future. Imagine a future in which there will be no call for creative criticism (might that come as a relief?), no need for the yoking together of what appear to be two writerly modes, two forms of thinking and – why not say it? – two forms of living. What manner of writing could bear the possibility of such an impossible promise? It would need to succeed in gesturing towards fulfilment, but fail to deliver, for to do so would be at once to betray the promise. To succeed would be to fail. For Schlegel, the possible impossibility in question was the union of poetry and philosophy, to achieve which would mean nothing less than the union of knowledge – including the knowledge that can at times make living so hard – and living, the felt experience of which can seem to be at odds with the forms of our thinking. The Romanticism of the time is marked in the call for such unifying promises and in the belief in the aesthetic as that realm in which they will best be made. And it is the fragment, a form 'complete in itself and separated from the rest of the universe like a hedgehog', which brought into play such impossible futures.[25] Hedgehog writing points outward in order to shut itself in and cut itself off; it gestures beyond itself in order to remain discrete; it is a bundle of energy whose edge is multiple, dispersed.

We should be wary of equating poetry and philosophy with, respectively, creative and critical writing, although clearly the former pair resonates with the senses of the latter. A guidebook can only indicate the territory in question. Derrida's aphorisms apart, the majority of the writing to which we lay claim is not fragmentary in the ways imagined by Schlegel and company, and yet it displays severally signs of interruption, of discontinuity, of a desire for the play of the interval. The rhythmic relation across discrete parts – numbered blocks; individual voices; mixed modes; turns of thought; bounded journal entries – is the promise in the writing of what is still to come, so of a necessary failure of mastery or completion, a strong failure. For who could imagine mastery to be the goal of writing? The break promises to keep things open.

CAN I USE THE FIRST PERSON?

A good question. It is roughly the same as asking whether or not I can write in my own voice – or should that be whether or not *one* can write in *one*'s own voice? For all its common-or-garden tone this is in fact a question close to the heart of much of the writing gathered here. It's a question we never really stop asking, each in our own voice. Held within the question is a mixture of desire and fear: desire for the supposed comforts of the first person, for a peculiar mix of the familiar and the unconstrained, and fear that such comforts may render any writing of this kind somehow inappropriate to the task at hand, that it might be somehow risky. Such fears are of course frequently borne out, for as any writer of criticism will attest – and we can, for sure – the first person can be rather more shifty than comfortable. I is not an easy place to be, and certainly not as simple as it sounds; and yet to say that the admittance of the first person really does not solve the problem is not to say, however ironically, 'I told you so', nor that the first person is not all it's cracked up to be. It is rather that the first person is only one part of the matter of voice in criticism.

Blithely to talk of critical writing as a matter of voice is to be already knee-deep in metaphor, or, as John Wilkinson has it, in the pitch where we find ourselves whenever we feel called on to write what we think we mean. That pitch is also one of the means by which we find ourselves only adds to the complications. Voice is a rich and fertile thing and we should stick with it, because it will keep us close to criticism as a matter of *writing* – ironically close, given that voice would appear to suggest a worldly yet intimate self-sound that is necessarily muted in our written words. It is in fact not so much a desire to cling to the vaguely felt comfort of such a sound that leads to the question of critical voice, as a fearful sense that criticism is precisely where one's I is disavowed, whisked away by the porters. Criticism is where I am not allowed to use my own voice: criticism is where I learn to ventriloquise.

The frustration and disappointment of criticism-as-ventriloquy is sounded most often in the academy by creative writers, precisely at that moment when an institutional requirement to pass from the creative to the critical is invoked. Creative writing is felt to be a matter of one's own voice whereas the voice of criticism is only ever that of someone else; and yet of course it is rather creative writing that tends to demand feats of ventriloquy, the animation of a voice that is an essential element in the making-in-writing of character. The sense that criticism requires a degree of forgery whereas creative writing does not arises from a more general feeling that the self is at stake in the latter but not in the former, because the language of creative writing is chosen by one's self whereas, again, the language of criticism has always already been chosen by another. The best *we* can do is practise our dummy runs. The question of voice in the sense of grammatical person – first, third, second – is thus a question not only of metaphor but also of metonym: voice as an animating sign of my self. Above all, it is a question of our relation to language and of how that relation is played out word-by-word in all that we write. Is it any wonder then that the matter of voice resonates forcefully through the pieces gathered here, from the unapologetic self-centredness of Geoff Dyer to John Cage's dispersed auto-polyphony?

When poet-critic Charles Bernstein speaks of 'Criticism's blindness to the meaning of its forms' he means in part blindness to the meaning of critical voice.[26] To avoid further muddying the metaphors we should call it instead a partial deafness to the meaning of voice and tone in criticism – to the meaning of register in the broadest sense. And we should say immediately by way of caveat that creative criticism is not a licence to use I, with all that would imply. That is not it, at all. Creative criticism is not a free play of so-called personal opinion, whether offered in the person of a first-year undergraduate or a seasoned commentator. It does however admit and acknowledge voice, and with it the likes of pitch and tone, as a question that sounds whenever writing is at stake; and in this it learns from creative prose and poetry. It should come as no surprise therefore to find that the frustrations of voice as experienced when we write criticism – and we do well to confess the frisson of recognition when we read of such moments – are registered with singular force in the writings of those such as Charles Bernstein; that is, by creative writers writing criticism. The rich store of critical writing by writer-critics – how we stumble as we mark the distinctions – is a body of work we should like here to call as evidence in support of the wide life of our catch-all ragbag of creative criticism. Not that all criticism by creative writers is grist for our mill; again, that is not it, at all. Our invocation is specifically of the reflective work of authors for whom the contiguity of creative and other forms of writing is lived as a matter of principle, a continued playing out of a relation with language allied with a refusal, faced with the content of criticism's forms, to accede to any measure of sensory deprivation. Such writing comes from far and wide, forms no kind of tradition and is amenable to no kind of historical corralling. In the words of the poet-critic Lisa Samuels, 'the absence of a common project leaves us little choice other than to group them [the writers in question] together as "Other". Individuality *is* their project.'[27] An 'Other' criticism, then: this critical writing of the creatives (to rescue for a moment that tarnished appellation) is a grouping capacious enough to allow for the inclusion in particular of works of gunslinger poetics from the likes of Laura Riding and Charles Olson, Louis Zukosky and William Carlos Williams, Robert Duncan and Lisa Robertson. To invoke such uncontainable spirits is passingly, and with a twinge of regret, to acknowledge those extraordinary acts of creative criticism that lie beyond the necessarily limited reach of the present volume. The spirits are here in spirit.

And yet before we get carried away with the outsider-pioneer rhetoric we should say that the writing called to here, some of it at least, is marked by a small number of common, hence shared, features, one of which is indeed the use of the first person. Hence, for instance, the tolling of 'I's in the opening of Part One of Olson's *Call Me Ishmael*: 'I am interested in . . . I am interested in . . . I am willing'; hence too Susan Howe making a case for *My Emily Dickinson*: 'For years I have wanted to find words to thank Emily Dickinson for the inspiration of her poetic daring'.[28] Each respondent begins by declaring an interest and staking a claim, in a register far from conventionally academic or professional. The Howe in particular has become something of a touchstone for poets wishing to commemorate an intimate affiliation with the words of another. As well as the plain statement of gratitude that runs through *My Emily Dickinson*, there is also the marking of an engagement over time; and then there is the first person, although not perhaps in the form expected. Howe has 'wanted to find words', a locution somewhat at odds with the promised immediacy of the first person. The first person is allegedly where we don't need to seek to *find* words: the first person is where the words already are, always to hand. Howe's profession of gratitude is voiced by a critical I seeking after words fit for the calling. As such, the admittance here of the first person is not a charter for speaking off the cuff but rather something else entirely: an acknowledgement that the matching of words with words is the very gist of the action, no matter how hard the task. It is in fact conventional critical prose that relies on and propagates a myth of immediacy, of a language to hand for any occasion; the same language, that is, available regardless of the grain of the reading and writing involved. It is a myth of a subject-less and transparent language with aspirations to objectivity, an off-the-peg register in which the contingencies of the writing I – chief amongst which is its entanglement with the felt self of the speaker – are comfortingly brushed aside. The cost of such myth-making is a tidying of tone, what Bernstein calls the '"tone lock"' of academic criticism; and it is a refusal to pay such a high price for what can appear to be so little that motivates flashes of first-person anger in such ostensibly unrelated writers as Robert

Duncan and Geoff Dyer. In fact, this anger at the academy might be one further motif tying together the works of Samuels' 'Other' criticism. The tenured wankers of the late twentieth century scorned by Dyer are the offspring of the professional scholar-critics of the American 1950s against whom Duncan rages – the 'new class . . . that now fills our departments of English', hell bent on 'setting up critical standards and grading responses to fit the anxieties and self-satisfactions of their professional roles'.[29] Duncan, faced with this newly established orthodoxy, marshals a crew comprising largely writer-critics, from H.D. and Edith Sitwell (Edith Sitwell!) to Zukofsky and Olson; a motley crew united in their concern for the 'inner nature and process of poetry itself', at odds with any attempt to 'weigh' or 'count' or 'assign' – at odds, that is, with any notion of 'disciplining'.[30] Duncan's *H.D. Book* is the most extraordinary working through of what a criticism of the type hymned in its pages might sound like writ large; an extended working out by one writer of the inspirational forces held in the words of another, self-justifyingly 'excited' and 'aroused' and resistant throughout to closure, lock or boundary.

To seek to name the visionary Romanticism in Duncan, so as to imply its other, a necessarily caricatured Classicism, is not only to repeat what is marked repeatedly in the work itself, but also to adopt the very disciplining tendency against which Duncan is writing. It is in the nature of such critical writing to profess an affiliation of one with another, hence to practise an unashamedly partisan poetics. We might read this tendency in part in relation to the familiar rhetorical move whereby a critical register is charged as both inadequate to and at worst falsifying of the real presence of the artwork: criticism as a kind of dead letter, a category mistake, life-sucking where it should be animating. If we're to make a claim for affiliation between creative criticism and the work of writer-critics such as those mentioned here – and surely we must – then it should be in terms not of an heroic truth-to-materials but rather of Howe's desire 'to find' words to acknowledge the life of those of another. Looking to find, we may be surprised or sidetracked or shocked or disappointed. To set out to find is to take our chances, and so to admit desire and to acknowledge the contingent. Creative criticism employs the first person because at times the first person is required for such a task, in order to account for the constitutively occasional nature of all such writing. Creative criticism is resistant to the tone lock of so much academic commentary because tone and register are not incidental to the occasion but rather part and parcel of its making, and of its essentially ventriloquial scenario. To suggest otherwise is to be blind, or deaf, perhaps even a little dumb. The dizzyingly different tones that sound in the pieces gathered here are testament to creative criticism as an essaying of voice, and as a resistance to critical register as necessarily pre-packaged and well-tempered. This goes as much for the stagey confessions of Dyer and the counterpointed auto-commentary of Riley and Wilkinson as it does for Benjamin Friedlander's voiceless procedure. Each is in its own way wide-eyed at the meaning of its chosen form, not least when that form is acknowledged as a vocal performance: from Barthes's framing set-up – 'So it is a lover who speaks and who says . . .' – to Kopelson's self-confessed 'Barthesian' turns: 'I'll try to understand . . . by acting like a typical student – and typical teacher, and typical writer. I'll *perform* comprehension.'[31] For the first person is something we need to perform, to act out, perhaps especially so when working to voice what is felt to be an incontrovertibly personal response. And this motif of performance, sounded repeatedly through the various parts of our introduction, invokes also the first-person plural, the very we that occurred only one sentence ago. I am only ever I to a you, real or imagined, outside or within; and my you is ever able to turn as other to an I, in which turn I become you. (We return to 'You' below.) But within the role-playing antics of this two-hander rests also the possibility not for two to become one, but rather for two to be the start of many. The conventional first-person plural of critical writing can serve merely as a faux-communal front for yet more professions of what I most definitely know; but this needn't be the case. How might an exploratory criticism animate a voice that is neither yours nor mine, but rather that is ours, genuinely shared and accepted thus as both within and without, never to be settled? Such an exploration might start with the idea of voice as a matter always of something found or made in-between.

On which note I should hand over to you.

ON

'Write an essay *on*.' 'What are you writing *about*?' The vocabulary of criticism tends to limit itself to these two prepositions. They position us as standing apart from a text or artwork, facing it, a subject confronting an object from which it is distinct and aloof. Turning intellectual-historical for a moment (as though one could simply write *about* the history one is still *in*) we might suggest that this model is indebted to the Enlightenment philosophical tradition, a tradition which celebrates human consciousness's capacity to explore, shed rational light on, and so get the measure of, its world. Enlightenment thought hasn't gone dark, but it has always been shadowed by its own dark sides and blindspots, and in intellectual work since the nineteenth century, in particular, these have been identified, criticised and made into the resource for new, perhaps less masterful, forms of thinking and writing. The Romantic philosophers and poets (discussed further in this introduction under 'Continuous prose' and 'Title') explore, and in their fragmentary and discontinuous writing also stage, the ways in which the writing and thinking of finite mortals might best render the infinite world of which they are but a small part. In the work of later thinkers such as Nietzsche and Freud, consciousness's own dark sides and hidden motivations have been remarked, and the subject starts to emerge as subject to forces and impulses she can never simply know or stand outside, and as made up of other people, things, bits of language and ideas. The twentieth-century philosopher Heidegger, working over the German word for being, *Dasein*, underscores the ways in which we human beings are already *da*, there *in* the world and a part of it, and suggests that the enlightened, knowing 'subject' violently effaces this before-the-beginning *inherence* in the world, in her claim to stand opposite it, know it, write on or about it.[32] This is no mere philosophical finagling or fine-tuning. A dark light indeed is shed on Enlightenment hubris by the current environmental crisis, produced by just that same deluded sense that we are masters of a world of objects, rather than involved a priori in, and responsible for, that world.

For all these reasons, creative critics invent a more flexible prepositional vocabulary, to capture the mesh of their involvement in and relationship to the art they encounter. Sedgwick's proposal of a criticism of 'beside' offers one instance of this. 'Beside' is pitched by Sedgwick as the prepositional aspiration for a revised critical practice, a shift away from 'beneath' and 'beyond', hence from 'the topos of depth or hiddenness, typically followed by a drama of exposure' that we know all too well.[33] While ostensibly spatial in orientation, 'beneath' and 'beyond' turn all too easily to the plotted rise and fall of origins and endings, thereby shutting down the enabling, if always contested, space of the encounter. Something else is at stake with 'beside', something less reliant on dualism or hierarchy, on narratives of priority or late-coming. And yet 'as any child knows who's shared a bed with siblings', being beside is likely still to involve some rough and tumble.

So what space is this? Let's say that it is neither the space of fine proportions and fixed vantage nor the clean and static space in which all appears just so, but something rather closer to home. It is this space right here: creative space criticism. Do you see it? Did you hear it? Will you sense it? It is the little space made in the bringing alongside, the making roughly coincident, of our two words: the space in creative criticism. Only roughly coincident, mind, for to make a space is to interrupt as well as to conjoin. The rough edge of interruption offers a manner of conjoining, a contretemps the formal adaption of which we find in the variously fragmented writing here vouched for: in Barthes's intermezzi; in Cage's polyphonic passage 'beyond our understanding'; in Derrida's thirty-nine steps towards aphorism; in the drifting turns of Carson's sleep reading; in Kopelson's 'miniature fiasco' of thirteen tones; in the counterpointing of prose and poetry in Riley and Wilkinson; in Friedlander's cut-and-paste job; and beyond our selection, in a bit-part writing of daybooks and diaries and dialogues and the like. The space in creative criticism is the opening in which the creative and the critical are at once brought together – pressed to collaborate – and, in appearing cut, kept apart. It is spacing between the words and the respective practices they hold dear in which these words are themselves found already to be turning otherwise, oscillating each towards the other as towards a recognition of themselves in the other, something akin to Pasternak's declaration: 'You in others: this is your soul'.[34] Hence it is better thought as a passage, a spacing which opens and which keeps open. A lot is happening in this space, happening already; and yet it is also the space necessary in order for something *to* happen, akin to what Sarah Wood nominates as 'the space between what I thought I understood and what I can't'. 'There I can *hear*,' says Wood; there we can anew again.

Sedgwick compares a critical practice of besideness with the childhood space of a shared bed – perhaps the very bed from the sleep side of which Anne Carson writes – and with a rough-and-ready repertoire of 'rivaling, leaning, twisting, mimicking, withdrawing . . . warping', a less muscle-bound rival to Richard Serra's *Verb List* (1967–8). Where Serra proposes 'Actions to Relate to Oneself', Sedgwick has actions to relate, and we know what she means. This is a realm and a series of moves that 'any child knows': it is child's play, hence the melodrama. To account for the creative in creative criticism requires that we acknowledge not only the historical baggage with which it necessarily arrives, and with which we contend as we write, but also the matter of an everyday impulse, a moment-by-moment attitude of inhabiting and experiencing in places as common as a shared bed. This is creativity conceived far away from the dizzy heights, away from narratives of decline, and, in its daily occurrence here-and-now-and-again, from the potential aggrandisements of the idea of the encounter. 'Making' is perhaps a more fitting word, closer in spirit to the secular magic turns of the everyday about which there is nothing ordinary; just as long as the stress is placed on something happening rather than on something made, hence on the creative imagined along the lines offered by D. W. Winnicott, as nothing short of 'a feature of life and total living';[35] 'a colouring of the whole attitude to external reality':

> The creative impulse is therefore something that can be looked at as a thing in itself, something that of course is necessary if an artist is to produce a work of art, but also something that is present when *anyone* – baby, child, adolescent, adult, old man or woman – looks in a healthy way at anything or does anything deliberately, such as making a mess with faeces or prolonging the act of crying to enjoy a musical sound. It is present as much in the moment-by-moment living of a backward child who is enjoying breathing as it is in the inspiration of an architect who suddenly knows what it is that he wishes to construct.[36]

Creativity is a matter of me, but it is a human self across and around and through which the creative cuts; a human self dispossessed in the making, 'in the area of transitional phenomena'. The creative is here a me-in-the-making, 'marionette-becoming', 'an invented someone, someone invented in part by not having been, someone suggested by someone else'.[37] Flux writing – let's say we name it thus, just this once – is generous in its admission of the through-flow of making, a scrappy affair that is nevertheless all that any of us has, held in all that we read and write. As we shall see, the desire neither to erase nor to delete such singularly common experience, which is to say the desire not to have the space in which it happens close up, figures variously in so much of what concerns us here.

The space in creative criticism is transitional and for this reason we are justified in leaning, gently and in passing, on Winnicott; which Sedgwick-esque leaning will lead us to Wilkinson's 'Imperfect Pitch', his rough-hewn tracking of how a thing-in-the-making arrives in language.[38] Stripped of the name-dropping, our sense is that creative criticism acknowledges in its own means and matter the creativity of the artwork as transitional, and that it sounds a response in kind to the artwork desirous itself of remaining on the common ground of this transitional space.

YOU

Who *are* you? Who will you have been? What might you become? Our rubric addresses you as though it knows – or rather, as though it doesn't care. And indeed all writing is to some extent indifferent to its addressee, insofar as it is legible by anyone. We certainly have no way of knowing who will happen upon this *Anthology*, in a library or a bookshop, say. But we do have certain readers in mind, several of whom we have acknowledged already. You might be someone studying creative writing, and obliged to write a 'critical essay' alongside your own 'creative work' – and you might feel that as an imposition. You might be a literature student, alienated by the language of conventional, academic critical prose. You might be an art student, engaged in the ever more various discipline of art criticism or art writing. You might be a tutor of one of these subjects, looking for helpful classroom material. You might be one of our parents or friends. Whoever you might be, this book is for *you*, and we hope you find in it something for you, something you can pirate away, reinvent, make your own.

Creative criticism itself is fascinated by the adventures and mis-adventures of address: by the ways in which, even as we address ourselves to writing about a text or artwork, our words are on the turn, tendered elsewhere, and readable by who-knows-whom.[39] See in this very *Anthology*, for example, the quick-fire dialogue between 'I' and 'you' in Ali Smith's 'Green'. This you is unnamed, and her (?) identity slips, sometimes an interlocutor, at other times an aspect of the speaker's self, always, possibly, the you who reads 'Green'. Criticism needs others if it is not simply to incorporate what it reads into the loop of its own solipsism. Perhaps for this reason, inventive thinking and writing since Plato has made use of the dialogue form. This very book has emerged from the endless, on-going, back and forth of a conversation, between us, its two editors, and also with others. It is in part to mark this that we conclude our introduction with a dialogue. Whether it is inventive or not – well, that's for you to say.

YOUR TITLE

Our title is *Creative Criticism*. We agreed it between ourselves and in discussions with colleagues and our publishers. But it could have been otherwise: *Inventive Criticism? Performative Criticism? The Making of Criticism?* They, and others, each have their attractions. We're by no means sure, in fact, that ours is the most appropriate, or even the most immediately helpful. It's certainly not very creative. It was first used as a title in 1917, by one Joel Elias Spingarn, who used it to mean something like close reading – 'creative' in this context, because it resisted philological or historical approaches to literature.[40] And Spingarn aside, our title is made entirely from found material, namely from two words which are much in the air at the institution at which we teach, as lecturers in literary criticism at a university in which creative writing is a signal success story.

But we'd like to suggest that the lack of 'creativity' in our title is its strength. Let's, then, say something about the histories and contexts of the two words which make it up. A squint at etymology will tell us that the word 'criticism' comes from the Greek *krinein* – to separate, judge or decide – and then further back from an Indo-European root 'krei-' which means to sieve, to discriminate and to distinguish. In English, Raymond Williams tells us, its 'predominant early sense was of fault-finding', and this remains its most obvious common-parlance, non-specialist meaning today, alongside a general feeling that to criticise is to be a carper and kill-joy, and to align oneself with all that is negative.[41] In the seventeenth century comes the more technical sense of criticism as judgement, and of the critic as the arbiter of taste, or as the judge of a work's merits. A critic of this ilk sorts the wheat from the chaff, according to some rule, principle or feeling of rightness. For Pope this feeling is Heaven-sent – 'Both must alike from Heav'n derive their light, / Those born to judge, as well as those to write'.[42] Whereas T. S. Eliot (as we discussed under 'Reading and writing') invokes rectitude and propriety as the basis for critical judgement, Pope appeals to a more transcendental origin. But for both, criticism anchors itself in the steadying ground of an elsewhere, some place apart from its own reading life and activity. The reference to Pope is no accident here. Criticism in the judicious and adjudicatory sense that we glimpse in its etymology flourished in the public places and periodicals of the eighteenth century, alongside the expansion of the forces of literary production, and the growth of a literate reading public. And the role of critic-as-judge today is filled – most overtly at least – primarily by the writers of *reviews* in newspapers and journals, rather than by the inhabitants of university literature departments.

Criticism, in these accounts, is irrevocably secondary, coming after the creative work both temporally and in importance, and attending upon it from a distance that is necessarily slightly servile. Eliot takes it as axiomatic that 'a creation, a work of art, is autotelic' – it is self-sufficient and autonomous – whereas 'criticism, by definition, is *about* something other than itself'.[43] But as with all such statements which set up guardrails and boundary lines, we might espy a certain defensiveness or anxiety here, a desire to keep things apart and in their correct place. And the fact that criticism doesn't always stay in its place but sometimes seems to borrow the energy and glamour of so-called 'creative' work is one that has long been acknowledged, sometimes approvingly and sometimes not. Matthew Arnold, in *his* 'The Function of Criticism', writes, for example, that 'criticism must be sincere, simple, flexible, ardent, ever widening its knowledge. Then it may have, in no contemptible measure, a joyful sense of creative activity.'[44] Arnold is keen to add, however, that criticism shouldn't get too uppity: 'in full measure, the sense of creative activity belongs only to genuine creation,' he says, a little tautologously.[45] Oscar Wilde, wild critic and arch over-turner, has no such right-thinking compunctions. In 'The Critic as Artist' he (or at least one of 'his' voices) makes the strong claim that criticism is *necessarily* inventive, in that it makes up the very concepts and ideas we think with, and remake our world with:

> it is the critical faculty that invents fresh forms. The tendency of creation is to repeat itself. It is to the critical instinct that we owe each new school that springs up, each new mould that art finds ready to its hand.[46]

Criticism and creation swap sides here then, a scandalous provocation. And yet the structural relation of one to the other remains unchanged: it is still a matter of sides. Creative criticism does not propose to do away with, even less to sidestep, this demarcation, but it does seek variously to test its workings and its reach, and to imagine innovative forms for the taking of sides.

And yet before any of this is possible we need to consider our other titular word: 'creative'. For all that the word means 'imaginative' or 'inventive', and implies the capacity to have 'original ideas as well as routine skill or intellect' (*OED*), 'the creative' itself isn't an original idea, but an inherited one, and comes marked with and shaped by the contexts and traditions from which it derives. Most obviously we think here of the long tradition of linking creativity with poetic, literary and other kinds of artistic making, and connecting this, in turn, with the arrogation or emulation of a god-like power. There are two creators, writes Tasso in the sixteenth century: God and the poet. Or – leaping over a few centuries – let's look at Wordsworth, pausing at a high point in his poetic autobiography, *The Prelude*:

And here, O friend, have I retraced my life
Up to an eminence, and told a tale
Of matters which not falsely I may call
The glory of my youth. Of genius, power,
Creation, and divinity itself
I have been speaking, for my theme has been
What passed within me.[47]

This is perhaps rather less obnoxiously cocky than it appears at first blush, though it is certainly not unaware of just how much of a double take that outrageously nonchalant 'for' will prompt in a reader. (And it's worth mentioning that the apostrophised reader-friend, Coleridge, is at once more extravagant and more modest in his own claims about the creative, figuring the 'primary imagination' impossibly as 'the repetition in the finite mind of the eternal act of creation in the infinite I AM'.[48]) For Wordsworth genius, power, creation and divinity traverse the poet – happen in and through and to him, and don't belong to him. Their passage might bless or authorise him, of course – there's 'me' there, for sure – but his theme is not the me, but what happens to or in it. While Wordsworth is writing not long after 'creative' first becomes an adjective, connoting a specifically human faculty of creation, creation here marks the crossing of the human by the divine, and so a kind of dispossession. The creative is not a private property but a force which cuts athwart all privacy and all property.

For Wordsworth, it's all down-hill after this. He descends to the flat lands of East Anglia, takes up a place at university and spends the following year in 'submissive idleness'.[49] Naysayers might suggest that this is the fate, too, of the 'creative' when it is invited into the university.[50] It's not only, so this story goes, that creative writing programmes will trammel invention into well-worn grooves, but also that the 'high and serious claim' the word itself embodies becomes banalised: 'thus any imitative or stereotyped literary work may be called, by convention, creative writing, and advertising copywriters officially describe themselves as creative,' says Raymond Williams, exploring how 'creative' has become a 'cant word'.[51] That's not the story we are interested in here: it is more its shape *as* a story that is worth remarking. 'Consciously or not,' Derrida quotes Georges Canguilhem as saying, 'the idea that man has of his poetic power corresponds to the idea he has about the creation of the world, and to the solution he gives to the problem of the radical origin of things.'[52] And Williams's account of a once authentic notion of creativity becoming commercial cant, as with the autobiographical trajectory Wordsworth traces from an eminence where he's shot through with creative forces, to a come down and a dulling in the university, does hook up with something more to our purpose. For the story of 'the idea of the creative' seems in some ways to be a classic Creation story, which is to say also the story of a fall. This could be the bathetic slide from the heights to the fens, from the divine to the human to the mechanical or industrialised, from the moment of creative inspiration to the finished and created object, from innovation to generic norms, force to form, defamiliarisation to weary recognition. But whether in terms of the trajectory of an individual writer, or the cultural and historical fate of the notion of creativity itself, nothing seems more common than this narrative of a lamentable lapse.

Creative criticism, at once more disabused and yet more wide-eyed, isn't having these hackneyed creation myths and fall stories. It views the act of artistic creation as something which didn't happen back 'in the beginning', but that is still at stake. Staying with the idea of creation as dispossession, it doesn't respect a work's composure so much as it participates in its abandonment. Creative critics get their hands dirty in what Frankenstein calls the 'workshop of filthy creation', tapping into the dynamism of a work at its roots and participating in its unmaking and rebinding energies.[53] They approach literature from what Anne Carson dubs 'the sleep side' where it is tousled and blurry but apt to dream still, and make odd, inspired connections.

For this reason, while what we are calling creative criticism is concerned with its own form and with its own writerliness or even poeticising, it's often far from being classically beautiful. This is not fine writing. It is messy and it judders. It begins again and again, moving not in sequence, but, to borrow from Derrida, aphoristically and counter-time. It is aware of its own contingency and occasional caprice, which is also the motive of its desire. 'I want to' begins Carson's essay, and then 'I think' and 'I don't know' and then 'let's': 'let's look', 'let's say', 'let's consider' – casual as you like, but intent, too, on staying with some movement, some coincidence of shape, feeling or thought. At its best, this staying with is the means by which writing comes to imagine its form; that is, the means by which writing comes to make a form in which to meet the peculiar provocation in the artwork. Creative-critical writing is performative: that much we know.

How easy it is to make such a generic statement, when it is in the very imagining and inhabiting of forms that such writing is at its strangest, its most unsettling, its most agitating.

QUOTATION

The challenge of critical writing lies in the finding of words in response to the work of another – 'to meet the work with writing', and so to engage in what we might call a form of 'continuing'.[54] There are myriad ways in which to continue, some more discontinuous than others, but it is a convention in all cases to establish and perform a relationship through the use of quotations: to have one's own words hold the words of others, whether those whose words are the occasion for one's own writing or those to whom we turn under neurotic instruction to 'back up' all we have said lest it should prove unfounded. In each case it is a question of authority. As little pockets of excitement, quotations are at once centripetal and centrifugal: in acknowledging continuity they bring and hold words together, yet in doing so provide evidence of the necessarily patchwork composition of writing, with its variously glossed hinges, brackets and joints. Quotation marks criticism as a play of forces akin to a balancing act. In the act of affiliation there is always the possibility of appearing to claim sovereignty, while carried within the illustrative or ornamental lies the possibility of viral infection. And of course, quotations make of all criticism something plural, the work of polyphony, however much we may strive for the one true line. We lose the security of our voice at that very moment in which we carefully select the lines of others imagined to be best suited for the showing of our own purpose.

And an anthology is a work made of quotations, albeit quotations permitted to stand free of those marks by which we notionally safeguard our words as property, as things to be owned:

He gave his wife a ring with keys on it and said: 'These are the keys to the two large storerooms where I keep my gold and silver. Here are the ones to the caskets where I store my jewels. And finally, this is the master key to all the rooms in my mansion. As for this particular key, it opens the small room at the end of the long gallery on the ground floor. Open anything you want. Go anywhere you wish. But I absolutely forbid you to enter that little room, and if you open it so much as a crack, nothing will protect you from my wrath.'[55]

The work of an anthology involves reaching into the writing of another, taking what is wanted for the occasion and then, within a new and unforeseeable place, pairing it up with what are claimed as like-minded partners. It is a gathering of materials, an act either of friendship or of defacement, depending on whether or not the rationale is felt to carry sufficient warrant. So we might say that the anthology in its purest form, and writ large, lays bare the quotation as a particular device of criticism, resonant with questions of decency and measure, to say nothing of the where, the when and the how. For to use quotations is always to call up the question of number and length, which is to say the question of the quota: how many will be allowed? How many is too many or too few? And how many will be just enough? How long should any one quotation be, or how short? And where should it go? 'Things have their due measure; there are ultimately fixed limits, beyond which, or short of which, something must be wrong.'[56]

Quotation allows us to take the measure of criticism, and to keep taking it. 'Still, in full measure, the sense of creative activity belongs only to genuine creation; in literature we must never forget that.'[57] It is never self-evident, the answer to the question of evidence. Too many quotations, especially if allowed to speak at length, and we run the risk of appearing to want to hide from the task, however much such generosity towards the words of another may stem from respect or high regard. Too few quotations, or too brief, and we risk not only suggesting that we made it all up, failed sufficiently to substantiate our claims, but also speaking over, hence silencing, those others we have ourselves invited in:

> Literary criticism and philosophy have a family resemblance to literature – and to this extent to one another as well – in their rhetorical advancement. But their family relationship stops right there, for in each of these enterprises the tools of rhetoric are subordinated to the discipline of a distinct form of argumentation.[58]

It is a question of discipline and, predictably, a question of authority. 'If so large a part of creation is really criticism, is not a large part of what is called "critical writing" really creative? If so, is there not creative criticism in the ordinary sense? The answer seems to be, that there is no equation.'[59] Yes, a question of authority, and of authority's place: 'We accept more easily the

idea of a creative element in the critical essay if its author is a poet or novelist: then his authority in the creative realm carries over into the critical.'[60]
And once again also a question of balance and proportion, of the balancing
or constellating of materials. Quotations are amongst the prime locations
of criticism, their ostensible neatness the result of a series of scrappy back-
stage negotiations during which the shape of our writing comes to appear.
Quotations are where criticism happens:

> So that each person may quickly find that
> Which particularly concerns him, certain metaphors
> Convenient to us within the compass of this
> Lesson are to be allowed. It is best I sit
> Here where I am to speak on the other side
> Of language. You, of course, in your own time
> And incident (I speak in the small hours.)
> Will listen from your side. I am very pleased
> We have sought us out.[61]

Or at least quotations *can* be where criticism happens, which is why
creative criticism is fully justified in sniffing an opportunity, the chance
of making something of quotation's possibilities. To do so will require
playing seriously with the matter of authority and affiliation, of speaking
of and speaking for, of those voices of others which over-reach the mark
as they haunt and echo and turn about; and will require also the possibility
of over-stepping the mark or of shirking, risking as we go the charge of
irresponsibility – 'The moment of irresponsibility, in itself an aspect of
every truth that does not exhaust itself in responsibility toward the status
quo' – in the interests of an expanded notion of a responsible writing that
knows no bounds, that stops at nothing, according to which everything is
a possible something over which to linger, into which to pry and on which
to lavish attention.[62] 'The work of criticism is superfluous unless it is itself
a work of art as independent of the work it criticises as that is independent
of the materials that went into it.'[63] As with each and every constituent part
of the writing of criticism, creativity is possible, an opening

> It is a question of producing a signifying structure, a producing
> that obviously cannot consist of reproducing, by the effaced and
> respectful doubling of commentary, the conscious, voluntary,
> intentional relationship that a writer institutes in his exchanges with

the history to which he belongs thanks to the element of language. This moment of doubling should no doubt have its place in a critical reading. To recognize and respect all its classical exigencies is not easy and requires all the instruments of traditional criticism. Without this recognition and this respect, critical production would risk developing in any direction at all and authorize itself to say almost anything. But this indispensable guardrail has always only protected, it has never opened, a reading.[64]

of the part in question as being *in question*, a thing in need of making:

One must be an inventor to read well. As the proverb says, 'He that would bring home the wealth of the Indies, must carry out the wealth of the Indies'. There is then creative reading as well as creative writing. When the mind is braced by labour and invention, the page of whatever book we read becomes luminous with manifold allusion.[65]

Whether we like it or not, quotation always exceeds its quota and says more than we think. To get its measure is to attempt to imagine where one thing starts and another begins, perhaps even where one starts and another begins.

With love's light wings did I o'er-perch these walls;
For stony limits cannot hold love out,
And what love can do that dares love attempt.[66]

THEORY

Theory with a capital 'T'. Pronounced to rhyme with 'weary' or 'dreary'. A term which 'since the 1960s . . . has belonged to the lexicon of the intra-academic ideological war'.[67] Pronounced to rhyme with 'beery' or 'leery'. Apt to be treated, in journalistic prose, as a matter of intellectual fashion or personal predilection, or else as a kind of circus where, to quote Derrida, different theories appear 'as little wooden horses on a merry-go-round where New Criticism, structuralism, poststructuralism, new socio-historicism, and then again formalism, nonformalism, and so on . . . follow one another'.[68] Object of considerable animus in some. Cause of intense intellectual excitement in others. A term which refers to 'an unbounded group of writings about everything under the sun'.[69] A term which risks suggesting that reading is a question of applying a set of precepts and procedures formulaically to this text or that – as in the injunction in our rubric to espouse a 'critical methodology'. Opposite of: proof. Opposite of: practice. Opposite of: unthinking purblind stupidity. Opposite of: common sense. Anagrammatises into: Eh Troy! . . . He Tory . . . Her toy . . . Thy ore. Taking flight from these anagrams, we might say that Theory has launched a thousand academic sallies; can lapse into its own forms of conservatism; is something to pin your colours to, or take up arms against; can be a play thing or a prompt for the most serious play; is a real treasure, an investment, a resource for speculation.

To put things more soberly, literary or critical theory has for the last half a century been an essential component of the academic study of literature and art. Its impetus is questing and radical, questioning and exploratory. Accounts of its origins tend to start with the names of the big discourse-launching decenterers – Marx, Freud and Nietzsche – writers whose accounts of the world, the psyche and language have effected a bouleversement in our ways of thinking about and describing those things, a conversion in the ways in which we relate to ourselves and our environment and culture. Theory draws on intellectual innovations and experiments across the range of the 'human sciences' and beyond – on philosophy, linguistics, psychoanalysis, historiography, sociology, for example – and is also inspired by civil rights movements and political activists and thinkers. Its aim is to explain, explore, analyse, appreciate, criticise, respond to or think about all aspects of cultural life, amongst which are included literature and art. Conversely theorists often find resources *in* literature and art to help account for other aspects of our world too. And what many of them share is, as Nicholas Royle has recently put it, 'a commitment to questioning, experimenting and tampering with language'.[70] Their texts, he continues, 'interfere with any straightforward distinction between creative and critical writing'. Amongst theoretical works whose very work of questioning and reflection requires such experimenting, tampering and interference, we might include Maurice Blanchot's *The Infinite Conversation*, with its shifts into dialogue form; Julia Kristeva's 'Stabat Mater', where the exploration of maternity and the figure of the Virgin Mary takes place through a text in which is enwombed and encradled another text, and where the writing is at times upright, fixed, orderly and dispassionate and at others fluid, pulsing, quick and corporeal; and Georges Bataille's *Inner*

Experience, where the nature of that experience is tracked and testified to in the first-person comings and goings, rhapsodies and reflections, of its thinking voice.[71] In none of these works is the form of the writing, and the troubling of its language, simply window-dressing. It is rather that the very nature of what is being theorised, conceptualised or written about demands an adjustment and an inventiveness in the writing through which the thinking is conducted.

For all these reasons, it might seem that Theory participates in the very energies and aspirations which also animate creative criticism. And it is certainly the case that a number of the writers in this book – notably Barthes, Derrida and Cixous – are usually amongst those named when a litany of Theorists is intoned, and that others – Sedgwick and Wood – draw on and reinvent the work of Theorists. But it is also true to say that Theory is often attended by an atmosphere of intellectual phobia and anxiety, and that many see it as offering nothing but tyrannical orthodoxies, cumbersome, ugly prose, and formulaic zombie-criticism, anathema to the life of the artworks it treats and utterly counter to any spirit of invention.[72] Think for example of the dry-as-a-bone but vicious dead-panning of Dyer. He's a guest just as welcome to the creative-critical party we're hosting here as is Derrida, but look what he writes:

> In my final year at university there was a great deal of fuss about
> course reform. Instead of ploughing through everything from
> *Beowulf* to Beckett, academics like Terry Eagleton were proposing
> a 'theory' option. I didn't know what theory was but it sounded
> radical and challenging. Within a few years 'theory', whatever it
> was, had achieved a position of domination in English departments
> throughout Britain. Synoptic works of theory were pouring through
> the presses. Fifteen years down the line these texts still appear
> radical and challenging except in one or two details, namely that they
> are neither radical nor challenging.[73]

A cutting account indeed. How to reconcile it with the inclusion in this *Anthology* of many so-called theorists? Should we just argue that creative criticism is a broad church, and that it takes all sorts to make a world? That sounds a bit soft: it denies the edge of the works gathered here, and also what they share. Better, perhaps, to say that there is good theory and bad theory, inventive theory and sclerotised theory; that inventive theory always bears an uneasy, critical relation to the notion of Theory itself; and indeed that the very notion that there is such a thing as Theory is a fabrication. Theory 'itself' is a force-field or battle-ground, not a monolith; and it's this, in part, that gives it its energy. Moreover, and this is perhaps the nub of the matter, any single 'theory', insofar as it is worthy of the name, has an inventive, game-changing thrust. But at the same time, even to have this thrust it must have a set of identifiable traits or properties, which can always be mindlessly taken up, ventriloquised, repeated robotically, and so on. Derrida, writing of the fate of the inventive processes of thinking and writing he has called 'deconstruction', suggests that this is just inevitable: 'even on the side where one generally tries to situate "deconstruction",' he writes, '"deconstructionists" and "deconstructionism" represent an effort to reappropriate, tame, normalize this writing in order to reconstitute a new "theory"'.[74] There's no simple choice – and that's true of the work gathered in the present volume too. You (for it is up to *you*) could choose simply to model yourself on one of the critics gathered here, taking up his or her writing as a 'methodology' to be applied willy-nilly to what you read or look at. But you would be missing what is best about it, namely the fact that *it* eschews the fatuously formulaic or the mindlessly methodological.

Creative critics – to put things in a nutshell – aren't afraid of theory, because they aren't afraid of thinking. Any creative critic worthy of that name is against sclerotised, necrotised, lobotomised -isming. Creative critics, that is to say, resist the instrumentalising of thought and the mechanising of criticism. But – and this is the crucial thing – they don't do so against theory, or in favour of some pure realm of aesthetic experience or blokey plain sense, or in the interests of more beautiful writing, or in the name of some non-existent Everyman reader. Such defences and evasions are as sclerotised, necrotised and lobotomised as the isms and posts they oppose.

PLAGIARISM

Be original – but not *too* original: thus the implicit counsel of our rubric. Acknowledge your sources, but make your own argument. If you've borrowed an argument, acknowledge that too. Be clear about what's yours and what's not. Keep the boundaries of intellectual property intact. Ignore the fact that when you read or look, those boundaries seem to dissolve; the fact that images haunt you like your own dreams, become the stuff of those dreams; the fact that words speak in you that aren't your own, and merge into the fabric of your own inner voice, a voice that is always made up of other voices.

Creative critics, in terms of intellectual property laws, are something like burglars, or perhaps communists. See in particular, in this *Anthology*, Benjamin Friedlander, whose 'Gertrude Stein: A Retrospective Criticism' steals a work of criticism by Edgar Allen Poe. Out goes Rufus Dawes, the original subject, and in comes Stein. In deferring absolutely to the authorised voice of another – there is little that is new here save for the swapping of the words of two ostensibly unrelated writers – something has been made to happen, to take shape, around the awkward matters of, precisely, voice, authority and property. Barthes's *Lover's Discourse* is another example. Barthes's writing, lover's writing, does a dawn raid on the literature it loves. Its relation to that literature is of a magpie acquisitiveness: he takes what he wants to voice his own needs and desires.

A licence to plagiarise, then? Yes and no. Property laws are certainly flouted here, but flouted in the name of a fidelity to the law of literature, or of thinking, or of art. These critics take responsibility for their thefts, singularly signing, offering something back in acknowledgement of the artwork's generosity, its giving itself up to whoever likes to pilfer it. In so doing, they point to the writing of criticism as an engagement with the question of responsibility, the variously pressing need to do justice to one's text or topic or discipline or occasion. In inheriting and adopting the received conventions of critical writing we allow ourselves to assume the matter of responsibility has been settled out of court, elsewhere, by others, when it is rather in the nature of the encounter with the artwork to call conventions to account: to ask again what responsibility might mean. The merest step away from convention in critical writing is liable to generate anxiety on the part of the critic; this is unavoidable, and, yes, it can be an unsettling experience, especially within the context of an institution dependent for its status and continuance on the tacit acceptance of normative protocol. There is no easy solution here. The best that can be said – and it is quite something to say – is that to attempt to work with the question of responsibility in one's writing is to be close to the heart of what such writing can be, which is to say close to the possibility of writing conceived in the most ambitious terms. For this is after all a question of politics – not the identity parade politics-by-rote that characterises so much critical prose, but a politics that begins, or rather has already begun, at the cellular level, the level of each of the countless small and seemingly insignificant moves we make as we conceive and compose; those moves we make as we make and which will be our making, several of which we have sought to anatomise in the course of our introduction. Creative criticism demands much of us, as writers and as readers. In that demand rests its promise.

WORD COUNT

Creative critics make their words *count*.

DEADLINE

There is a limit to our writing (thankfully?), a line drawn, usually by others, to mark an end after which we shall need to let go and let it be. Running up to this finish line, egg in spoon, is what we shall come to recognise as the timeline of the writing, during whose course will happen all the reading and the thinking, not to say all the living into and out of which the task at hand intrudes. How much critical writing is done in the early hours, fuelled by the promise of next-day delivery? How much is done through the course of a quiet day as our attention moves variously in the vicinity of the materials at hand? And how much happens piecemeal over weeks and months, perhaps longer, as the words of another turn their way round and about our days and nights?

Deadlines and submission dates mark in bold the always time-bound state of our writing, and in so doing signal also the convention according to which such bounds tend to remain unstated within the writing itself. Deadlines mark the erasure of the time in which writing will turn out to have happened. But while there is much to be said for getting things in on time, it does not follow that we should therefore keep quiet about how we have spent our days. Introducing his diaristic account of six fortunate months spent on-and-off in the company of two Poussin paintings, T. J. Clark is surprised to find no point of comparison for his chosen form: 'a record of looking taking place and changing over time', hence of the 'slow work' of 'coming to terms'.[75] This is the same slow work acknowledged in Dyer's ambulatory narration of time spent with Lawrence, although Dyer writes in a less stately register, the slowness being here a case of self-confessed slacker tactics. Paintings have a different relation with time to that of novels, and yet critical writing on each tends to share in common a forgetting of how that relation figures variously in our own attention: a tendency 'to have always embedded in the *form* of the narrative the (false) suggestion that once upon a time, back there and in the present, at the end and the beginning, the picture lived everlastingly here and now' – and not only the picture, or the novel.[76] The convention of criticism is to present our findings after the manner of a *fait accompli*, and so to keep below stairs our distracted comings and goings. The implication is that all was always already running like clockwork.

An acknowledgement of the hidden time, the counter-time, of critical writing marks creative criticism. Clark's process form and Dyer's dilatory confessions are only the most obvious instances of this. Neither attempts to tidy away the timeline of their respective engagements, making of the writing a record of something being made rather than of a made something: the finding rather than the found, or rather the finding within the found. On the flip side of such processual tactics is Barthes's refusal of order, in particular the received time of story, indeed of anything '*classified*: organized, hierarchized, arranged with a view to an end (a settlement)'.[77] Just as Dyer's reluctance to settle down to the task is a calculatedly Lawrentian move, so is Barthes's resistance to order a mark of respect for the accidental nature of his subject, which is our always untimely being in love, with the many incidents that befall us on such occasions. To maintain the incidental nature of the lover's discourse 'it was necessary to choose an *absolutely insignificant* order', an alphabeticised naming of figures entirely arbitrary in its workings, and felt as such by the reader. Barthes declares the book to be 'fragments', a favoured form, as we have seen – 'so many fragments, so many beginnings, so many pleasures' – the time of which is discontinuous, an intermezzo in which *timbre* takes the place of 'development'.[78]

Allied to writings of process and discontinuity are those performative exercises in which the time of our reading is more pointedly disrupted and divided: by the division of the space of the page, for example, or through the use of experiments with typography.[79] Lines are disrupted here: juxtaposed, multiplied, crossed. No doubt we need to submit to deadlines, but not in such a way as to naturalise or internalise a logic of the straight, the true and the final. Speaking of which . . .

We are working to our own deadline, a date by which we have to submit our manuscript. We confess that we have had to ask for several extensions. Will we make this one? Time is against us. And there is always more to say. Perhaps the best way to frustrate the impending sense of an ending would be to turn our attention, and yours, back to before the beginning of this co-written venture into the possibility of a pairing – creative criticism. For our venture has been twinned all along with a singular twosome . . .

> SB: The cover of this book is the image of an object made by the artists Kimberley and Karl Foster – working as hedsor – in response to their reading of Sarah Wood's writing, in 'Anew Again', of what there is to be made of looking at and listening to Picasso and Wallace Stevens.
>
> CC: OK, let's look at it then. Whatever its prehistory – the Fosters' fostering of Wood's sounding of Stevens's rhyming of Picasso's paintings of guitars – it nevertheless comes out of the blue. Nevertheless: and despite 'out of the blue' being a cliché, and despite its being one quoted and reinvented already in Sarah Wood's essay. Something old, something new. It comes out of the blue, the old-new blue.
>
> SB: You're saying 'it'. Yes, there's a single image, but what comes here is two things in relation, two in-themselves complicated things. Together they don't form a whole but nor are they simply separate. They're an odd couple, though not entirely unlike or unlikely.
>
> SB and CC (almost in unison): Such friends as never.
>
> CC: Luminously strange, they reflect the light and so irradiate and open up the space, the twilight or even outer-space blue-black dark, in which they appear.
>
> SB: These things are already-made, ungainsayably there.
>
> CC: And they weren't there before –
>
> SB: – or rather, there is a before in which they weren't, and they make their own before, cast it back behind them.
>
> CC: They ob-trude, and arrest us. There's no missing them. They are objects – a word which in light of them starts to take on a stroppily obstinate force: ob- ob- ob- madly prepositional: in the direction of, towards, against, in the way of, in front of, in view of, on account of – but whichever way you take it jettisoned, thrust, thrown, like a gauntlet. Creative criticism registers the way works of art don't just passively lie there, all before us, as the world did to Adam and Eve, but come at us in some way. We are surprised, or stolen up upon, find ourselves caught. It needn't be immediate; it is what turns out to have happened. It could take the form of an obsession, perhaps. We have to keep going back.

SB: Back. What I pick out first is the guitar, simple as that. It's the most solid-looking and also familiar thing here, and made thingier in its oddity. It's a Narnia guitar, still with the magic of its making in it, like the lamppost sprouting in the clearing in the wood. Next – though it happens almost at the same time; it's the glitch or stutter in my looking, the double take – I see the uncanny hand, a hand where a headboard should be. This is an encreatured-instrument, puppet-contraption, faintly monstrous hybrid, a sorcerer's apprentice guitar. There's something sinister here –

CC: – and that's a left hand, isn't it?

SB: But it's not a living hand, warm and capable, though it resembles one closely enough to be a bit spooky. It is at once the poised, string-holding, string-twitching hand of a puppeteer, all cool, calling-the-shots command, and, at the same time, a puppet hand too, itself strung by the strings it appears to wield, and which its fingers seem poised to fret yet will never touch. It's as though the guitar foolishly or hubristically imagines it can play itself; an instrument yearning to become automaton. It dreams of being self-moving and self-sufficient yet is hamstrung by its very desire. I think of Midas – all he touches turned to gold, strung up like a kipper. Be careful what you wish for. Perhaps this is what Eliot's auto-telic art object might look like? Caught in its own loop with nothing to love or link with, all taut restraint, but utterly vulnerable too. Still unravish'd.

CC: Hang on a minute. Hold the pathos. It's not all about that Thing, that Instrument, the one that wants to touch itself but can't. Instead it's nudged, jostled, budged and bumpsy daisied from the side. We get a new angle on it, a quizzical askance relation – and how silly and po-faced it looks for a moment, thanks to this second thing, this second object come to object to the first. What *is* that?

SB: A hanging frame? An outline? A bauble or Christmas tree decoration?

CC: Whatever it is, it's its own thing, turned elsewhere, outwards, towards us and apart. No mimic, iterated or air guitar this. Or rather – it just doesn't give a fig for secondariness, *it* doesn't get hung or strung up on such things. It's a cheeky take on the guitar, but it's there in front, for God's sake. Can we say that *this* is what plays the guitar, then, or plays on it – this and the invisible hand that hung it here, set it echoing?

SB: I think so, but then what we mean by 'play' would have to change. We'd have to play with 'play'. This second-first airy-object plays the guitar but in its own idiom. Impatient with the inarticulate macho tragedy of unheard melodies, it hugs and twines and cups the guitar's curves in places only, and at tangents, in a sinuous language of shapes and softs and rounds and arcs and cs –

CC: – *and* esses.

SB: Back. To look at the ensemble again. I see its lines and curves, its shapes and sections, its lights and darks, its apples and pears, its spiral stairs.

CC: Oh, *yes*! It rhymes, talks Cockney. Didn't expect to find that kind of slang, here where, marionettes and monsters notwithstanding, some classical restraint prevails, some held-back orderliness, a sense of things placed. Placed but – I squint again – suspended – impossibly, mid-air. No strings visible, just a hovering. And we suspend our disbelief along with them. We don't need there to be supports; it holds us there, in the air.

SB and CC (together): And it is this ether that our *Anthology and Guide* inhabits. We end our introduction here, but the dialogues, correspondences, connections, discontinuities, breaks, calls and responses continue in what follows. It's all still happening.

NOTES

1. Gregory L. Ulmer, 'The Object of Post-Criticism', in Hal Foster (ed.), *Postmodern Culture* (London: Pluto, 1985), pp. 83–110; Lisa Samuels and Jerome J. McGann, 'Deformance and Interpretation', *New Literary History* 30 (1999): 25–56; Stephen Collis, *Through Words of Others: Susan Howe and Anarcho-Scholasticism* (Victoria, BC: University of Victoria Department of English, 2006); Heather Kerr and Amanda Nettlebeck (eds), *The Space Between: Australian Woman Writing FictoCriticism* (Perth: University of Western Australia Press, 1998); Daniel T. O'Hara, *The Romance of Interpretation: Visionary Criticism from Pater to de Man* (New York: Columbia University Press, 1985); Lisa Samuels, 'Creating Criticism: An Introduction to *Anarchism Is Not Enough*', in Laura Riding, *Anarchism Is Not Enough* (1928) (Berkeley: University of California Press, 2001); Geoffrey Hartman, *Criticism in the Wilderness: The Study of Literature Today*, 2nd edn (New Haven: Yale University Press, 2007).

2. Harper Lee, *To Kill a Mockingbird* (1960) (London: Arrow Books, 2010), p. 20.

3. Marcel Proust, 'On Reading: Translator's Preface to *Sesame and Lilies*' (1906), in *Marcel Proust and John Ruskin On Reading*, trans. and ed. Damion Searls (London: Hesperus Press, 2011), p. 18.

4. T. S. Eliot, 'The Perfect Critic' (1920), in *The Sacred Wood: Essays on Poetry and Criticism* (London: Faber, 1997), pp. 1–13, p. 6; and Eliot, 'The Function of Criticism' (1923), in *Selected Essays 1917–1932*, rev. edn (New Jersey: Houghton Mifflin Harcourt, 1950), pp. 12–24, p. 20.

5. See for example Terry Eagleton, *Literary Theory: An Introduction* (Oxford: Blackwell, 1983), pp. 30–53; and Clare Connors, *Literary Theory: A Beginner's Guide* (Oxford: Oneworld, 2010), pp. 33–9.

6. W. K. Wimsatt, *Hateful Contraries: Studies in Literature and Criticism* (Kentucky: University of Kentucky Press, 1965), p. 244.

7. Cleanth Brooks, *The Well-Wrought Urn: Studies in the Structure of Poetry* (1947) (London: Harcourt, Brace & Co., 1970), p. 203.

8. Robert Duncan, 'The Law I Love Is Major Mover', *The Opening of the Field* (1960) (New York: New Directions, 1973), pp. 10–11.

9. Michel de Montaigne, *The Complete Essays*, trans. M. A. Screech (London: Penguin, 2003).

10. Virginia Woolf, 'The Modern Essay' (1925), *The Common Reader: Volume 1* (London: Vintage, 2003), pp. 211–22, p. 211.

11. Brian Dillon, 'Energy and Rue', *Frieze* 151 (Nov–Dec 2012), <https://www.frieze.com/issue/article/energy-rue> (last accessed 1 May 2013).

12. Montaigne, 'On Experience', *Essays*, pp. 1,207–69, p. 1,222.

13. Erich Auerbach, *Mimesis: The Representation of Reality in Western Literature*, trans. Willard R. Trask (Princeton: Princeton University Press, 1953), p. 292.

14. Montaigne, *Essays*, p. 1,207.

15. Jean Starobinski, 'Can One Define the Essay?' (1983), excerpted in Carl H. Klaus and Ned Stuckley-French (eds), *Essayists on the Essay: Montaigne to our Time* (Iowa: University of Iowa Press, 2012), pp. 110–15, pp. 110–11.

16. T. W. Adorno, 'The Essay as Form' (1958), trans. Bob Hullot-Kentor and Frederic Will, *New German Critique* 32 (1984), pp. 151–71, p. 152.

17. Jacques Derrida, *Of Grammatology*, trans. Gayatri Chakravorty Spivak (Baltimore: Johns Hopkins University Press, 1976), p. 162.

18. Adorno, 'The Essay as Form', p. 154.

19. Ibid. p. 171.

20. Rachel Blau DuPlessis, 'f-Words: An Essay on the Essay', *American Literature* 68: 1 (1996), pp. 15–45, pp. 16–17.

21. Barthes is the arch-fragmenter. See the run of three entries on the subject – 'The circle of fragments'; 'The fragment as illusion'; 'From the fragment to the journal' – in *Roland Barthes by Roland Barthes* (1975), trans. Richard Howard (London: Macmillan, 1977), pp. 92–5.

22. See Frank Kermode, *The Sense of an Ending: Studies in the Theory of Fiction*, 2nd edn (Oxford: Oxford University Press, 2000).

23. Wayne Koestenbaum, 'Heidegger's Mistress', in *My 1980s and Other Essays* (New York: Farrar, Straus and Giroux, 2013), pp. 15–25, p. 19.

24. See especially Philippe Lacoue-Labarthe and Jean-Luc Nancy, *The Literary Absolute: The Theory of Literature in German Romanticism* (1978), trans. Philip Barnard and Cheryl Lester (New York: State University of New York Press, 1988); and Simon Critchley, *Very Little . . . Almost Nothing: Death, Philosophy, Literature* (London: Routledge, 1997), pp. 105–17.

25. Friedrich Schlegel, *Lucinde and the Fragments* (1798), trans. Peter Firchow (Minneapolis: University of Minnesota Press, 1971), p. 189.

26. Charles Bernstein, 'The Revenge of the Poet-Critic, or The Parts are Greater Than the Sum of the Whole', in *My Way: Speeches and Poems* (Chicago: University of Chicago Press, 1999), pp. 3–17, p. 12.

27. Samuels, 'Creating Criticism: An Introduction to *Anarchism Is Not Enough*', p. xiv.

28. Charles Olson, *Call Me Ishmael* (1947), in *Collected Prose*, ed. Donald Allen and Benjamin Friedlander (Berkeley and Los Angeles: University of California Press, 1997), pp. 1–105, pp. 17–18; Susan Howe, *My Emily Dickinson* (Berkeley: North Atlantic Books, 1985), p. 35.

29. Robert Duncan, *The H.D. Book*, ed. Michael Boughn and Victor Coleman (Berkeley: University of California Press, 2011), p. 224 and p. 434.

30. Ibid. p. 343.

31. Roland Barthes, *A Lover's Discourse* (1977), trans. Richard Howard (London: Vintage, 2002), p. 9; Kevin Kopelson, 'Music Lessons', in *Beethoven's Kiss: Pianism, Perversion, and the Mastery of Desire* (Stanford: Stanford University Press, 1996), pp. 117–36, p. 118 (also in Chapter 9 of this *Anthology*).

32. See Martin Heidegger, *Being and Time*, trans. John Macquarrie and Edward Robinson (Oxford: Blackwell, 1962): 'The question of whether there is a world at all and whether its Being can be proved makes no sense if it is raised by *Dasein* as Being-in-the-world; and who else would raise it? . . . The question of the "Reality" of the "external world" gets raised without any previous clarification of the *phenomenon of the world* as such. Factically, the "problem of the external *world*" is constantly oriented with regard to entities within-the-world (Things and Objects)' (pp. 246–7).

33. Eve Kosofsky Sedgwick, *Touching Feeling: Affect, Pedagogy and Performativity* (Durham, NC: Duke University Press, 2003), p. 8.

34. Boris Pasternak, *Doctor Zhivago* (1957), trans. Max Hayward and Manya Harari (New York: Ballantine Books, 1981), part 3, p. 68.

35. D. W. Winnicott, 'Playing: Creative Activity and the Search for the Self', in *Playing and Reality* (1971) (London and New York: Routledge, 2006), pp. 71–86, p. 73.

36. D. W. Winnicott, 'Creativity and its Origins', in *Playing and Reality*, pp. 87–114, p. 87 and pp. 92–3.

37. Sarah Wood, 'Anew Again', in Sarah Wood and Jonathan Tiplady, *The Blue Guitar* (London: Artwords, 2007), pp. 18–36, p. 20; also in Chapter 14 of this *Anthology*.

38. Cf. John Wilkinson, 'Following the Poem', in *The Lyric Touch: Essays on the Poetry of Excess* (Cambridge: Salt Publishing, 2007), pp. 195–212.

39. For a good account of some of the adventures of the 'you', especially in lyric poetry but elsewhere too, see Jonathan Culler's 'Apostrophe' in his *The Pursuit of Signs: Semiotics, Literature and Deconstruction*, 2nd edn (London: Routledge, 2002), pp. 149–71.

40. Joel Elias Spingarn, *Creative Criticism and Other Essays* (New York: Kennikat Press, 1964). For a discussion of Spingarn, see Gerald Graff, *Professing Literature: An Institutional History* (Chicago: University of Chicago Press, 1987), pp. 126–8. Graff's book is also worth consulting more generally, for its account of the history of academic literary studies in the United States, and the tensions and interactions played out therein, between scholars and 'creative writers'.

41. Raymond Williams, *Keywords: A Vocabulary of Culture and Society*, rev. edn (London: Fontana, 1983), p. 85.

42. Alexander Pope, 'An Essay on Criticism' (1744), *Poetical Works*, ed. Herbert Davis (Oxford: Oxford University Press, 1989), pp. 62–86, p. 64, lines 13–14.

43. Eliot, 'The Function of Criticism', p. 19.

44. Matthew Arnold, 'The Function of Criticism at the Present Time' (1864), in *Culture and Anarchy and Other Writings*, ed. Stefan Collini (Cambridge: Cambridge University Press, 1993), pp. 26–51, p. 51.

45. Ibid. p. 51.

46. Oscar Wilde, 'The Critic as Artist: A Dialogue in Two Parts' (1891), in *De Profundis, The Ballad of Reading Gaol, and Other Writings* (Ware: Wordsworth Classics, 1999), pp. 101–71, p. 119.

47. William Wordsworth, *The Prelude* (1805), ed. Jonathan Wordsworth, M. H. Abrams and Stephen Gill (London and New York: Norton, 1979), book 3, lines 168–74.

48. Samuel Taylor Coleridge, *Biographia Literaria: or, Biographical Sketches of My Literary Life and Opinions* (1817) (Montana: Kessinger Publishing, 2005), chapter 13, p. 144.

49. Wordsworth, *The Prelude*, book 3, line 669.

50. Two good accounts of the installation of creative writing as a university discipline are D. G. Myers, *The Elephants Teach: Creative Writing since 1880* (Chicago: University of Chicago Press, 2006), and Paul Dawson, *Creative Writing and the New Humanities* (New York: Routledge, 2005).

51. Williams, *Keywords*, p. 84.

52. Jacques Derrida, 'Force and Signification' (1963), in *Writing and Difference*, trans. Alan Bass (London: Routledge, 2005), pp. 1–35, p. 10.

53. Mary Shelley, *Frankenstein, or The Modern Prometheus – The 1818 Text* (Oxford: Oxford World's Classics, 2008), p. 36.

54. Susan Howe, 'BIRTH-MARK', quoted in Collis, *Through Words of Others*, p. 10 and p. 13.

55. Charles Perrault, 'Bluebeard', in *The Annotated Classic Fairy Tales*, trans. and ed. Maria Tatar (New York: W.W. Norton, 2002), pp. 145–57, p. 149.

56. Horace, *Satires, Epistles, Ars Poetica*, trans. H. R. Fairclough (Harvard: Loeb, 1989), I, i, 106.

57. Arnold, 'The Function of Criticism', p. 51.

58. Jürgen Habermas, *The Philosophical Discourse of Modernity*, trans. Frederick G. Lawrence (Cambridge, MA: MIT Press, 1998), pp. 209–10.

59. Eliot, 'The Function of Criticism', p. 19.

60. Hartman, *Criticism in the Wilderness*, p. 190.

61. W. S. Graham, 'Johann Joachim Quantz's Five Lessons', *Implements in Their Places* (London: Faber and Faber, 1977), p. 48.
62. Adorno, 'The Essay as Form', p. 154.
63. Friedrich Schlegel, quoted in Hartman, *Criticism in the Wilderness*, p. 159.
64. Derrida, *Of Grammatology*, p. 158.
65. Ralph Waldo Emerson, 'The American Scholar' (1849), in *Collected Works of Ralph Waldo Emerson, Volume 1*, ed. Robert E. Spiller and Alfred R. Ferguson (Harvard: Harvard University Press, 1971), pp. 49–70, p. 58.
66. William Shakespeare, *Romeo and Juliet*, ed. Jill L. Levenson (Oxford: Oxford University Press, 2000), II, i, 109–11.
67. Hélène Cixous, 'Post-word', trans. Eric Prenowitz, in Martin McQuillan, Graeme Macdonald, Stephen Thomson and Robin Purves (eds), *Post-Theory: New Directions in Criticism* (Edinburgh: Edinburgh University Press, 1999), pp. 209–13, p. 211.
68. Jacques Derrida, 'Some Statements and Truisms about Neologisms, Newisms, Postisms, Parisitisms, and Other Small Seismisms', in David Carroll (ed.), *The States of Theory* (New York: Columbia University Press, 1990), pp. 63–94, p. 78.
69. Jonathan Culler, *Literary Theory: A Very Short Introduction* (Oxford: Oxford University Press, 2000), p. 3.
70. Nicholas Royle, 'Composition and Decomposition', in *Times Higher Education*, 28 March 2013, <http://www.timeshighereducation.co.uk/features/composition-and-decomposition/2002751.fullarticle> (last accessed 24 May 2013).
71. Maurice Blanchot, *The Infinite Conversation* (1969), trans. Susan Hanson (Minneapolis and London: University of Minnesota Press, 1993); Julia Kristeva, 'Stabat Mater' (1977), trans. Léon S. Roudiez, in *The Kristeva Reader*, ed. Toril Moi (Oxford: Blackwell, 1996), pp. 161–86; Georges Bataille, *Inner Experience*, trans. Leslie Ann Boldt (Albany: State University of New York Press, 1988).
72. On the subject of the quality as writing of theoretically informed academic prose, see the essays collected in Jonathan Culler and Kevin Lamb (eds), *Just Being Difficult? Academic Writing in the Public Arena* (Stanford: Stanford University Press, 2003).
73. Geoff Dyer, *Out of Sheer Rage: In the Shadow of D. H. Lawrence* (London: Abacus, 1998), pp. 99–100; also in Chapter 6 of this *Anthology*.
74. Derrida, 'Some Statements and Truisms', p. 75.
75. T. J. Clark, *The Sight of Death: An Experiment in Art Writing* (New Haven: Yale University Press, 2006), p. 5.
76. Clark, *The Sight of Death*, pp. 8–9.
77. Barthes, *Lover's Discourse*, p. 8.
78. Barthes, *Roland Barthes by Roland Barthes* (1975), p. 94.
79. For example, Wayne Koestenbaum, *Hotel Theory* (New York: Soft Skull Press, 2007); Juliana Spahr, 'Spiderwasp or Literary Criticism' (1998), in Mark Wallace and Steven Marks (eds), *Telling It Slant: Avant-Garde Poetics of the 1990s* (Tuscaloosa: University of Alabama Press, 2001), pp. 405–28; and John Cage, 'Where Are We Going? And What Are We Doing?', included in the present volume.

SUGGESTED FURTHER READING

The following is an unashamedly personal selection from the writing that we have found inspiring and challenging, and which has had a particular influence on our thinking about this *Anthology*. It is offered here as a supplement to those works cited in our introduction and in the headnotes to the fourteen anthologised pieces. There are many more texts we might have included; no doubt there are texts whose absence you will feel as a significant omission. As we've found during the preparation of our book, there is always another striking instance of creative criticism waiting to be encountered, always another account that promises to be the final word. And so it goes. The open and the provisional are two of the presiding conditions of the anthology as a form, nowhere more conditionally than in the following suggestions.

Creative criticism

For the sake of sanity we have limited this selection to works from the twentieth and twenty-first centuries.

Antin, David, *Talking* (1972) (Champagne: Dalkey Archive, 2001).

Baker, Nicholson, *U & I: A True Story* (London: Granta, 1991).

Bal, Mieke, *Louis Bourgeois' Spider: The Architecture of Art Writing* (Chicago: University of Chicago Press, 2002).

Barthes, Roland, *Camera Lucida: Reflections of Photography* (1980), trans. Richard Howard (London: Jonathan Cape, 1982).

Barthes, Roland, *Roland Barthes by Roland Barthes* (1975), trans. Richard Howard (New York: Hill & Wang, 2010).

Bartlett, Neil, *Who Was That Man? A Present for Mr Oscar Wilde* (London: Serpent's Tail, 1988).

Bernstein, Charles, *Content's Dream: Essays 1975–1984* (1986) (Evanstown: Northwestern University Press, 2001).

Bonnefoy, Yves, *The Arrière-pays* (1972), trans. Stephen Romer (Calcutta: Seagull Books, 2012).

Brenner, Gerry, *Performative Criticism: Experiments in Reader Response* (New York: State University of New York Press, 2004).

Briggs, Kate, *Exercise in Pathetic Criticism* (York: information as material, 2011).

Cage, John, *Empty Words: Writings '73–'78* (Middletown, CT: Wesleyan University Press, 1981).

Cage, John, *I–VI* (1990) (Middletown, CT: Wesleyan University Press, 1997).

Carson, Anne, *Eros the Bittersweet* (Champagne: Dalkey Archive, 1998).

Cascella, Daniela, *En Abîme: Listening, Reading, Writing: An Archival Fiction* (London: Zero Books, 2012).

Cha, Teresa Hak Kyung, *Dictée* (New York: Tanam Press, 1982).

Cixous, Hélène, *Hyperdream*, trans. Beverley Bic Brahic (Cambridge: Polity, 2009).

Cixous, Hélène, *Zero's Neighbour: Sam Beckett*, trans. Laurent Milesi (Cambridge: Polity, 2010).

Clark, T. J., *The Sight of Death: An Experiment in Art Writing* (New Haven: Yale University Press, 2006).

Derrida, Jacques, *Glas* (1974), trans. John P. Leavey, Jr, and Richard Rand (Lincoln, NE: University of Nebraska Press, 1986).

Derrida, Jacques, *The Postcard: From Socrates to Freud and Beyond* (1980), trans. Alan Bass (Chicago: University of Chicago Press, 1987).

Derrida, Jacques, 'Tympan', in *Margins of Philosophy* (1972), trans. Alan Bass (Chicago: University of Chicago Press, 1982), pp. ix–xxix.

Doolittle, Hilda, *Tribute to Freud* (1956) (Manchester: Carcanet, 1985).

Duncan, Robert, *The H.D. Book*, ed. Michael Boughn and Victor Coleman (Berkeley: University of California Press, 2011).

Dyer, Geoff, *Zona: A Book about a Film about a Journey to a Room* (Edinburgh: Canongate, 2012).

Glossator: Practice and Theory of Commentary, <http://glossator.org>.

Halsey, Alan, *The Text of Shelley's Death* (1995) (Sheffield: West House Books, 2001).

Harryman, Carla, *Adorno's Noise* (Ithaca, NY: Essay Press, 2008).

Howe, Susan, *My Emily Dickinson* (Berkeley: North Atlantic Books, 1985).

Johnson, Kent, *A Question Mark Above the Sun: Documents on the Mystery Surrounding a Famous Poem 'By' Frank O'Hara* (Buffalo: Starcherone Books, 2012).

Josipovici, Gabriel, *Touch* (New Haven: Yale University Press, 1996).

Koestenbaum, Wayne, *Hotel Theory* (New York: Soft Skull Press, 2007).

Koestenbaum, Wayne, *Humiliation* (London: Notting Hill Editions, 2011).

Koestenbaum, Wayne, *The Queen's Throat: Opera, Homosexuality and the Mystery of Desire* (1993) (Cambridge, MA: Da Capo Press, 2001).

Mars-Jones, Adam, *Noriko Smiling* (London: Notting Hill Editions, 2011).

Mavor, Carol, *Black and Blue: The Bruising Passion of* Camera Lucida, La Jetée, Sans Soleil, *and* Hiroshima mon amour (Durham, NC: Duke University Press, 2012).

Morlock, Forbes, and Sharon Kivland, *Freud and the Gift of Flowers* (York: information as material, 2009).

Morris, Simon, Forbes Morlock and Liz Dalton, *Interpretation Vol. I* (York: information as material, 2002).

Myles, Eileen, *The Importance of Being Iceland: Travel Essays in Art* (Los Angeles: Semiotext(e), 2009).

Olson, Charles, *Call Me Ishmael* (1947), in *Collected Prose*, ed. Donald Allen and Benjamin Friedlander (Berkeley and Los Angeles: University of California Press, 1997), pp. 1–105.

Ratcliffe, Stephen, *Listening to Reading* (New York: State University of New York Press, 2000).

Riding, Laura, *Anarchism Is Not Enough* (1928), ed. Lisa Samuels (Berkeley: University of California Press, 2001).

Robertson, Lisa, *Nilling: Prose* (Toronto: Bookthug, 2012).

Ronnell, Avital, *The Telephone Book: Technology, Schizophrenia, Electric Speech* (Lincoln, NE: University of Nebraska Press, 1989).

Royle, Nicholas, *The Uncanny* (Manchester: Manchester University Press, 2003).

Royle, Nicholas, *Veering: A Theory of Literature* (Edinburgh: Edinburgh University Press, 2012).

Schad, John, and Oliver Tearle (eds), *Crrritic!: Sighs, Cries, Lies, Insults, Outbursts, Hoaxes, Disasters, Letters of Resignation, and Various Other Noises Off in These First and Last Days of Literary Criticism* (Eastbourne: Sussex Academic Press, 2011).

Sedgwick, Eve Kosofsky, *Touching Feeling: Affect, Pedagogy, Performativity* (Durham, NC: Duke University Press, 2003).

Smith, Ali, *Artful* (London: Hamish Hamilton, 2012).

Spahr, Juliana, 'Spiderwasp or Literary Criticism' (1998), in Mark Wallace and Steven Marks (eds), *Telling It Slant: Avant-Garde Poetics of the 1990s* (Tuscaloosa: University of Alabama Press, 2001), pp. 405–28.

Spahr, Juliana, Mark Wallace, Kristin Prevallet and Pam Rehm (eds), *A Poetics of Criticism* (Buffalo: Leave Books, 1994).

Stein, Gertrude, *Selections*, ed. Joan Retallack (Berkeley and Los Angeles: University of California Press, 2008).

Wallace, Mark, and Steven Marks (eds), *Telling It Slant: Avant-Garde Poetics of the 1990s* (Tuscaloosa: University of Alabama Press, 2001).

Wilkinson, John, *The Lyric Touch: Essays on the Poetry of Excess* (Cambridge: Salt Publishing, 2007).

Williams, William Carlos, *Spring and All* (1923) (New Directions, 2011).

Wood, Sarah, 'All the Way to Writing', *Angelaki* 12 (2007): 137–47.

Wood, Sarah, 'Edit', *Mosaic* 39 (2006): 47–57.

Zukofsky, Louis, *Bottom: On Shakespeare* (1963) (Middletown, CT: Wesleyan University Press, 2002).

On creative criticism

Adorno, T. W., 'The Essay as Form' (1958), trans. Bob Hullot-Kentor and Frederic Will, *New German Critique* 32 (1984): 151–71.

Bensamaïa, Reda, *The Barthes Effect: The Essay as Reflective Text*, trans. Pat Fedkiew (Minneapolis: University of Minnesota Press, 1987).

Butt, Gavin (ed.), *After Criticism: New Responses to Art and Performance* (London: Blackwell, 2005).

Collis, Stephen, *Through Words of Others: Susan Howe and Anarcho-Scholasticism* (Victoria, BC: University of Victoria Department of English, 2006).

DuPlessis, Rachel Blau, 'f-Words: An Essay on the Essay', *American Literature* 68: 1 (1996): 15–45.

Hartman, Geoffrey, *Criticism in the Wilderness: The Study of Literature Today*, 2nd edn (New Haven: Yale University Press, 2007).

Hartman, Geoffrey, 'Crossing Over: Literary Commentary as Literature', *Comparative Literature* 28 (1976): 257–76.

Jarvis, Simon, 'An Undeleter for Criticism', *diacritics* 32: 1 (2002): 3–18.

Lukács, György, 'On the Nature and Form of the Essay: A Letter to Leo Popper' (1910), in *Soul and Form*, trans. Anna Bostock, ed. John T. Sanders and Katie Terezakis (New York: Columbia University Press, 2010), pp. 16–34.

McDowell, Frederick P. W. (ed.), *The Poet as Critic* (Evanstown: Northwestern University Press, 1967).

McGann, Jerome, *The Point Is to Change It: Poetry and Criticism in the Continuing Present* (Tuscaloosa: University of Alabama Press, 2007).

O'Hara, Daniel T., *The Romance of Interpretation: Visionary Criticism from Pater to de Man* (New York: Columbia University Press, 1985).

Pope, Rob, *Creativity: Theory, History, Practice* (London: Routledge, 2005).

Remein, Daniel C., '*Kinesis* of Nothing and the *Ousia* of Poetics (Part Review Essay, Part Notes on a Poetics of Auto-Commentary)', *Glossator: Practice and Theory of the Commentary* 3 (2010), <http://solutioperfecta.files.wordpress.com/2011/10/remein-kinesis-of-nothing.pdf> (last accessed 6 September 2013).

Samuels, Lisa, and Jerome McGann, 'Deformance and Interpretation', *New Literary History* 30 (1990): 25–56.

Sedgwick, Eve Kosofsky, 'Teaching "Experimental Critical Writing"', in Peggy Phelan and Jill Lane (eds), *The Ends of Performance* (New York: New York University Press, 1997), pp. 104–15.

Sontag, Susan, 'Against Interpretation' (1964), in *Against Interpretation and Other Essays* (London: Penguin, 2009), pp. 3–14.

Turley, Richard Marggraf (ed.), *The Writer in the Academy: Creative Interfrictions* (Cambridge: D.S. Brewer, 2011).

Ulmer, Gregory L., 'The Object of Post-Criticism', in Hal Foster (ed.), *Postmodern Culture* (London: Pluto, 1985), pp. 83–110.

CHAPTER I

Roland Barthes, from *A Lover's Discourse: Fragments*

A Lover's Discourse is one of three extraordinary late works by Roland Barthes, the other two being *Camera Lucida* and *Roland Barthes by Roland Barthes*. Each is entirely singular and each practically invents a new form of critical writing. For this reason Barthes has some claim to be the patron saint of creative criticism, a claim borne out in his formative influence on three of the writers gathered here – Sedgwick, Kopelson and Dyer – and in the extent to which we can follow the traces of Barthes's preoccupations in many of the other pieces in this *Anthology*.

A Lover's Discourse is a book about a shared repertoire of 'figures' (Barthes uses this term) by and through which we experience and voice our experience of being in love. And yet it is not *about* this repertoire: the figures are inhabited and performed, according to what Barthes calls a 'dramatic' method. For to be in love is to perform, to ourselves and to the thought of our loved other, and it is this performance which Barthes is out to name. To imagine a position safely outside the performance would be to risk mishearing, and so misnaming, the repertoire at hand. As with so much creative criticism, the writing acknowledges its own prior entanglement in the subject about which it proposes to speak.

A Lover's Discourse is a singular exercise in each of its constituent parts: method, mode, form, layout, allusions to and quotations from others. As such, it is unrepeatable. *A Lover's Discourse* uses a first person that is neither Barthes's own nor that of a character but is rather each of ours to the extent that we play to ourselves the role of the lover. The book is structured alphabetically so as to avoid any suggestion of intentional ordering – of narrative or of hierarchy. And its rather confusing referencing of the names and words from elsewhere is an attempt not to demonstrate knowledge or provide examples, but rather to hold true to the flashes of recognition, the momentary sense of being understood, that is part of the imaginative experience of being the lover, and so part of its discourse. Hence the very form, mode and frame of reference of our writing may find themselves shaped by the subject about which we wish to speak. To learn from Barthes we need first to find our own subject – at the moment I can think of three: the father, the face, the teacher; to consider the discourse through which our subject appears to us *as a subject*; and then to think how best to speak of it from within, as a matter already implicated in the means by which it can be said to be known.

Roland Barthes, from *A Lover's Discourse: Fragments* (1977), trans. Richard Howard (London: Vintage, 2002), pp. 59–61, 67–8, 75–9, 129–31, 167–8 and 220–3.

'*I want to understand*'

comprendre / to understand

Suddenly perceiving the amorous episode as a knot of inexplicable reasons and impaired solutions, the subject exclaims: 'I want to understand (what is happening to me)!'

1. What do I think of love? – As a matter of fact, I think nothing at all of love. I'd be glad to know *what it is*, but being inside, I see it in existence, not in essence. What I want to know (love) is the very substance I employ in order to speak (the lover's discourse). Reflection is certainly permitted, but since this reflection is immediately absorbed in the mulling over of images, it never turns into reflexivity: excluded from logic (which supposes languages exterior to each other), I cannot claim *to think properly*. Hence, discourse on love though I may for years at a time, I cannot hope to seize the concept of it except 'by the tail': by flashes, formulas, surprises of expression, scattered through the great stream of the Image-repertoire; I am

in love's *wrong place*, which is its dazzling place: 'The darkest place, according to a Chinese proverb, is always underneath the lamp.'

Reik

2.   Coming out of the movie theater, alone, mulling over my 'problem,' my lover's problem which the film has been unable to make me forget, I utter this strange cry: not: *make it stop!* but: *I want to understand* (what is happening to me)!

3.   Repression: I want to analyze, to know, to express in another language than mine; I want to represent my delirium to myself, I want to 'look in the face' what is dividing me, cutting me off. *Understand your madness*: that was Zeus' command when he ordered Apollo to turn the faces of the divided Androgynes (like an egg, a berry) toward the place where they had been cut apart (the belly) 'so that the sight of their division might render them less insolent.' To understand – is that not to divide the image, to undo the *I*, proud organ of misapprehension?

Symposium

4.   Interpretation: no, that is not what your cry means. As a matter of fact, that cry is still a cry of love: 'I want to understand myself, to make myself understood, make myself known, be embraced; I want someone to take me with him.' That is what your cry means.

A.C.

5.   I want to change systems: no longer to unmask, no longer to interpret, but to make consciousness itself a drug, and thereby to accede to the perfect vision of reality, to the great bright dream, to prophetic love.
(And if consciousness – such consciousness – were our human future? If, by an additional turn of the spiral, some day, most dazzling of all, once every reactive ideology had disappeared, consciousness were finally to become this: the abolition of the manifest and the latent, of the appearance and the hidden? If it

etymology

REIK: Quoted in *Fragments of a Great Confession*.
A.C.: Letter.
ETYMOLOGY: The Greeks opposed ὄναρ (*onar*), the vulgar dream, to ὕπαρ (*hypar*), the prophetic (never believed) vision. Communicated by J.-L.B.

were asked of analysis not to destroy power (not even to correct or to direct it), but only *to decorate* it, as an artist? Let us imagine that the science of our *lapsi* were to discover, one day, its own *lapsus*, and that this *lapsus* should turn out to be: a new, unheard-of form of consciousness?)

'When my finger accidentally . . .'

contacts / contacts

The figure refers to any interior discourse provoked by a furtive contact with the body (and more precisely the skin) of the desired being.

Werther

1.   Accidentally, Werther's finger touches Charlotte's, their feet, under the table, happen to brush against each other. Werther might be engrossed by the meaning of these accidents; he might concentrate physically on these slight zones of contact and delight in this fragment of inert finger or foot, fetishistically, *without concern for the response* (like God – as the etymology of the word tells us – the Fetish does not reply). But in fact Werther is not perverse, he is in love: he creates meaning, always and everywhere, out of nothing, and it is meaning which thrills him: he is in the crucible of meaning. Every contact, for the lover, raises the question of an answer: the skin is asked to reply.

(A squeeze of the hand – enormous documentation – a tiny gesture within the palm, a knee which doesn't move away, an arm extended, as if quite naturally, along the back of a sofa and against which the other's head gradually comes to rest – this is the paradisiac realm of subtle and clandestine signs: a kind of festival not of the senses but of meaning.)

Proust

2.   Charlus takes the narrator's chin and slides his magnetized fingers up to the ears 'like a barber's fingers.' This trivial gesture,

PROUST: *The Guermantes' Way.*

which I begin, is continued by another part of myself; without anything interrupting it physically, it branches off, shifts from a simple function to a dazzling meaning, that of the demand for love. Meaning (destiny) electrifies my hand; I am about to tear open the other's opaque body, oblige the other (whether there is a response, a withdrawal, or mere acceptance) to enter into the interplay of meaning: I am about *to make the other speak*. In the lover's realm, there is no *acting out*: no propulsion, perhaps even no pleasure – nothing but signs, a frenzied activity of language: to institute, on each furtive occasion, the system (the paradigm) of demand and response.

The Dedication

dédicace / dedication

An episode of language which accompanies any amorous gift, whether real or projected; and, more generally, every gesture, whether actual or interior, by which the subject dedicates something to the loved being.

1.   The amorous gift is sought out, selected, and purchased in the greatest excitement – the kind of excitement which seems to be of the order of orgasm. Strenuously I calculate whether this object will give pleasure, whether it will disappoint, or whether, on the contrary, seeming too 'important,' it will in and of itself betray the delirium – or the snare in which I am caught. The amorous gift is a solemn one; swept away by the devouring metonymy which governs the life of the imagination, I transfer myself inside it altogether. By this object, I give you my All, I touch you with my phallus; it is for this reason that I am mad with excitement, that I rush from shop to shop, stubbornly tracking down the 'right' fetish, the brilliant, successful fetish which will *perfectly* suit your desire.

The gift is contact, sensuality: you will be touching what I have touched, a third skin unites us. I give X a scarf and he wears it: X *gives* me the fact of wearing it; and, moreover, this is how he, naïvely, conceives and speaks of the phenomenon. *A contrario*:

any ethic of purity requires that we detach the gift from the hand which gives or receives it: in Buddhist ordination, personal objects and the three garments are offered to the bonze on a pole; the bonze accepts them by touching them with a stick, not with his hand; thus, in the future, everything which will be given to him – and on which he will live – will be arranged on a table, on the ground, or on a fan.

Zen

2.   I have this fear: that the given object may not function properly because of some insidious defect: if it is a box (selected very carefully), for example, the latch doesn't work (the shop being run by society women; and, moreover, the shop is called '*Because I love*' – is it *because I love* that the latch doesn't work?). The delight of giving the present then evaporates, and the subject knows that whatever he gives, he does not have it.

Ph.S.

(One does not give merely an object: X being in analysis, Y wants to be analyzed too: analysis as a gift of love?)

The gift is not necessarily excrement, but it has, nonetheless, a vocation as waste: the gift I receive is more than I know what to do with, it does not fit my space, it encumbers, it is too much: 'What am I going to do with your present!'

3.   A typical argument of a 'scene' is to represent to the other what you are giving him or her (time, energy, money, ingenuity, other relations, etc.); for it is invoking the reply which makes any scene 'move': *And what about me! Haven't I given you everything?* The gift then reveals the test of strength of which it is the instrument: 'I'll give you more than you give me, and so I will dominate you' (in the great Indian potlatches, whole villages were burned, slaves slaughtered with this intention).

To declare what I am giving is to follow the family model: *look at the sacrifices we're making for you*; or again: *we gave you the gift of life* (– *But what the fuck do I care about life!* etc.). To speak of the

PH.S.: Conversation.

gift is to place it in an exchange economy (of sacrifice, competition, etc.); which stands opposed to silent expenditure.

4.   'To that god, O Phaedrus, I dedicate this discourse . . .'
One cannot give language (how to transfer it from one hand to the other?), but one can dedicate it – since the other is a minor god. The given object is reabsorbed in the sumptuous, solemn utterance of the consecration, in the poetic gesture of the dedication; the gift is exalted in the very voice which expresses it, if this voice is *measured* (metrical); or again: *sung* (lyrical); this is the very principle of the *Hymn* or *Anthem*. Being unable to give anything, I dedicate the dedication itself, into which is absorbed all I have to say:

Symposium

R.H.

> *A la très chère, à la très belle,*
> *Qui remplit mon coeur de clarté,*
> *A l'ange, à l'idole immortelle . . .*
> To the beloved, the beautiful being
> who fills my heart with light, to
> the angel, the immortal idol . . .

Song is the precious addition to a blank message, entirely contained within its address, for what I give by singing is at once my body (by my voice) and the silence into which you cast that body. (Love is mute, Novalis says; only poetry makes it speak.) *Song means nothing*: it is in this that you will understand at last what it is that I give you; as useless as the wisp of yarn, the pebble held out to his mother by the child.

5.   Powerless to utter itself, powerless to speak, love nonetheless wants to proclaim itself, to exclaim, to write itself everywhere: *all'acqua, all'ombra, ai monti, ai fiori, all'erbe, ai fonti, all'eco, all'aria, ai venti* . . . And once the amorous subject creates or puts together any kind of work at all, he is seized with a desire to dedicate it. What he makes he immediately,

The Marriage of Figaro

R.H.: Conversation.
The Marriage of Figaro: Cherubino's aria (Act I).

and even in advance, wants to give to his beloved, for whom he has worked, or will work. The addition of the name will take its place as a way of uttering the gift.

Yet, except for the case of the Hymn, which combines the dedication and the text itself, what follows the dedication (i.e., the work itself) has little relation to this dedication. The object I give is no longer tautological (I give you what I give you), it is *interpretable*; it has a meaning (meanings) greatly in excess of its address; though I write your name on my work, it is for 'them' that it has been written (the others, the readers). Hence it is by a fatality of writing itself that we cannot say of a text that it is 'amorous,' but only, at best, that it has been created 'amorously,' like a cake or an embroidered slipper.

And even: less than a slipper! For the slipper has been made for your foot (your size and your pleasure); the cake has been made or selected for your taste: there is a certain adequation between these objects and your person. But writing does not possess this obligingness. Writing is dry, obtuse; a kind of steamroller, writing advances, indifferent, indelicate, and would kill 'father, mother, lover' rather than deviate from its fatality (enigmatic though that fatality may be). When I write, I must acknowledge this fact (which, according to my Image-repertoire, lacerates me): there is no benevolence within writing, rather a terror: it smothers the other, who, far from perceiving the gift in it, reads there instead an assertion of mastery, of power, of pleasure, of solitude. Whence the cruel paradox of the dedication: I seek at all costs to give you what smothers you.

(We often notice that a writing subject does not have his writing 'in his own image': if you love me 'for myself,' you do not love me for my writing (and I suffer from it). Doubtless, loving simultaneously two signifiers in the same body is too much! It doesn't happen every day – and if it should happen, by some exception, that is Coincidence, the Sovereign Good.)

6.   Hence I cannot give you what I thought I was writing for you – that is what I must acknowledge: the amorous dedication is impossible (I shall not be satisfied with a worldly or mundane

signature, pretending to dedicate to you a work which escapes us both). The operation in which the other is to be engaged is not a signature. It is, more profoundly, an inscription: the other is inscribed, he inscribes himself within the text, he leaves there his (multiple) traces. If you were only the dedicatee of this book, you would not escape your harsh condition as (loved) *object* – as god; but your presence within the text, whereby you are unrecognizable there, is not that of an analogical figure, of a fetish, but that of a force which is not, thereby, absolutely reliable. Hence it doesn't matter that you feel continuously reduced to silence, that your own discourse seems to you smothered beneath the monstrous discourse of the amorous subject: in *Teorema* the 'other' does not speak, but he inscribes something within each of those who desire him – he performs what the mathematicians call a catastrophe (the disturbance of one system by another): it is true that this mute figure is an angel.

Pasolini

Identifications

identification / identification

The subject painfully identifies himself with some person (or character) who occupies the same position as himself in the amorous structure.

1.   Werther identifies himself with every lost lover: he is the madman who loved Charlotte and goes out picking flowers in midwinter; he is the young footman in love with a widow, who has just killed his rival – indeed, Werther wants to intercede for this youth, whom he cannot rescue from the law: 'Nothing can save you, poor wretch! Indeed, I see that nothing can save us.' Identification is not a psychological process; it is a pure structural operation: I am the one who has the same place I have.

Werther

2.   I devour every amorous system with my gaze and in it discern the place which would be mine if I were a part of that system. I perceive not analogies but homologies: I note, for instance, that I am to X what Y is to Z; everything I am told about Y affects me powerfully, though Y's person is a matter of

indifference to me, or even unknown; I am caught in a mirror which changes position and which reflects me wherever there is a dual structure. Worse still: it can happen that on the other hand I am loved by someone I do not love; now, far from helping me (by the gratification it implies or the diversion it might constitute), this situation is painful to me: I see myself in the other who loves without being loved, I recognize in him the very gestures of my own unhappiness, but this time it is I myself who am the active agent of this unhappiness: I experience myself both as victim and as executioner.

(It is because of this homology that the love story 'works' – sells.)

Werther

3.   X is more or less desired, flattered, by others than by me. Hence I put myself in their place, as Werther is in the same place as Heinrich, the madman with the flowers, who has loved Charlotte to the point of madness. Now, this structural analogy (certain points are arranged in a certain order around one point) is readily imaginable in terms of personality: since Heinrich and I occupy the same place, it is no longer merely with Heinrich's place that I identify myself, but with his image as well. A hallucination seizes me: *I am Heinrich!* This generalized identification, extended to all those who surround the other and benefit from the other as I do, is doubly painful to me: it devalues me in my own eyes (I find myself *reduced* to a certain personality), but it also devalues my other, who becomes the inert object of a circle of rivals. Each, identical with the others, seems to be shouting: *Mine! mine!* Like a mob of children arguing over a ball or any other object; in short, over the fetish thrown into their midst.

The structure has nothing to do with persons; hence (like a bureaucracy) it is terrible. It cannot be implored – I cannot say to it: 'Look how much better I am than H.' Inexorable, the structure replies: 'You are in the same place; hence you are H.' No one can *plead* against the structure.

Werther

4.   Werther identifies himself with the madman, with the footman. As a reader, I can identify myself with Werther. Historically, thousands of subjects have done so, suffering, killing themselves, dressing, perfuming themselves, writing as

if they were Werther (songs, poems, candy boxes, belt buckles, fans, colognes à la Werther). A long chain of equivalences links all the lovers in the world. In the theory of literature, 'projection' (of the reader into the character) no longer has any currency: yet it is the appropriate tonality of imaginative readings: reading a love story, it is scarcely adequate to say I project myself; I cling to the image of the lover, shut up with this image in the very enclosure of the book (everyone knows that such stories are read in a state of secession, of retirement, of voluptuous absence: in the toilet).

Proust

No Answer

mutisme / silence

The amorous subject suffers anxiety because the loved object replies scantily or not at all to his language (discourse or letters).

1.   'When you were talking to him, discussing any subject at all, X frequently seemed to be looking away, listening to something else: you broke off, discouraged; after a long silence, X would say: 'Go on, I'm listening to you'; then you resumed as best you could the thread of a story in which you no longer believed.'

(Like a bad concert hall, affective space contains dead spots where the sound fails to circulate. – The perfect interlocutor, the friend, is he not the one who constructs around you the greatest possible resonance? Cannot friendship be defined as a space with total sonority?)

2.   This evasive listening, which I can capture only after some delay, involves me in a sordid calculation: desperately trying to seduce, to divert, I imagined that by talking I was

PROUST: (The orris-scented toilet, in Combray) 'Intended for a more particular and more vulgar purpose, this room . . . long served as a refuge for me, doubtless because it was the only one where I was allowed to lock the door, a refuge for all my occupations which required an invincible solitude: reading, daydreaming, tears, and pleasure.'

lavishing treasures of ingenuity, but these treasures have produced only indifference; I am spending my 'qualities' for nothing: a whole program of affects, doctrines, awareness, and delicacy, all the brilliance my ego can command dies away, muffled in an inert space, as if – culpable thought – my quality exceeded that of the loved object, as if I were *in advance* of that object. Now, the affective relation is an exact machine; coincidence, *perfect pitch* in the musical sense are fundamental to it; what is out of phase is immediately *de trop*: my language is not, strictly speaking, a discard but rather an 'overstock': what is not consumed in the moment (in the movement) and is therefore remaindered.

(This distracted kind of listening generates an anxiety of decisions: should I continue, go on talking 'in the void'? This would require precisely the assurance which amorous sensibility does not permit. Should I stop, give up? This would seem to show anger, accusation of the other, producing a 'scene.' The trap all over again.)

François
Wahl

Freud

3. 'This is what death is, most of all: everything that has been seen, will have been seen for nothing. Mourning over what we have perceived.' In those brief moments when I speak for nothing, it is as if I were dying. For the loved being becomes a leaden figure, a dream creature *who does not speak*, and silence, in dreams, is death. Or again: the gratifying Mother shows me the Mirror, the Image, and says to me: 'That's you.' But the silent Mother does not tell me what I am: I am no longer established, I drift painfully, without existence.

Thus

tel / thus

Endlessly required to define the loved object, and suffering from the uncertainties of this definition, the amorous subject dreams of

FRANÇOIS WAHL: '*Chute.*'
FREUD: 'The Three Caskets.'

a knowledge which would let him take the other *as he is*, thus and no other, exonerated from any adjective.

1.   Narrow-mindedness: as a matter of fact, I admit nothing about the other, I understand nothing. Everything about the other which doesn't concern me seems alien, hostile; I then feel toward him a mixture of alarm and severity: I fear and I reprove the loved being, once he no longer 'sticks' to his image. I am merely 'liberal': a doleful dogmatic, so to speak.

(Industrious, indefatigable, the language machine humming inside me – for it runs nicely – fabricates its chain of adjectives: I cover the other with adjectives, I string out his qualities, his *qualitas*.)

2.   Through these iridescent, versatile judgments, a painful impression subsists: I see that the other perseveres in himself; he is himself this perseverance, against which I stumble. I realize with hysteria that I cannot *displace* him; whatever I do, whatever I expend for him, he never renounces his own system. I contradictorily experience the other as a capricious divinity who keeps changing his moods in my respect, *and* as a heavy, *inveterate* thing (this thing will age just as it is, and that is what I suffer

etymology from). Or again, I see the other *in his limits*. Or finally, I question myself: Is there even a single point as to which the other might *surprise me?* Thus, curiously, the other's 'freedom to be himself' I experience as a cowardly stubbornness. I see the other *thus* – I see the other's *thusness* – but in the realm of amorous sentiment this *thus* is painful to me because it separates us and because, once again, I refuse to recognize the division of our image, the other's alterity.

3.   This first *thus* is wrong because I leave on the blotter, as an internal point of corruption, an adjective: the other is *stubborn*: he still derives from *qualitas*. I must get rid of any impulse to draw up accounts; the other must become, in my eyes, pure of any attribution; the more I designate him, the less I shall utter

ETYMOLOGY: *Inveterare*, to age, to grow old.

him: I shall be like the *infans* who contents himself with a blank
word to show something: Ta, Da, Tat (says Sanskrit). *Thus*, the

Zen   lover will say: *you are thus, thus and so, precisely thus.*

Designating you as *thus*, I enable you to escape the death of classification, I kidnap you from the Other, from language, I want
you to be immortal. *As he is*, the loved being no longer receives
any meaning, neither from myself nor from the system in which
he is caught; he is no more than a text without context; I no
longer need or desire to decipher him; he is in a sense the *supplement of his own site*. If he were only a site, I might well, someday,
replace him, but I can substitute nothing for the supplement of
his site, his *thus*.

(In restaurants, once the last service is over, the tables are set
again for the next day: same white cloth, same silverware, same

J.-L.B.   salt and pepper shakers: this is the world of site, of replacement:
no *thus*.)

4.   So I accede, fitfully, to a language without adjectives. I
love the other, not according to his (accountable) qualities, but
according to his existence; by a movement one might well call
mystical, I love, not what he is, but *that he is*. The language in
which the amorous subject then protests (against all the nimble
languages of the world) is an *obtuse* language: every judgment is
suspended, the terror of meaning is abolished. What I liquidate
in this movement is the very category of merit: just as the mystic
makes himself indifferent to sanctity (which would still be an
attribute), so, acceding to the other's *thus*, I no longer oppose
oblation to desire: it seems to me that I can make myself desire
the other less and delight in him more.

(The worst enemy of *thus* is Gossip, corrupt manufacturer of
adjectives. And what would best resemble the loved being *as he
is, thus and so*, would be the Text, to which I can add no adjective: which I delight in without having to decipher it.)

J.-L.B.: Conversation.

5.   Or again: is not *thus* the friend? He who can leave for a
while without his image crumbling? 'We were friends and have
become estranged. But this was right, and we do not want to
conceal and obscure it from ourselves as if we had reason to feel
ashamed. We are two ships each of which has its goal and course;
our paths may cross and we may celebrate a feast together, as we
did – and then the good ships rested so quietly in one harbor and
one sunshine that it may have looked as if they had reached their
goal and as if they had one goal. But then the mighty force of our
tasks drove us apart again into different seas and sunny zones,
and perhaps we shall never see each other again; perhaps we
shall meet again but fail to recognize each other: our exposure to
different seas and suns has changed us.'

Nietzsche

NIETZSCHE: 'Star Friendship,' *The Gay Science.*

CHAPTER 2

John Cage, from 'Where Are We Going? And What Are We Doing?'

Creative-critical writing can be thought of in terms of performance: as an incident, an event, what might once have been called a happening. Whatever the nature of writer and of subject, something happens in the writing, is brought into play. John Cage's 'Where Are We Going? And What Are We Doing?' started out life as a lecture, or rather as 'four simultaneous lectures'. Transferring them to the page, Cage opts to signify the individual lines by means of different typefaces, with suggestions as to speed, volume of delivery and use of pre-recorded readings. The experience of viewing the piece is akin to a kind of dance of the eye and the mind. The words are a light mix of statement, rumination, anecdote and manifesto. Cage is called to speak as an artist; rather than seek to justify or explain, he exemplifies, refusing the loaded distinction between practice and theory, art and life, showing and telling, and, we might now say, between the creative and the critical. In his own words, it is a piece 'in the course of which, by various means, meaning is not easy to come by even though lucidity has been my constant will-of-the-wisp'.

Cage's provocation is twofold. First, he uses the space of the page as a site comparable with the location of a performance, hence the possibility that the materials of writing – typography and page layout – can be brought into play as integral to the piece in question, a possibility which marks his affiliation with the Black Mountain poets (we might compare Cage's piece with the 'talk poems' of David Antin). By means of playing with these materials, this particular piece seeks to offer a visual analogue for the polyphony of a performance; as such, it is an example of an aspiration to polyphony evident in much creative-critical writing, most obviously those pieces composed from two or three separate columns of text (Derrida's 'Tympan'; Juliana Spahr's 'Spiderwasp'; Wayne Koestenbaum's *Hotel Theory*).

The second provocation is again a feature shared with much of the writing gathered here. Cage's piece is performative, in the sense that its form is an enactment of its content; or put another way, rather than tell us what we should be doing, Cage does it: the answer to the two titular questions *are* the performance. To experiment along the lines of Cage we need to consider not only the possibilities inherent in our materials, but also the ways in which our writing might exemplify rather than explain.

John Cage, from 'Where Are We Going? And What Are We Doing?', in *Silence: Lectures and Writings* (1961) (Middletown, CT: Wesleyan University Press, 1973), pp. 194–259 (pp. 194–213).

When I was invited to speak in January 1961 at the Evening School of Pratt Institute in Brooklyn, I was told that the burning questions among the students there were: Where are we going? and What are we doing? I took these questions as my subjects and, in order to compose the texts, made use of my Cartridge Music.

The texts were written to be heard as four simultaneous lectures. But to print four lines of type simultaneously – that is, superimposed on one another – was a project unattractive in the present instance. The presentation here used has the effect of making the words legible – a dubious advantage, for I had wanted to say that our experiences, gotten as they are all at once, pass beyond our understanding.

A part of this lecture has been printed, in a different typographical arrangement, in Ring des Arts, *Paris, summer 1961. The entire lecture has been recorded by C. F. Peters, New York, in the form of four single-track tapes (7½ ips, forty-five minutes each). The following is a set of directions: Four independent lectures to be used in whole or in part – horizontally and vertically. The typed relation is not necessarily that of a performance. Twenty-five lines may be read in 1 minute, 1¼ minutes, 1½ minutes, giving lectures roughly 37, 47, 57 minutes long respectively. Any other speech speed may be used.*

A performance must be given by a single lecturer. He may read 'live' any one of the lectures. The 'live' reading may be superimposed on the recorded readings. Or the whole may be recorded and delivered mechanically. Variations in amplitude may be made; for this purpose, use the score of my composition WBAI *(also published by C. F. Peters).*

I was driving out to the country once with Carolyn and Earle Brown. We got to talking about Coomaraswamy's statement that the traditional function of the artist is to imitate nature in her manner of operation. This led me to the opinion that art changes because science changes — that is, changes in science give artists different understandings of how nature works.

A Phi Beta Kappa ran in the other day and said, 'Your view is that art follows science, whereas Blake's view is that art is ahead of science.'

Right here you have it: Is man in control of nature or is he, as part of it, going along with it? To be perfectly honest with you, let me say I find nature far more interesting than any of man's controls of nature. This does not imply that I dislike humanity. I think that people are wonderful, and I think this because there are instances of people changing their minds. (I refer to individuals and to myself.)

Not all of our past, but the parts of it we are taught, lead us to believe that we are in the driver's seat. With respect to nature. And that if we are not, life is meaningless. Well, the grand thing about the human mind is that it can turn its own tables and see meaninglessness as ultimate meaning.

I have therefore made a lecture in the course of which, by various means, meaning is not easy to come by even though lucidity has been my constant will-of-the-wisp. I have permitted myself to do this not out of disdain of you who are present. But out of regard for the way in which I understand nature operates. This view makes us all equals — even if among us are some unfortunates: whether lame, blind, stupid, schizoid, or poverty-stricken.

Here we are. Let us say Yes to our presence together in Chaos.

If we set out to catalogue things

.

.

.

today, we find ourselves rather

.

.

.

endlessly involved in cross-

.

.

.

referencing. Would it not be

Those of us who don't agree are going

.

.

less efficient to start the other

around together. The string Duchamp dropped.

.

.

way around, after the fashion of

He took the apartment without being able to

.

.

some obscure second-hand bookstore?
pay for it. They danced on a concrete floor.

.

.

.

.

The candles at the Candlelight Concert are
.

One New Year's Eve I had too
electric. It was found dangerous
.

.

many invitations. I decided to
for them to be wax. It has not yet
.

.

go to all the parties, ending up
been found dangerous for them to
.

.

at the most interesting one. I
be electric – and this in spite of
.

.

arrived early at the one I was
the air-conditioning. If I were
.

.

sure would be dull. I stayed there

able to open my windows, I think

.

.

the whole evening – never got to the others.
I would do it often, and for no reason at all.

.

.

.

I would have written sooner but

.

.

.

I picked up the book and

.

.

.

could scarcely put it down. It is absolutely

.

.

.

charming. I'm going to write to the author.
How can we go over there when

.

.

.

we haven't the least idea of

.

.

.

what we will find when we

.

.

.

get there? Also we don't

.

Three birds and a telephone ringing. Does

.

know how to land, and we

.

that relate to where we are going? Does

.

have no way of trying it

.

it tell us the direction to take: out

.

out beforehand. Perhaps we

.

the window and down the hall?

.

will sink into a huge mile-

.

I take a sword and cut off my

.

thick pile of dust. What then?

.

head and it rolls to where we

.

.

.

are going. The question is: Do they

.

.

.

mean it when they say No Trespassing?

.

.

.

.

.

.

.

.

.

.

In a sense we are going to extremes.

.

.

You want to know what we're doing?
That is what we are doing. In fact

.

.

We're breaking the rules, even our
we don't need to go to bring that

.

.

own rules. And how do we do that?
into our action. We tend to rush

.

.

By leaving plenty of room for X quantities.
to what we think are the limits
The house had been so well built that

.

only to discover how tamed our
even though it burned, it did not
After we have been going for some

.

ambitions were. Will we ever learn
burn down. The fire gutted it.
time, do we mellow? (They used to

.

that it is endless? What then
We're not going to become less
say we would.) Mellowing is sof-

.

is an extreme? The very low sounds,
scientific, but more scientific. We
tening. Left to ourselves, if the

.

extremely low, are so little available
do not include probability in science.
birds didn't get us, we'd putrefy.

We're putting art in museums, getting it out
to us and yet we rush to them
Do I thank you or the one who's
Of course, our air-conditioning

of our lives. We're bringing machines
and don't get them. We find
opening and closing the door? On days when
is such that if we just managed

home to live with us. Now that

them too soft. We want them
nobody answers, we stop telephoning. We are
to die under its influence we'd

the machines are here so to say to
extremely loud. If you announced
going and then coming back and going and
not putrefy: we'd dry up.

stay with us, we've got to find
that there was going to be a low
coming back again. Eventually we
But since the windows won't

ways to entertain them. If we don't,
and loud sound, I imagine
will go and not come back at all.
open, we could scarcely be ex-

they'll explode, but as for going, we're
quite a number of us would

.

pected to blow away. I've always

going out. Did we just notice the moon
rush to hear it. What about an

had my heart set on cremation

or was it there always? Where we're
extremely loud high sound? Hear!

.

but now I see the reason for earth,

going is not only to the moon but out into
Anxiety enters. Some of us would stay

.

it frees the air from dead influences.

space. Home is discrete points. Space is an
put and say, 'Tell me about it.'
The house is built around a large
.

infinite field without boundaries. We are
Once someone's done something,
chimney, so large that on a good
.

leaving the machines home to play the
it's no longer his responsibility.
day when the flue is open, the sun
.

old games of relationships, addition and
It's someone else's. It could of
shines on the hearth. We're getting into
.

who wins. (We're going out.) A teen-ager –
course be his again, but what
our heads that existence, the existence of
.

served custard that had wheyed – said, 'My
would he do? I asked the three girls
a sound, for instance, is a field
At the beginning of our going, it seems

mother bakes custard too, but she
what they would take with them
phenomenon, not one limited to
that we are going our separate ways,

doesn't put water in it.' Let us admit,
to the Caribbean. The third was
known discrete points in that field – the
that we have nothing further to say

once and for all, that the lines
going to take some fish and a
conventionally accepted ones – but capable
to one another, and we leave behind

we draw are not straight.
bird which she cannot because
of appearance at any point in the field.
in particular the ways we learned to

.

they're being housed by friends when
This brings about a change in our heads.
communicate. Later on

.

she and her family go away. I
.

we won't bother about any of that.

.

pointed this out: 'Since you can't

.

We'll be one happy anarchistic family.

.

take the bird and the fish, what
.

We haven't any time left to stay: we

.

will you take? Your sisters
.

must go now. Though his ears are

.

have said what they'll take.'
.

extraordinarily sensitive and he's a Quaker,

.

There was no answer. Shortly,

.

he recommended a restaurant with Muzak.

.

but after her sisters, she ran up-

.

.

Small telephones for those near the

.

stairs to bed. 'Tuck me in.'

.

.

central telephone and large telephones

.

.

.

She drives rapidly; her life is shorter.

.

for those farther away following

.

Everything is ready for tomorrow morning.

.

.

what one calls a law of nature.

.

I must remember to turn out her lights.

.

.

.

.

.

.

If there are as many ways as

there are of looking, there must

be at least three ways of going – not

so much ways as wheres. Well,

there you have it: If I go over

there and stop, could I not have

The trouble with Denver is its past.
gone slightly to the left? As I

San Francisco used to have the same
go, direction changes. It is not

problem. But how are we going to know
measurable. But it is precise

where to go when it doesn't make
going. One moved off to the south,

the least difference to us where we
and when I measured he was going

go? The problem is simple: You
north. Or I crossed the stream at the
'Powdered eggs are good enough for me.'

either stay put until you get
point where the water was going both
It's not the air-conditioning; it's the

an invitation or you make your-
ways. They say how fast and there
radiant heating in the ceiling: it makes

a certain obligation to go we

self an invitation written in such
is no way to answer. Tempo is out
me think someone's up on the roof.

.

to see someone. It turns out it wasn't
Do you remember the story of his

.

may very likely not be able to.

a way that you couldn't know,
but comes back in. You might add:
They played a game in which she
At the present time it seems

anybody: it was a machine. I'm as
hanging his shoes out of his own
Whether or not we want it, we

.

when you wrote it, what you
There was no need for us to have gone.
was the sun. One man was the
reasonable not to go. The weather

crazy as a loon: I'm invited out to
reach, so that rather than taking
are insured. And we say it is a

.

were writing, and where it would

.

earth and the other was the moon: a
is not made for adult affairs

dinner. I keep telling myself: Before
the trouble of getting them down,
good thing. The thing to do is not to

.

be sending you going. And other ways.

.

choreography. Now what shall we do?
(and the furtherance of the national

you go to bed, be sure to close the
he would simply go on doing what
have one policy but many and then

.

.

.

.

bathroom door; if you don't, you'll
he was doing and not go out? From
there is the possibility that the central

.

economy) but for the games of

.

.

.

just have to get up and close it
what I hear, there are ideas that
office will get confused. (It happens.)

.

children. Even if we sense

I wander out in the hall expecting

.

later. We are going stupidly to places
we have not yet had simply be-

We are going to realize that our

.

we have never been. Going away from
cause we don't yet have the language
analytic method of approaching

.

home, sometimes lost, we come by
to have them. But even in our
the material we are working with

.

circle, home again. We're surprised:
own language, it seems, there
(sound, I mean) which was so

.

it's changed. Did it slip – out
are ideas that are confined
useful is going to give place to
What we do is not utterly different from

from under us? The day in the
to systems, each to a single one,
some other means, some other
what we used to do. That is: we

woods I took a compass was the
which means there would be
useful means. Its awkwardness led us
used to get an idea and do it and

day I got lost for sure. Two years
times when it would be reason-
willy-nilly into a certain sloppiness.
then someone else had to do more

later when I was throwing it out,

able to say Yes and other times
(That was not without its hilarious
or less what he was told to do.

a child to whom I'd given a bass
when it would be absurd to say
effects which we in our deadliness
Now we get an idea and present

drum asked whether he might also have
that same word. Ideas take on
did not notice.) There is a lingering
it in such a way that it can

the compass. The first thing she said
a kind of material reality
confusion, paying heed to results
be used by him who is going to

was: 'Everyone's confused; there isn't
but essentially they are intangible.
rather than actions (the only solution
do it. Someone once raised the

anyone now who isn't confused.'
My question is: Why do we, as
is to stay where you are: it's you acting).
question who gets the credit. The

Or was that the first thing she said?
it were, imprison them? Of

.

listener gives it to himself when

.

all things, they are best equipped,

.

he gets it. All the people have

.

wouldn't you say, to fly in and
People always want to know what
become active and enjoy what you

.

out of the most unlikely places?
we're doing and the last thing we
might call individual security.

.

Off hand, for instance, we can do
want to do is keep it a secret. But
The composer also has ears on his head.

.

one thing at a time. But we
the truth is we don't know what
.

.

used to admire those artists of
we're doing and that is how we
.

.

vaudeville who did several
manage to do it when it's lively.
.

.

at once. To their three, say,
I believe, of course, that what we're
.

.

we could add our one. But at
doing is exploring a field, that the
.

.

a circus, three rings, though
field is limitless and without
.

.

high up, I remember I
qualitative differentiation but with
.

.

could only look at one ring
multiplicity of differences,
.

.

at a time. I kept missing or
that our business has changed
.

.

thinking I was missing some-
from judgment to awareness –
.

.

thing. On the other hand, if
I believe all this and it makes
Travel was not only possible.

.

what I'm doing is digging the
me speechless, for there is nothing
It was widely engaged in. On

.

hog peanut, then it actually happens
to say. For if I say I am

both sides of the streets, the two–

.

that I can converse, notice changes
especially active in the
way ones, there were long lines

.

in temperature, take as perfectly
amplifications of small sounds
of traffic proceeding, to be sure,

.

natural the discovery of geasters
and work with the voice, it
slowly, but getting, one assumed,

.

growing underneath the surface
doesn't tell you what the others
eventually where they were going.

.

of the earth when I knew
(who are also us) are doing. Would
People also were walking and a

It's very curious. I remember recording
perfectly well the books don't men–
it be accurate to say then that
very large crowd attended the

machines with dials and clutches.
tion they do or can. Perhaps a live
we are all off in separate corners
Candlelight Concert. Was it because

Then later there were push buttons. Now
ghost might have made an ap–

engaged in our special concerns?
it was a tradition? It must

one has the feeling we're going to
parition and I would have
No. It is more to the point to talk
be that that is the case: the lady

have dials again. We need
found it perfectly unremarkable.
about the field itself, which
beyond the one sitting next to me

desperately when it comes to a
Is this the effect of concentration?
is that it is and enables us
whispered to my neighbor that

machine to be able to go at any speed.
If only, she said, I have a
all to be doing the same thing
the program this year was not

.

thread, I can then take the
so differently. And about this
as entirely appreciated by her

.

rest, hanging on as it were.
field, nothing can be said. And
as the one last year. And

.

We also discussed the mortality of
yet one goes on talking, in order
when they first came in, they

.

birds in connection with modern architecture.
to make this clear. Suzuki Daisetz
sat down in the reverse relation

Instead of living and learning, don't we
.
laughed many times quietly: once
to me that I have just described

live by learning we're not learning?
.
it was when he was discussing
so that the one who was later

For instance: When I moved to the
.
the quality of not being explicable
my neighbor was then at the

country I no sooner found myself
They have curious regulations for
and pointing out that he had
beginning beyond my neighbor.

insatiably involved in tramping
pedestrians. After the light turns
come from Japan with the inten-
She whispered her approval of

through the woods than summer
red, there is a white one and
tion of making explicit this
the wreaths and ropes of greenery

passed through fall into an
then the people walk wherever
quality which was of not being clear.
which decorated the chapel

icy winter. I made some
they wish, crossing the intersection
(My words, it goes without saying,
along with the electric lights and

inquiries and finally got to
even diagonally. One begins to think
are not the ones he used.) We
electric candles. She found them

a municipal office where I
it's better when we're going not
don't any more take vacations. Or
more beautiful than last year.

filled out blanks that led to
to pay attention to the signs.
if through special circumstances we
Very rarely do people any more

my getting a license for hunting
It is as though we were looking
are obliged to take a vacation, we
flock to a public occasion.

and fishing. Then I bought some
with other eyes than our own. I mean
take what we're doing with us.
Apparently if you keep some-

ingenious paraphernalia for fishing
the way we are going is transform-
There is, in fact, no way to get away
thing traditional they'll still do

on an ice-covered body of water.
ing our vision. And the profound-
.
it, providing the weather permits.

Dressed as warmly as possible,
est changes take place in the

.

One thing I found a bit jarring

I drove up to the lake, chopped
things we thought the most

.

was the switching on of the electric lights that

holes in the ice, fixed hooks
familiar. On the first trip when

.

suddenly gave the effect of sun–

and lines and waited for
the cat was taken up to that

.

light streaming through the

little red flags, popping up,
town near Boston (because they were going

.

stained glass windows high above

to signal success. I heard
away) it got sick; they nursed it back.

.

the chorus and orchestra. I glanced

the sounds that travel through
On the second trip, the cat died.

.

along the sides of the chapel. The

the ice as it freezes; I was

.

.

windows there were not illuminated.

astonished. Later, I was on the

.

.

The tradition of focusing one's

ice as the sun, setting, colored

.

.

attention was being observed. The

both it and the sky. I was

.

.

electric candles were some white and

amazed. I remember I shrank

.

.

some a sort of highway brownish yellow.

in my own estimation. Before

.

.

.

I nearly froze, I collected all

.

.

.

my traps, no fish. I made a

.

What we do, we do without purpose.

.

mental note not to go ice-fishing

.

We are simply invited

.

again without a bottle of cognac.

.

to do it, by someone else

.

On the other hand, there are certain

.

or by ourselves. And so we do this or that.

.

things I am taught (and I do want
The day before yesterday towards the

.

.

to learn them); for instance: if
middle of the afternoon I noticed

.

.

I will remember not just to touch
I was running out of matches.

.

.

wood but to rub my hand on
I went through pockets, under

.

.

it before I touch metal, then I
papers on tables and finally

.

.

won't get a shock. I had pre-

found a single match. Having

.

.

viously thought that if I picked
lit a cigarette, I decided to

.

We are not doing very much

up my feet as I walked
keep one lit constantly whether

.

of any one thing. We are continually

across the carpet or if I even
I was smoking or not. Oppressed

.

dropping one thing and picking

hopped through the room
by this obligation, I went down-

.

up another. We are, you might

before turning a doorknob or
stairs to the kitchen, found

.

say, concentrated inside and idiotic out.

a light switch that I
nothing, but picked up an

.

.

wouldn't get a shock. That
article by the man at the

.

.

doesn't work. The wood-rubbing
other end of the hall that happened

.

.

does work. The crux of the
to catch my eye. I read it,

.

.

matter is: will I remember
cooked dinner, went on working,

.

.

to rub wood first and, even
and managed through all of this

.

.

so, just in case I sometime
to light another cigarette be-

.

.

find myself in a situation
fore the burning one burned out.

.

.

where there isn't any wood
I determined to go to the movies

.

.

to rub, shouldn't I just
in order to get some matches.

.

.

decide, here and now, no
However, in the car, I found

.

.

matter where I go, to carry
some partly used folders of them

.

.

a piece of wood with me?
and just went to the movies uselessly.

.

.

Although we speak about going,
The next afternoon, the secretary

.

.

I notice that we spend a lot
came in and asked for a

.

.

of time waiting; that is, I wait.
match. I still had a few

.

.

And when I tell others about it,
left from those I'd found in the

.

He was afraid all along that he

.

they say they wait too.
car. I realized the situation

.

.

might lose his mind. He had no

.

was growing ticklish. I left and

.

fear of the cancer which killed him.

.

with the single purpose of getting
He gave rise to two schools, and repudiated

.

.

matches. I came back with an
them both. That is partly true. We are

.

Talking about death, we began
artichoke, a sweet potato, an onion
not just going: we are being swept away.

.

laughing. There had even been an
I didn't need (for I already
How was it she managed to teach me

.

attempted suicide. Which are
had one), three limes, two per-
that the play of her emotions needn't involve

.

you supposed to read: the
simmons, six cans of ale, a box
me? Christmas is here and then

.

article or the advertisements?
of cranberries and an orange, eggs,

shortly we'll be filling out the income tax.

.

I felt so miserable I went to
milk, and cream, and fortunately

.

.

sleep even though I'd just
I remembered the matches. That

.

.

gotten up. I decided to
evening the possibility of lighting

.

.

cancel everything. Instead
a cigarette on an electric stove

.

.

I went out in the woods and
was mentioned, an action

.

.

revived. Going into the unknown
with which I am fully familiar.
You remember the seeds? Well, today,

.

we have no use for value
It is fairly clear that we have
it was rubber bands (not flying

.

judgments. We are only greedy:

changed our direction, but it

through the air, but littering the

There are those who go part way

we want more and more while

is not so clear when we

sidewalk). It would be so much

but can't go any farther. And

there's still time. We're getting

did it. Was it in 1913 when

simpler if we were expressing

there is a great interest in going

around to the usefulness of science

Duchamp wrote his piece of music?

ourselves. In that case all you'd

and staying at the same time:

(I don't mean probability) (I mean

And since he didn't tell us, how

need for an understanding of

naturally not in the physical

seeing things just as they are in

did we know? Is what we're

what we're doing would be a

world, but in the world of art.

their state of chaos). And so, if

doing in the air or on the land?

large collection of city directories.

These people want somehow to

you were writing a song, would

When did competition cease?

.

keep alive the traditions and

you write music, or would you

Looking back, it all seems to

.

yet push them forward. It gets

write for a singer? 'I can't even

have been done the way we are

.

rather superhuman as a

try,' she said, 'I can't whistle.'

doing it. Even the old bridges.

.

project. The others don't care

.

.

.

so much about tradition, but hang on anyway.

.

.

.

.

.

.

.

.

.

.

.

.

.

.

CHAPTER 3

Anne Carson, 'Every Exit Is an Entrance (A Praise of Sleep)'

This is an encomium to sleep whose own writing is far from soporific. Generically, Carson's 'Every Exit Is an Entrance (A Praise of Sleep)' is perhaps the truest example in this *Anthology* of the essay form in the relatively strict sense – that form which, to reach once again for the bit of Adorno we quoted in our introduction, 'does not begin with Adam and Eve but with what it wants to discuss' and whose writing 'reflects a childlike freedom that catches fire, without scruple, on what others have already done'. Carson moves easily between texts, including Keats's 'Sonnet to Sleep', Bishop's 'Man-moth', *To the Lighthouse*, the *Odyssey* and *Rosencrantz & Guildenstern Are Dead*, a discussion of one melding into and calling up another. Here, then, it is Carson's 'theme' – rather than a particular literary text – which redounds on the forms of her writing, and there is a sleepy, dreamy logic to the way the piece moves. Try to mark, as you read it, the turns and switch-points in her argument. Where is a new idea introduced, and how? Freud is alluded to though never quoted in this essay, but his *Interpretation of Dreams* – with its account of the sly ways dreams make their meanings, seizing on odd conjunctions and coincidences in the material they work over – can be felt in both the 'content' and the 'form' of Carson's writing. Sleep fascinates Carson as a kind of blindness and unknowingness which is an intimate part of our everyday lives, and of the life of much literature, but is at the same time deeply strange. Through a tenacious pursuit of what we might too-easily dismiss simply as the 'theme' of sleep, Carson dreams up a new way of writing about the intimate strangeness, the uncanniness, of literature itself.

Write an essay plan on a 'theme' of your choice, tracing that theme across a number of texts or artworks. And write out in full the 'topic sentences' – the connecting sentences that help the reader leap nimbly from point to point. Think about how the connections you make themselves arise *from* the theme you are pursuing. Does literature on love mate amorously with other literature on love, for example? Try to make these intertwinings between your theme and the form of your writing legible to your reader.

Anne Carson, 'Every Exit Is an Entrance (A Praise of Sleep)', in *Decreation: Poetry, Essays, Opera* (London: Jonathan Cape, 2006), pp. 17–42.

EVERY EXIT IS AN ENTRANCE
(A Praise of Sleep)

I want to make a praise of sleep. Not as a practitioner – I admit I have never been what is called 'a good sleeper' and perhaps we can return later to that curious concept – but as a reader. There is so much sleep to read, there are so many ways to read it. In Aristotle's view, sleep requires a 'daimonic but not a divine' kind of reading.[1] Kant refers to sleep's content as 'involuntary poetry in a healthy state.'[2] Keats wrote a 'Sonnet to Sleep' invoking its powers against the analytic of the day:

> O soft embalmer of the still midnight!
> . . .
> Then save me, or the passed day will shine
> Upon my pillow, breeding many woes;
> Save me from curious conscience, that still lords
> Its strength for darkness, burrowing like a mole;
> Turn the key deftly in the oiled wards,
> And seal the hushed casket of my soul.[3]

My intention in this essay is to burrow like a mole in different ways of reading sleep, different kinds of readers of sleep, both those who are saved, healthy, daimonic, good sleepers and those who are not. Keats ascribes to sleep an embalming action. This means two things: that sleep does soothe and perfume our nights; that sleep can belie the stench of death inborn in us. Both actions are salvific in Keats' view. Both deserve (I think) to be praised.

My earliest memory is of a dream. It was in the house where we lived when I was three or four years of age. I dreamed I was asleep in the house in an upper room. That I awoke and came downstairs and stood in the living room. The lights were on in the living room, although it was hushed and empty. The usual dark green sofa and chairs stood along the usual pale green walls. It was the same old living room as ever, I knew it well, nothing was out of place. And yet it was utterly, certainly, different. Inside its usual appearance the living room was as changed as if it had gone mad.

Later in life, when I was learning to reckon with my father, who was afflicted with and eventually died of dementia, this dream recovered itself to me, I think because it seemed to bespeak the situation of looking at a well-known face, whose appearance is exactly as it should be in every feature and detail, except that it is also, somehow, deeply and glowingly, strange.

The dream of the green living room was my first experience of such strangeness and I find it as uncanny today as I did when I was three. But there was no concept of madness or dementia available to me at that time. So, as far as I can recall, I explained the dream to myself by saying that I had caught the living room sleeping. I had entered it from the sleep side. And it took me years to recognize, or even to frame a question about, why I found this entrance into strangeness so supremely consoling. For despite the spookiness, inexplicability and later tragic reference of the green living room, it was and remains for me a consolation to think of it lying there, sunk in its greenness, breathing its own order, answerable to no one, apparently penetrable everywhere and yet so perfectly disguised in all the propaganda of its own waking life as to become in a true sense something *incognito* at the heart of our sleeping house.

It is in these terms that I wish to praise sleep, as a glimpse of something *incognito*. Both words are important. *Incognito* means 'unrecognized, hidden, unknown.' Something means not nothing. What is *incognito* hides from us because it has something worth hiding, or so we judge. As an example of this judgment I shall cite for you two stanzas of Elizabeth Bishop's poem 'The Man-Moth.' The Man-Moth, she says, is a creature who lives most of the time underground but pays occasional visits to the surface of the earth, where he attempts to scale the faces of the buildings and reach the moon, for he understands the moon to be a hole at the top of the sky through which he may escape. Failing to attain the moon each time he falls back and returns to the pale subways of his underground existence. Here is the poem's third stanza:

> Up the façades,
> his shadow dragging like a photographer's cloth behind him,
> he climbs fearfully, thinking that this time he will manage
> to push his small head through that round clean opening
> and be forced through, as from a tube, in black scrolls on the light.
> (Man, standing below him, has no such illusions).
> But what the Man-Moth fears most he must do, although
> he fails, of course, and falls back scared but quite unhurt.[4]

The Man-Moth is not sleeping, nor is he a dream, but he may represent sleep itself – an action of sleep, sliding up the facades of the world at night on his weird quest. He harbours a secret content, valuable content, which is difficult to extract even if you catch him. Here is the poem's final stanza:

> If you catch him,
> hold up a flashlight to his eye. It's all dark pupil,
> an entire night itself, whose haired horizon tightens
> as he stares back, and closes up the eye. Then from the lids
> one tear, his only possession, like the bee's sting, slips.
> Slyly he palms it, and if you're not paying attention
> he'll swallow it. However, if you watch, he'll hand it over,
> cool as from underground springs and pure enough to drink.

To drink the tear of sleep, to detach the prefix 'un-' from its canniness and from its underground purposes, has been the project of many technologies and therapies – from the ancient temple of Asklepios at Epidauros, where sick people slept the night in order to dream their own cure, to the psychoanalytic algebras of Jacques Lacan, who understands sleep as a space from which the sleeper can travel in two directions, both of them a kind of waking. If I were to praise either of these methods of healing I would do so on grounds of their hopefulness. Both Asklepiadic priests and Lacanian analysts posit a continuity between the realms of waking and sleeping, whereby a bit of something *incognito* may cross over from night to day and change the life of the sleeper. Here is an ancient account of one of the sleep cures at Epidauros:

> There came as a suppliant to the god Asklepios a man who was
> so one-eyed that on the left he had only lids, there was nothing,
> just emptiness. People in the temple laughed at him for thinking
> he would see with an eye that was not there. But in a vision that
> appeared to him as he slept, the god seemed to boil some medicine
> and, drawing apart the lids, poured it in. When day came the man
> went out, seeing with both eyes.[5]

What could be more hopeful than this story of an empty eye filled with
seeing as it sleeps? An analyst of the Lacanian sort might say that the one-
eyed man has chosen to travel all the way in the direction of his dream and
so awakes to a reality more real than the waking world. He dove into the
nothingness of his eye and is awakened by too much light. Lacan would
praise sleep as a blindness, which nonetheless looks back at us. What does
sleep see when it looks back at us? This is a question entertained by Virginia
Woolf in *To the Lighthouse*, a novel that falls asleep for twenty-five pages
in the middle. The story has three parts. Parts I and III concern the plan-
ning and execution of a trip to the lighthouse by the Ramsay family. Part
II is told entirely from the sleep side. It is called 'Time Passes.' It begins
as a night that grows into many nights then turns into seasons and years.
During this time, changes flow over the house of the story and penetrate
the lives of the characters while they sleep. These changes are glimpsed
as if from underneath; Virginia Woolf's main narrative is a catalogue of
silent bedrooms, motionless chests of drawers, apples left on the dining
room table, the wind prying at a window blind, moonlight gliding on floor-
boards. Down across these phenomena come facts from the waking world,
like swimmers stroking by on a night lake. The facts are brief, drastic and
enclosed in square brackets. For example:

> [Mr. Ramsay, stumbling along a passage one dark morning,
> stretched his arms out, but Mrs. Ramsay having died rather
> suddenly the night before, his arms, though stretched out, remained
> empty.]

or:

> [A shell exploded. Twenty or thirty young men were blown up in
> France, among them Andrew Ramsay, whose death, mercifully, was
> instantaneous.]

or:

> [Mr. Carmichael brought out a volume of poems that spring, which
> had an unexpected success. The war, people said, had revived their
> interest in poetry.][6]

These square brackets convey surprising information about the Ramsays
and their friends, yet they float past the narrative like the muffled shock of a
sound heard while sleeping. No one wakes up. Night plunges on, absorbed
in its own events. There is no exchange between night and its captives,
no tampering with eyelids, no drinking the tear of sleep. Viewed from the
sleep side, an empty eye-socket is just a fact about a person, not a wish to
be fulfilled, not a therapeutic challenge. Virginia Woolf offers us, through
sleep, a glimpse of a kind of emptiness that interests her. It is the emptiness of things before we make use of them, a glimpse of reality prior to its
efficacy. Some of her characters also search for this glimpse while they are
awake. Lily Briscoe, who is a painter in *To the Lighthouse*, stands before her
canvas and ponders how 'to get hold of that very jar on the nerves, the thing
itself before it has been made anything.'[7] In a famous passage of her diaries,
Virginia Woolf agrees with the aspiration:

> If I could catch the feeling I would: the feeling of the singing of
> the real world, as one is driven by loneliness and silence from the
> habitable world.[8]

What would the singing of the real world sound like? What would the thing
itself look like? Such questions are entertained by her character Bernard, at
the end of *The Waves*:

> 'So now, taking upon me the mystery of things, I could go like a spy
> without leaving this place, without stirring from my chair . . . The
> birds sing in chorus; the house is whitened; the sleeper stretches;
> gradually all is astir. Light floods the room and drives shadow
> beyond shadow to where they hang in folds inscrutable. What does
> this central shadow hold? Something? Nothing? I do not know . . .'[9]

Throughout her fiction Virginia Woolf likes to finger the border between
nothing and something. Sleepers are ideal agents of this work. So in her
first novel, *The Voyage Out* (a story in which Clarissa Dalloway and six

other people travel to South America on a boat), she places her heroine in a remarkable paragraph afloat between waking and sleep:

> 'I often wonder:' Clarissa mused in bed, over the little white volume
> of Pascal which went with her everywhere, 'whether it is really
> good for a woman to live with a man who is morally her superior, as
> Richard is mine. It makes one so dependent. I suppose I feel for him
> what my mother and women of her generation felt for Christ. It just
> shows that one can't do without *something*.' She then fell into sleep,
> which was as usual extremely sound and refreshing, but visited by
> fantastic dreams of great Greek letters stalking round the room,
> when she woke up and laughed to herself, remembering where she
> was and that the Greek letters were real people, lying asleep not
> many yards away . . . The dreams were not confined to her indeed,
> but went from one brain to another. They all dreamt of each other
> that night, as was natural, considering how thin the partitions were
> between them and how strangely they had been lifted off the earth to
> sit next each other in mid ocean.[10]

I think Virginia Woolf intends us to enjoy the gentle marital experiment in which Clarissa condenses her husband (Richard) with Christ and then Christ with *something* – put in italics to remind us of its proximity to *nothing*. But I am not sure how 'natural' it is for dreams to go stalking from brain to brain on an ocean liner, or for ancient Greek letters of the alphabet to be identified with real people. Something supernatural is beginning to be conjured here. Slightly more spooky is a story Virginia Woolf published in 1921 called 'A Haunted House,' which features a pair of ghosts sliding from room to room of a house where they had lived centuries ago. The ghosts seem happy but their transit through the house is disturbing, not least of all in its pronouns. The narrative voice shifts from 'we' to 'one' to 'you' to 'they' to 'I,' as if no one in the story can keep a stable skin on, and the story ends with a sleeper startled awake by the ghosts leaning over her bed:

> Waking, I cry 'Oh is this *your* buried treasure? The light in the
> heart.'[11]

I don't exactly know what the last two sentences mean. A transaction of some importance seems about to take place. Between the realms of sleep and waking, life and death, Virginia Woolf throws open a possibility of dispossession, and then leaves it standing ajar, as if she isn't sure which side she wants to be on. The story, although light and almost comical, leaves a dark aftertaste. Let us compare the supernatural effects of an earlier author. Homer locates the psychological climax of the *Iliad* in a scene at the start of the twenty-third book where Achilles falls asleep and is visited by the *psyche* of his dead friend Patroklos. Achilles converses with Patroklos and vainly tries to embrace him. As he reaches out his arms in sleep towards his dead friend, Achilles may remind us of poor Mr. Ramsay in *To the Lighthouse*, stretching out his arms in square brackets to his dead wife. Yet Homer's metaphysic of sleep is much less dark than Virginia Woolf's. Ghosts in epic are sad but they are also efficacious. While Patroklos goes gibbering off to his place in the underworld, Achilles jumps out of bed to perform the funeral rites enjoined on him by the dream, with this careful comment:

'Soul and ghost are certainly *something*!'[12]

Sleepers in Virginia Woolf do not negotiate sublime transactions in this way. Her narrative advises us to place no hope in them:

> . . . and should any sleeper, fancying that he might find on the
> beach an answer to his doubts, a sharer of his solitude, throw off his
> bedclothes and go down by himself to walk on the sand, no image
> with semblance of serving and divine promptitude comes readily
> to hand bringing the night to order and making the world reflect
> the compass of his soul. Useless in such confusion to ask the night
> those questions as to what and why and wherefore, which tempt the
> sleeper from his bed to seek an answer.[13]

In Homer on the other hand, we find answers, beds and sleepers often intertwined, especially in the *Odyssey*. You could say the *Odyssey* is a saga of who sleeps with whom, in its driving mythic impulse towards Penelope and away from Helen, in its fantastic elaboration of kinds of beds, culminating in the famous 'trick of the bed' whereby Penelope and Odysseus prove who they are. Throughout the poem, Homer orchestrates a master sleep plan that pulls all the major characters into a nocturnal rhythm lying just under the surface of the awake narrative. Let's look more closely at how people sleep and where their beds are in this epic.

Telemachos, to begin with, is an insomniac. On the seven occasions in the *Odyssey* when we observe him going to bed, only once does he 'take the gift of sleep' in Homer's phrase. Usually he lies awake worrying, as at the close of Book 1:

> There all night long, wrapped in a sheep fleece,
> he deliberated in his mind the road Athene had shown him.[14]

or at the beginning of Book 15:

> Sweet sleep did not get hold of Telemachos but in his heart
> throughout the ambrosial night, cares for his father kept him awake.[15]

Cares for his father include, not least of all, cares for who his father is. When Athene asks him if he is Odysseus' son he gives a tough teenage answer:

> Well my mother says I'm his but I'm dubious
> myself: no one ever knows his own begetting.[16]

Yet he would certainly like to know. Sexual knowledge ripples everywhere in this story just out of Telemachos' reach. He sits amid the suitors 'biting his heart' as they cavort before his mother. He travels to the houses of other married couples, Nestor and his wife, Menelaos and Helen, where he passes the night on a couch aligned with the marital bed. Thus pursued by primal scenes and primary doubts he makes his way to the sixteenth book and to the hut of Eumaios, the swineherd, where he finally meets and knows his father. Here Telemachos 'takes the gift of sleep' lying down in the swineherd's hut beside Odysseus. This idyllic, impossible night as substitute Penelope beside his own father is Telemachos' happiest moment in the *Odyssey*. The very next evening sees him returned to his childhood and to insomnia: back at Penelope's house, as Odysseus plans the rout of the suitors, he sends Telemachos upstairs to bed alone:

> Then there Telemachos laid himself down
> and waited for radiant dawn.[17]

Meanwhile Odysseus: no question the man of many turns is a master of waking reality, yet his relation to sleep is troubled. He frequently feels the need to force himself awake, as when predatory animals or rapacious humans surround him (5.473; 8.445), or because a roomful of eager listeners wants to hear one more chapter of his adventures (11.379). Whenever he does nod off, catastrophes occur. Sailing from the island of Aiolos, whose king has given him a bag containing all the winds, Odysseus dozes on deck and his companions get curious:

> 'So they loosened the bag and the winds all rushed out together.
> Storm winds seized them and carried them wailing their hearts out,
> over the sea away from their homes. But I
> awakened from sleep, considered in my excellent heart
> whether to drop from the deck and die right there in the sea
> or to endure, keep silent, go on being one of the living.'[18]

Odysseus has another suicidal moment occasioned by sleep, in Book 12 when slumber overtakes him on the beach of Thrinakia and his companions slaughter the cattle of the sun. Odysseus wakes up and cries out:

> 'O father Zeus and you other gods who live forever,
> how to my ruin you have lulled me in pitiless slumber!'[19]

So let's say in general Odysseus and sleep are not friends. Whatever this may mean for the hero's characterization overall, I'm struck by how Homer uses it in subjugating Odysseus to Penelope at the end of the poem. For no one can deny that Penelope is a master of sleep. She goes to bed dozens of times in the course of the story, has lots of sleep shed on her by gods, experiences an array of telling and efficacious dreams and evolves her own theory of how to read them. Moreover, Homer shows us as early as Book 4 that sleep is the deepest contract she shares with her husband. Miles apart, years apart, consciously and unconsciously, they turn the key of each other. So Penelope in Book 4, lying awake in her chamber while the suitors carouse below, is compared by Homer to a lion cornered in a circle of huntsmen. Then she falls asleep, to dream of her husband, 'noble Odysseus who has the heart of a lion,'[20] and wake up profoundly soothed. Sleep *works* for Penelope. She knows how to use it, enjoy it, theorize it and even to parody it, should need arise. As in her famous 'recognition scene' with Odysseus (which occupies Books 19–23 of the poem).

Penelope's purpose in this scene is to seduce and overcome Odysseus, i.e., to seduce *by* overcoming Odysseus. She goes at it from the sleep side, because there she can win. As we have already seen, and as she probably knows, sleep is not his country. Her seduction has two aspects, first a practical one, the bed question: Who sleeps where? This question culminates in Book 23 in the so-called 'trick of the bed:' whereby Penelope manoeuvres Odysseus (still disguised as a stranger) into betraying his identity. For she alludes to the bed in her marriage chamber as one that can be moved out into the corridor to accommodate a guest. Odysseus is outraged: as he alone knows, the bed in her chamber was one he carved himself twenty years ago out of an oak tree in the middle of their house. His outrage is the final proof she needs of who he is. But before this recognition quite a bit of sleeping goes on, or is prevented from going on, in noteworthy ways.

Let's look at Book 19, which takes the form of a long conversation between husband and wife before they retire to separate beds, on the night before the climax of the plot. After they have conversed, Penelope instructs her maid-servants to give Odysseus a bath and prepare a luxurious bedstead for him. Odysseus rejects these arrangements, insists on being bathed by an old woman and being given a place on the bare ground to sleep. So Odysseus goes off, has his bath, then returns and sits down beside his wife. Whereupon, instead of saying goodnight, she launches into Penelope's Interpretation of Dreams (to which we'll return in a moment). Finally they do say goodnight and retire – she upstairs to her chamber, he to the ground in the forecourt. So there they are, in separate rooms of the same house, each lying awake. Athene sheds sleep on Penelope at the end of Book 19, then sheds sleep on Odysseus at the beginning of Book 20. No sooner does Odysseus fall asleep than Penelope awakes, weeping and crying out. Her voice carries through the house to where Odysseus is sleeping, enters his dream and convinces him that his wife is standing over him in the flesh, recognizing and welcoming him home. Odysseus wakes up, receives an omen from Zeus and rejoices in the forecourt. Homer has woven a strange symbiosis between these two people, together and apart in the same night, entering and exiting each other's minds, almost sharing one consciousness – especially at that moment when Penelope penetrates the membrane of her husband's sleep and fills him with joy. I would call that a successful seduction.

For the theoretical aspect of this seduction, let's return to the long conversation of Book 19. It has two parts. First, husband and wife exchange narratives of what they've been doing for the last twenty years; here Odysseus mainly lies, Penelope tells the truth. Then there is a pause while Odysseus has his bath. Now a bath in epic is often a mechanism of transition to new conditions.[21] After the bath, Penelope takes the conversational initiative and offers a complex (and almost certainly fictitious) narrative about a dream she has had, demanding that Odysseus interpret the dream. Surely this demand is peculiar. The dream is of an eagle who flies down from the sky, slaughters Penelope's twenty pet geese, then announces that he is not an eagle at all, nor a dream, but the real Odysseus returned to save his household. The dream is as blatant as an English movie with English subtitles and Odysseus politely says so. But why does Penelope require his complicity in reading it?

Because it is her game they are playing now: they are reasoning from the sleep side, where she is a master. Look what she does next. Broaches her theory of dreams. Dreams are double, she says, some true, some false. True ones emerge from the gates of horn, false from the gates of ivory. This theory is as bogus as the dream of geese. Penelope is talking through her hat. But all of a sudden, out of her hat, Penelope drops a bombshell. Tomorrow, she announces, I'm going to set up a contest, see which of the suitors can shoot through twelve axes with Odysseus' bow. The winner will take me home as his wife. Here is a sudden practical solution to the whole domestic dilemma. Odysseus hastily agrees it is a great idea. Penelope has orchestrated the conversation so the great idea seems to drop out of a dream – or indeed to shoot out through the very gates of horn. She has involved Odysseus in the interpretive necessity of dreams as he earlier involved her in the autobiographical necessity of lies. She has matched his ambiguities and used her sleep knowledge to wrap him in an act of seduction that he cannot outwit – that he will not wish to outwit. She invites him into the way her mind works. Rather like the moon in the mirror in Elizabeth Bishop's poem 'Insomnia':

> The moon in the bureau mirror
> looks out a million miles
> (and perhaps with pride, at herself,
> but she never, never smiles)
> far and away beyond sleep, or
> perhaps she's a daytime sleeper.

By the Universe deserted,
she'd tell it to go to hell,
and she'd find a body of water,
or a mirror, on which to dwell.
So wrap up care in a cobweb
and drop it down the well

into that world inverted
where left is always right,
where the shadows are really the body,
where we stay awake all night,
where the heavens are shallow as the sea
is now deep, and you love me.[22]

As far as love goes, Penelope's only real rival among the female personnel of
the *Odyssey* is Nausikaa, the *very* unmarried girl whom Odysseus meets in
Book 6 on the island of the Phaiakians. She is asleep when we first meet her:

. . . the girl
lay sleeping in form and image like to immortals,
Nausikaa, daughter of great-hearted Alkinoos,
and alongside her two attendants having beauty from the Graces
on either side of the pillars. But the brilliant doors were shut.[23]

Homer shows us the sleeper in all her layers of defense. He shows us the
doors, pillars, attendants, behind which the she lies. Then he shows us how
to pass through doors, in the person of Athene, who traverses the house as
a blast of wind and stands over Nausikaa's bed, whispering:

'*Nausikaa* – how is it your mother bore so slack a girl as you?
Look, your shining clothes lie in a mess.
But for you marriage is near, when you will need beautiful things
to wear yourself and to give to those who attend you.
. . . let's go do laundry as soon as dawn appears.'[24]

Athene puts into Nausikaa a word that condenses laundry with marriage
(cleanliness with sex), a word whose dream logic names Nausikaa's perfect
purity at the very moment we see it most exposed to violation. For there
is another motionless presence on this page. Nausikaa lies sleeping side by

side with Odysseus, not in the space of her room but in narrative juxta-
position. Two verses describing Odysseus (who is lying naked in a pile of
leaves on the outskirts of Nausikaa's city) immediately precede our view of
Nausikaa in her bed:

> So there he lay much-enduring goodly Odysseus
> overwhelmed by sleep and exhaustion.[25]

Odysseus' exhaustion subtends and embraces Nausikaa's dream (she rises
at v.50 but he does not wake until 117). Their sleep prefigures everything
that will occur between the man and the girl in the days to follow – a system
of contradictions curving in and out of impossibility without arriving at
refutation, oxymoron of male and female – as the old, wild, dirty; naked,
married, shelterless man of many turns coils himself around a girl who lies
straight in her nine frames of safety dreaming of laundry.

She is the cleanest girl in epic. And his dirt emphasizes that, not to say
the brutal opacity of his sleep – whereas she lies transparent: we watch the
dream in her head, we know her action before she does, we see her desire
prior to itself. Her desire is to find a pretext and travel far from the city, to
where the washing pools lie. But this is precisely where Odysseus lies. The
night before, at the end of Book 5, he laid himself down 'on the edge of the
land' to sleep the sleep of elemental life. Life is all he has left. Wife, child,
parents, home, ship, comrades, possessions, clothing, youth, strength and
personal fame are all lost. He had to cover himself in a pile of leaves to
survive the night:

> And when he saw [the leaf pile]
> much-enduring goodly Odysseus laughed
> and lay in the middle and heaped a big bunch of leaves over himself.
> As when someone hides a firebrand in black embers
> on the edge of the land, who has no other neighbours near,
> preserving the seed of fire, lest he have to kindle a light
> from somewhere else,
> so Odysseus wrapped himself in leaves.[26]

'On the edge of the land' is a symbolic description. 'Land' means farm-
land, cultivated space. Odysseus is stranded at the margin of culture: he
has come back in from the wilderness and preserves within himself (just

barely) the means to begin civilization again. But no one can begin civilization alone. And the sleep of fire needs careful waking. Homer seems to
enjoy assigning this task to a girl whose chief concerns are cold water and
aristocratic hygiene.

Once he is awake, Odysseus finds the island of the Phaiakians a perplexing
place. Almost everyone he meets presumes he has come there to marry
Nausikaa, inherit her father's kingdom and live happily ever after. It is as
if he has waked up inside someone else's dream, only to find himself the
protagonist of it. For these dreamlike Phaiakians know who Odysseus is,
although he withholds as long as possible from them the news that *he* is
Odysseus. And as their local poet performs songs from the epic tradition
that tell of Odysseus' exploits at Troy, he sits and weeps to hear himself
acclaimed in the third person. He has backed into his own heroic *persona*,
like a shadow finding its body.

Or, like Rosencrantz and Guildenstern in Tom Stoppard's play *Rosencrantz
and Guildenstern Are Dead*, where two Shakespearean courtiers find themselves in the midst of the tragedy of *Hamlet* without quite understanding who wrote them into the script. Yet they scramble to play their
part, manage to produce the right lines and end up dead in England, as
Shakespeare's scenario requires. It is not clear whether they are awake or
asleep – they talk about having been roused at dawn yet act like people
stuck in a bad dream. It is a familiar dream. Stoppard uses the familiarity
of Shakespeare's play to lock us into the badness of the bad dream. He
puts us, as audience, on the sleep side of the play, alongside Rosencrantz
and Guildenstern, while the other characters of *Hamlet* wander in and out
muttering passages of Shakespeare's text. Stoppard uses Shakespeare's text
to capture Rosencrantz and Guildenstern within his own, in somewhat the
same way Virginia Woolf used square brackets to capture the Ramsays and
their friends in a long night of sleep. As readers we take a guilty pleasure
in these arrangements. For we would almost like to see Rosencrantz and
Guildenstern escape their predicament, except it would spoil the plot
of *Hamlet*. Good sleepers that we are, we do not quite want to wake up.
Stoppard's play praises sleep, functionally, for its necessity. No other experience gives us so primary a sense of being governed by laws outside us. No
other substance can so profoundly saturate a story in compulsion, inevita-
bility and dread as sleep can. Mr. Ramsay in square brackets has no option
to snatch his wife back from death, nor Rosencrantz and Guildenstern to

rewrite the tragedy of *Hamlet*. It is, as Virginia Woolf says, useless to ask the night these questions. Stoppard allows his character Guildenstern to ask them anyway. Guildenstern is a kind of amateur philosopher; he derives consolation in the middle of the play from a well-known Taoist parable about waking and sleeping:

> Guildenstern: Wheels have been set in motion, and they have their own pace, to which we are . . . condemned. Each move is dictated by the previous one – that is the meaning of order. If we start being arbitrary it'll just be a shambles: at least let us hope so. Because if we happened, just happened to discover, or even suspect, that our spontaneity is part of their order, we'd know we were lost. *(He sits.)* A Chinaman of the T'ang dynasty – and by which definition a philosopher – dreamed he was a butterfly, and from that moment he was never quite sure that he was not a butterfly dreaming it was a Chinese philosopher. Envy him; in his two-fold security.[27]

There is something cheesy about Guildenstern's envy, about his use of the parable of the butterfly and the sage (traditionally ascribed to Zhuang Zi, who was not of the T'ang dynasty), about his philosophizing in general, that makes me happy to turn to a different amateur philosopher for my final example of the praise of sleep. Sokrates, arguably the most amateur and the most different of the philosophers of the Western tradition, exhibits, in the Platonic dialogues describing the final days of his life, a certain regard for that sublime residue, the tear of sleep.

Let's consider the *Krito*. Plato begins this dialogue in the dark, with Sokrates starting up sheer from sleep and his dream still wet on its back. Here are the opening lines of the dialogue:

> Sokrates: Why are you here? Isn't it early?
> Krito: Yes pretty early.
> Sokrates: What time?
> Krito: Near dawn.
> Sokrates: I'm surprised the guard let you in.
> Krito: Oh he knows me by now. Anyway I tip him.
> Sokrates: So did you just arrive or have you been here awhile?
> Krito: Quite awhile.
> Sokrates: Why didn't you wake me?[28]

And so it emerges that Krito sat watching Sokrates sleep because he looked
happy sleeping and Krito had nothing to wake him for but his death day.
Perhaps I should call to mind the situation here. The *Krito* is the third of
a tetralogy of dialogues concerned with Sokrates' trial, imprisonment and
death. Sokrates has by now been judged guilty and is in jail awaiting execution. His death is postponed because his trial coincided with the annual
Athenian mission to Delos, during which no prisoners could be executed.
Krito has come to announce to Sokrates that the ship from Delos has
been sighted and so his death will take place the next day. To which news
Sokrates responds:

> Sokrates: You know I don't think so. It won't be tomorrow.
> Krito: What are you talking about?
> Sokrates: I had a dream last night – lucky you didn't wake me!
> Krito: What dream?
> Sokrates: A beautiful woman came up to me, dressed in white, called
> to me and said: *Sokrates, on the third day you shall reach rich Phthia.*
> Krito: Weird dream, Sokrates.
> Sokrates: Well it seems obvious to me.[29]

Plato has constructed the opening of this dialogue in such a way as to
align the realms of waking and sleeping, drawing our attention to an active
boundary between them – active because it leaks. Sokrates brings a bit of
difference back with him from the sleep side. The words of the woman in
white contain a hint of the argument that will carry Sokrates all the way
from these sleepy sentences to his death at the end of the *Phaedo*. She tells
Sokrates he will reach Phthia on the third day. It is a line from Homer.
In the ninth book of the *Iliad* Achilles receives an embassy of Greeks sent
by Agamemnon to persuade him to return to war, promising tons of gifts
if he does. He responds with a 114-line denunciation of gifts, war and
Agamemnon, including a threat to leave for home at once:

> 'On the third day I could reach rich Phthia.'[30]

Phthia is Achilles' homeland. It is also a name cognate with a Greek verb
for death (*phthiein*) but that may be incidental. Let us observe some analogies between these two heroes heading for Phthia on the third day: both
Sokrates and Achilles are eccentric gentlemen who find themselves defying
the rules of life of their society and disappointing the hopes of a circle of
intense friends. For, as Achilles is surrounded by Achaians urging him

to resume life as a warrior, Sokrates is surrounded by Athenians urging him to escape prison and take up life in exile. Both of them say *no* to their friends. Both argue this choice on the basis of an idiosyncratic understanding of the word *psyche*, 'soul, spirit, principle of life.' So Achilles repudiates Agamemnon's offer of gifts in these terms:

'All the gifts and treasure in Troy aren't worth as much as my own soul!'[31]

And Sokrates explains his choice for death at the end of the *Phaedo* by saying,

'Since the soul seems to be immortal . . . a man [who has lived a good life] might as well be cheerful as he makes his exit into Hades.'[32]

Who knows what either of them means by *psyche* or whether 'soul' is a reasonable translation of it. Still we can say they both use this word to indicate some kind of immortal value, some sort of transcendent attractor, that exerts such a strong pressure on their mortal lives and thinking as to pull them into a choice that strikes everyone around them as insane. I reckon that Plato in his dialogues involving Sokrates had somewhat the same literary problem as Homer in his *Iliad*, namely to convey a hero in his *difference* from other people, a hero whose power over other people arose in part from something *incognito* in his very being. In the dialogues that record his last days, the Platonic Sokrates seems increasingly a person ungraspable in ordinary sentences, a person who is (to use a current expression) *coming from somewhere else*.

Plato shows him coming from the sleep side in the *Krito*. As if he had slept in the temple of Asklepios, Sokrates emerges from his dream 'seeing with both eyes.' And he does not hesitate to trust what the woman in white has let him see, although Krito dismisses it. The woman in white will turn out to be correct. Sokrates is inclined to trust, and to be correct about trusting, different sources of knowledge than other philosophers do – like his crazy *daimon*, or the oracle of Apollo, not to say the good sentences of sleep. Sokrates also puts a fair amount of faith in his own poetic imagination – his power to turn nothing into something. So in the latter half of the *Krito*, since Krito can think of nothing further to say, Sokrates conducts both sides of an imaginary conversation between himself as Sokrates and a ventriloquized projection of the *Nomoi*, the Laws of Athens. These ventriloquized Laws are as weird as the ghosts that Virginia Woolf sent rustling and whispering around the rooms of her 'Haunted House,' looking for their buried treasure. If you recall, that story of the haunted house ends with a spooky moment of dispossession, as the ghosts lean over the sleeper's bed and discover *their* treasure buried in *her* heart. Sokrates also suffers a moment of dispossession at the end of the *Krito*. The voices of the Laws, he says, fill his prison cell and drown out all other sound. He has to stop talking:

> 'O beloved friend Krito, these voices are what I seem to hear – as
> Korybantic worshippers imagine they hear flutes – and the sound of
> their words is so loud in me, I am deaf to everything else.'[33]

So Sokrates falls silent, overcome by what Virginia Woolf might call 'the singing of the real world.'

To sum up.
I shall state my conclusions in the form of an 'Ode to Sleep.'

ODE TO SLEEP
Think of your life without it.
Without that slab of outlaw time punctuating every pillow – without
pillows.
Without the big black kitchen and the boiling stove where you
snatch morsels
of your own father's legs and arms
only to see them form into a sentence
which – you *weep with sudden joy* – will save you
if you can remember it
later! Later,
not much left but a pale green *upsilon* embalmed between *butter* and fly –
but what's that stuff he's dabbing in your eye?
It is the moment when the shiver stops.
A shiver is a perfect servant.
Her amen sootheth.
'As a matter of fact,' she confides in a footnote, 'it was
a misprint for *mammoth*.'
It hurts me to know this.
Exit wound, as they say.

NOTES

1. In his essay *On Prophecy in Sleep*, Aristotle reads sleep as part of nature and dreams as messages from the realm of the daimonic, which lies between divine and human being (463b12–15): Aristotle, *Parva Naturalia*, ed. W. D. Ross (Oxford: Clarendon Press, 1955). Translations are my own unless otherwise noted.

2. Immanuel Kant, *Anthropology from a Pragmatic View*, trans. M. J. Gregor (The Hague: Martinus Nijhoff, 1974), p. 85.

3. John Keats, *Complete Poems*, ed. J. Stillinger (Cambridge, MA: The Belknap Press of Harvard University Press, 1978, 1982).

4. Elizabeth Bishop, *The Complete Poems: 1927–1979* (New York: Farrar, Straus and Giroux, 1979, 1983), p. 14.

5. *Inscriptiones Graecae: vol. IV Inscriptiones Argolidis*, ed. M. Fraenkel (Berlin: Berlin Academy, 1902), pp. 223–4.

6. Virginia Woolf, *To the Lighthouse* (New York: Harcourt, Brace, 1927), pp. 128; 133; 134.

7. Ibid. p. 193.

8. Virginia Woolf, *The Diary of Virginia Woolf*, ed. A. O. Bell and A. McNeilhie (London: The Hogarth Press, 1980), 3.260: Oct. 11, 1929.

9. Virginia Woolf, *The Waves* (New York: Harcourt Brace Jovanovich, 1931), p. 292.

10. Virginia Woolf, *The Voyage Out* (London: Duckworth, 1915), p. 59.

11. Virginia Woolf, *A Haunted House and Other Stories* (London: The Hogarth Press, 1944), p. 11.

12. Homer, *Iliad*, ed. W. Leaf and M. A. Bayfield (London, 1895), 23.103.

13. Woolf, *To the Lighthouse*, p. 128.

14. Homer, *Odyssey*, ed. W. B. Stanford (London: Macmillan, 1947) 1.433–4.

15. Ibid. 15.7–8.

16. Ibid. 1.215–16.

17. Ibid. 19.50.

18. Ibid. 10.47–52.

19. Ibid. 12.371–2.

20. Ibid. 4.514.

21. This scene, where Odysseus is recognized by his old nurse Eurykleia because of the scar on his leg, is analyzed by Eric Auerbach in *Mimesis*, trans. W. Trask (Garden City: Doubleday, 1957); Penelope seems unaware.

22. Bishop, *The Complete Poems*, p. 70.

23. Homer, *Odyssey*, 6.15–19.

24. Ibid. 6.25–30.

25. Ibid. 6.1–2.

26. Ibid. 5.486–91.

27. Tom Stoppard, *Rosencrantz and Guildenstern Are Dead* (London: Faber and Faber, 1967), p. 51.

28. Plato, *Krito*, 43a–b, in *Platonis Opera*, ed. J. Burnet (Oxford: Clarendon Press, 1976), vol. 1.

29. Ibid. 43d–44b.

30. Homer, *Iliad*, 9.363.

31. Ibid. 9.401.

32. Plato, *Phaedo*, 114d–115a, in *Platonis Opera*, vol. 1.

33. Plato, *Krito*, 54d.

CHAPTER 4

Hélène Cixous, 'Without end, no, State of drawingness, no, rather: The Executioner's taking off'

How often do you feel that the early stages of any project are the best? That's the time when you scribble notes excitedly and wake in the small hours to jot down new ideas. It's the time when everything seems possible – and when what you plan to make or write or do might, just might, turn out to be the best of its kind *ever*. Later, everything closes down, time presses, pursuing one route precludes taking another, and the final result seems at once inadequate and deathly in its ostensible completion. It's out of feelings such as these that Cixous writes 'Without end, no, State of drawingness, no, rather: The Executioner's taking off' – a piece whose title, in its auto-revisions, plays out the very desire to keep earliness in play that the succeeding essay explores. Its focus is on drawings, sketches and notebooks, by da Vinci, Picasso, Rembrandt, Kafka, Lispector and others. It attends to and loves these inchoate documents because they archive the processes and the flux from which works – finished articles – are born. It's the 'to-be-in-the-process of writing or drawing' that impassions Cixous; and it's in the midst of that process, in the present continuous of its making, that she herself writes. 'I wanted to call this text: "For the Instant," or "At the instant," but I changed my mind,' she writes at one moment, quickly, and in one of the many instances in this piece where the drafting of its own composition is made legible.

Quick! write a piece of criticism in which you register the traces of the revisions, edits, decisions, second thoughts and paths not travelled that go into its making. (Sarah Wood's 'Edit' might provide further inspiration here. We'd wondered about including it in this *Anthology*, but decided in the end on her 'Anew Again'. Oh to have had both!) As you write, think too – and register in your writing – the ways in which this less composed form of critical composition might speak to what remains alive, quick, early-feeling, unfinished and in the making, in the texts or artworks you are exploring.

Hélène Cixous, 'Without end, no, State of drawingness, no, rather: The Executioner's taking off', trans. Catherine A. F. MacGillivray, in *Stigmata: Escaping Texts* (London: Routledge, 1998), pp. 20–31.

'I want the beforehand of a book.' I just wrote this sentence, but before this sentence, I wrote a hundred others, which I've suppressed, because the moment for cutting short had arrived. It's not me, it's necessity which has cut the text we were on the way to writing. Because the text and I, we would continue on our way.

'I've learned to tear up nothing of what I write,' Clarice Lispector tells me. But then comes the time for separation. The time for publication.

I would like so much this unknown untorn page. Everything we read: remains.

I want the forest before the book, the abundance of leaves before the pages, I love the creation as much as the created, no, more. I love the Kafka of the Journals, the executioner-victim, I love the process a thousand times more than the Trial process (no, a hundred times more). I want the tornados in the atelier.

And what I love best are Dostoevsky's notebooks, the crazy and tumultuous forge, where Love and Hate embrace, rolling around on the ground in convulsions which thwart all calculation and all hope: no one knows who will be born of this possessed belly, who will win, who will survive.

I want the world of pulses, before destiny, I want the prenatal and anonymous night. I want (the arrival) to see arriving.

Acts of birth, potency, and impotency mingled are what I'm passionate about. The to-be-in-the-process of writing or drawing. (*Mais pourquoi avons-nous perdu le gérondif en français? Le vrai temps de ce texte est le gérondif.*)

There is no end to writing or drawing. Being born doesn't end. Drawing is a being born. Drawing is born.

– When do we draw?

– When we were little. Before the violent divorce between Good and Evil. All was mingled then, and no mistakes. Only desire, trial, and error. Trial, that is to say, error. Error: progression.

As soon as we draw (as soon as, following the pen, we advance into the unknown, hearts beating, mad with desire) we are little, we do not know, we start out avidly, we're going to lose ourselves.

Drawing, writing, what expeditions, what wanderings, and at the end, no end, we won't finish, rather time will put an end to it.

(N.B. I'm saying writing-or-drawing, because these are often twin adventures, which depart to seek in the dark, which do not find, do not find, and as a result of not finding and not understanding, (draw) help the secret beneath their steps to shoot forth.)

I write this accompanied by seeking drawings.

It is the dead of night. I sense I am going to write. You, whom I accompany, you sense you are going to draw. Your night is waiting.

The figure which announces itself, which is going to make its appearance, the poet-of-drawings doesn't see it. The model only appears to be outside. In truth it is invisible, but present, it lives inside the poet-of-drawings. You who pray with the pen, you feel it, hear it, dictate. Even if there is a landscape, a person, there outside – no, it's from inside the body that the drawing-of-the-poet rises to the light of day. First it exists at the torment state in the chest, under the waist. See it now as it precipitates itself in spasms, in waves, the length of the arm, passing the hand, passing the pen. Eyes open wide in the night, staring wide-eyed with hope, the one who draws follows the movement. S/he obeys. Ecstasy: technique. Because not seeing doesn't impede the pen from noting. To the contrary.

I write before myself by apprehension, with noncomprehension, the night vibrates, I see with my ears, I advance into the bosom of the world, hands in front, capturing the music with my palms,

until something breathes under the pen's beak.

(I've just written these lines eyelids closed as usual, because the day and its huge light keeps us from seeing what is germinating.)

Now we turn on the lights, and lean over to see the work born. Then, surprise before what, passing through us, was drawn; and if it is *I* who drew this unknown child then who are I?

The drawing is without a stop. I mean to say the true drawing, the living one – because there are dead ones, drawn-deads. Look and you shall see.

Barely traced – the true drawing escapes. Rends the limit. Snorts. Like the world, which is only a perennial movement, the drawing goes along, befuddled and staggering, with a natural drunkenness.

All that exists is naturally drunk: the boat, the Egyptian pyramids, the executioner's coldness, the iron. Who said that? If it's not Rembrandt or Rimbaud, it's one Montaigne or the other.

To think there are those who seek the finished. Those who seek to portray cleanly, the most properly!

But some portray passing. The truth. The passing (of the) truth. This is what gives to their drawing that panting and unstable allure.

Look at the child barely seated on his mother's knees: on the one hand the little arms are in the drawing, in the circle, but on the other hand the legs sketch the escapade. This little one doesn't stay put.

You will recognize the true drawing, the live one: it's still running. Look at the legs. I'll come back to that.

For the moment, I am, following, the error, without fear but with respect. To what extent we need error which is the promise of truth, to what extent we can't do without the silvery burst of error, which is the sign, all those who go by pen don't cease to marvel at this in a similar way, from century to century.

Felix culpa, St Augustine calls it, and then *portal of discovery*, says Joyce, *submissão ao processo*, says Clarice Lispector, the writing process is made up of errors . . . And before that, 'naïve and essential submission,' said our wandering grandfather Montaigne; and we're all in agreement, how to draw other than by groping in the night, 'inquiring and ignorant.'

Necessary error, school mistress, faltering essential companion, we love her, because she is the only way we have on this earth to feel the truth, which is always a little farther, exists, a little farther away.

And repentance? No repentance. We who draw are innocent. Our mistakes are our leaps in the night. Error is not lie: it is approximation. Sign that we are on track.

And: to not become gloomy from not 'attaining.' We don't lose anything by erring, to the contrary.

The unhappy thing would be to believe we had found.

As long as we are seeking we are innocent. We are in naïve submission. In prenatality.

I advance error by error, with erring steps, by the force of error. It's suffering, but it's joy.

I seek the truth, I encounter error. How do I recognize error? It is obvious, like truth. Who tells me? My body. Truth gives us pleasure. It makes us burst out laughing, trembling. Blushing. It's hot. It's like this: I grope. I try the word 'hesitation.' I taste it. No pleasure. No taste. I cross out. I try: 'correction.' I taste. No. I taste ten words. Finally I fall on the word: 'essay.' Before even trying I already sense a pretaste . . . I taste. And, that's it! Its taste is strong and fine and rich in memories of pleasure.

Truth strikes us. Opens our heart. Our lips. Error makes us sense the absence of taste. Drops us like a dead person, apathetic tongue, dry eyes. Error really can't fool us.

We've just drawn an executioner. Just a little while ago he was amassing in our entrails, in our lungs, we felt his storm rumbling. Now we look at him standing on the paper, and we don't feel anything. In us the storm is always alive, on paper, no. I submit myself to the invisible truth of my vision, I obey the strange and foreign voice in my body.

– A little farther! Go on! Start again! Forward!

– To the right? Shall I draw to the right?

– Try . . .

– I'm trying.

– I'm still trying.

See why I guard against effacing my first steps. I need to lean on, to start again from my error.

In order to be able to draw a crime, Dostoevsky began again a hundred times. It was such a subtle crime, which escaped him, so profound. He felt it. Missed it. Approached it. The other escaped. The essays accumulated. The scene was turning, the pen, trying, a door – a victim – Here? – That's not it – was distancing itself, shall I knock? and if that wasn't it, the drawing wouldn't take, its heart wouldn't beat, the knife was rising, the victim was falling – Is that it? – Not yet,

then is it in the stairway? – take note, D. told himself, but that wasn't it, was there someone behind the door? N.B., D. noted, N.B., N.B., annotating his notes. These notebooks were a joyous carnage. N.B. – You have to have found the key by midnight. With the result that wanting to discover the invisible heart of his crime before midnight, he managed to play four books at the same time and one against the other – one barring the other, one killing the other, one chasing the other, one haunting the other denying – four books from only one hand, on the same page we go straight to the confession. Three words later we leave running.

These notebooks so many failures! Before the midnight scissors what fecundity.

What do we want to draw?

What are we trying to grasp between the lines, in between the strokes, in the net that we're weaving, that we throw, and the dagger blows?

Figure 4.1. Leonardo da Vinci, *Vierge à l'Enfant*. Paris, Musée du Louvre.

Not the person, but the precious in that person, not the Virgin, not the child, but what is between them in this very moment, linking them – a secret, that which mysteriously renders those two unforgettable. I sense: it's not divinity, it's whim. That little grain of meanness which *makes* the little boy. Do you see?

It's not a question of drawing the contours, *but of what escapes the contour*, the secret movement, the breaking, the torment, the unexpected.

The drawing wants to draw what is invisible to the naked eye. It's very difficult. The effort to write is always beyond my strength. What you see here, these lines, these strokes, are rungs on the ladder of writing, the steps which I have cut with my fingernails in my own wall, in order to hoist myself up above and beyond myself.

And drawing '*the living of life*' (what else is there to want to draw?) – is maddening; it's exactly what none *knows* how to draw, the quick of life. But it's not impossible.

It's something small, precise – I'm guessing – it must be red, it's, I'm guessing, the fire speck – or the blood speck – it's – I'm searching – the point which nails this drawing, this page, this verse, in our memory, the unforgettable stroke – the needle planted in the heart of eternity – I'm searching – a minuscule fatality, a point which hurts my heart and hurts the world's heart, it's no bigger than the red spider which continues on while Stavroguine thinks about the crime, thinks about the crime, and doesn't repent . . .

(– I'm advancing, I'm approaching, be careful because if I see what it is, just as quickly I won't see anymore –)

the trace of the quick of life hidden beneath the rounded appearances of life, life which remains hidden because we wouldn't bear seeing it as it is, in all the brilliance of horror that it is, it is without pity, like the drawing must be.

This morning in the museum, I was passing in front of the drawings, in the slight alarm of the reading which doesn't know from where the blow will come, and I was looking, distracted, at these morsels of worry, these stuttered avowals of nothing, nothing clearly delivered.

It was then that the blow came from whom I wasn't expecting it at all. What is this moment called when we suddenly recognize what we have never seen? And which gives us a joy like a wound? This is the woman who did that to me: the Woman Ironing.

This Woman Ironing hurts us. Because the drawing catches 'the secret' in its (contrary) enmeshed threads. 'The thing,' that sharp thing, 'life.' We thought we were drawing a Woman Ironing. But it's worse. This Woman Ironing is a tragedy. A needle blow right in the middle of eternity's chest. But in order to pull the needle out, to strike the blow, one had to scribble furiously. We struggled. Against what or whom?

Against the *idea* of Woman Ironing. The drawing carries traces of blows, of bruises and even of blood. She's tumefied.

By dint of passing and ironing over the body of the woman ironing, what ended up appearing – is – one would say a crime. From the body broken and streaked with strokes comes the body hidden in the body of the woman ironing, or more precisely the soul's head, and, neck exposed, she bellows.

I don't want to draw the idea, I don't want to write being, I want what happens in the Woman Ironing, I want the nerve, I want the Revelation of the broken Woman Ironing.

And I want to write what passes between us and the Woman Ironing, the electric current. The emotion. Because as a result of drawing her with my eyes, I felt: *it's death* that is passing through the Woman Ironing, our mortality in person. I want to draw our mortality, this quiver.

The emotion is born *at the angle* of one state with another state. At the passing, so brusque. Accident. Instant of alteration that takes us by surprise. And the body which expresses itself before the word. First the cry, then the words.

When it's not entirely clear, what is being felt or being thought in the body – of Christ, of the woman ironing – that's the moment we seek to draw. Are we going to die? Kill? The hand rises, the head, the pen falls once more.

The drawing feels death passing.

We believe we're drawing (going to) the Beheading of St John the Baptist. But it's worse. At the moment of Beheading, suddenly, there's been a change of heart. Or rather of life. Something unpredictable has happened between the two characters *during* the drawing. We were bending over the saint in horror, and at the moment we contemplated his body with curiosity, that is to say the two parts of his body, suddenly so contrary

our entire attention was diverted and carried away in the opposite direction by the executioner. Because, at the moment the drawing wanted to draw the body's pain and the head's mourning, there was a sudden rise of life in the executioner, which the drawing was unable to resist. The executioner's joy burst out. This couldn't have occurred *before* the drawing executed the saint. Because the saint had to have been properly beheaded in order for the executioner to have suddenly been transfigured, and become

Figure 4.2. Pablo Picasso, *Etude pour 'La Repasseuse.'* Paris, Musée Picasso.

one, on the spot, body with saber. At the instant we were describing the saint's collapse (and at the sight of the decapitated body trying to get up, pushing with its arms), the executioner straightened up like a spring, I mean the pen, and with a grand full stroke signed the executioner's strong and sudden jubilation.

We want to write the torment, and we write the joy. At the same time. At each moment I am another myself. The one in and on the other.

What was the first stroke of the pen? And before the first line there were many others. In truth the first line is the survivor of the mêlée: everything starts in the middle.

Figure 4.3. Rembrandt, *Décollation de Saint Jean Baptiste*. Paris, Musée du Louvre.

One must jump into the middle of the sheet of paper, fell the quill, as soon as the race begins, or else it's battle.

And now I see what the Woman Ironing, the Executioner, the Saint, the little boy, have in common: it's Violence. It's about combat.

Drawings of combat, these drawings which, fatally, touch me, wounded though they are, and therefore similar to us.

Drawings par excellence: because every drawing (is) combat(s) itself. Drawing is the emblem of all our hidden, intestine combats. There we see the soul's entrails.

What is the page of a book? What remains of a sheet of paper becomes a field of battle on which we, writing, drawing, have killed each other ourselves. A flagstone of paper under which a carnage effaces itself. In writing, all is disputed, and sacrificed. As soon as Kafka took his pen in his right hand, his left hand jumped on it (on his right) and the combat raged. This made for such drafts that, in the inability to give reason to the one hand or the other, Kafka dreamed of dragging into the fire, with himself, the innumerable traces of his hostilities. And if he didn't do it himself that's just because he tried to repent. We try to repent, but we never repent. One doesn't repent. One doesn't manage. One makes essays.

When Rembrandt wanted to draw *The Beheading of St John the Baptist* there was an explosion, and the two men, the executioner and the victim, fought one another for the paper with ferocity, Rembrandt, the executioner, the victim, moaned with long cutting wails. What was drawing itself between himself *is the decapitation exploding in the body of the executioner.* The pen has captured the transfer, the brutal and rapid explosion in the process of instantaneously transforming the two adversaries. Everything, drawn from the point of view of the executor. The drawing was called: *The Executioner's Taking Off,* but subsequently this name was crossed out and replaced . . . N.B. And precisely in this scene where Rembrandt became an executioner, *no repentance.* I mean to say: no Christian repentance. (The executioner is searching for his accomplishment, and in a few strokes, becomes the incarnation of the cutting blade.)

Because our soul has no firm footing.
Agitation reigns in these drawings. This is perhaps why painters draw? Because drawing is the right to tumult, to frenzy. The right to: no. The drawing cries out. But painting, even frenetic, even Van Gogh, paints all the same after the tempest. It takes a little time. But the drawing is: essay: before. 'Work in which the author treats his or her matter without pretending to say the last word . . .' We don't have the last word: truth always has the word before, and we run out of breath at its heels. In the essay entitled 'Of Repentance' Montaigne recounts how he always in fact guarded against all (Christian) repentance, while at the same time giving himself up to the Essay, the only form of writing faithful to the truth, the desirable unseizable. *'If my mind could gain a firm footing, I would not make essays, I would make*

decisions,' but it is always 'in apprenticeship and on trial.' Our soul never has its footing on this earth. Graze the paper with the soul's foot, and immediately the foot slips. It's always this same story of the foot and the ground, one and the other in motion, the one missing the other. How then to draw a firm footing, when our soul is merely a staggering? Our drawings, our books and us, we all go along at the same pace, with an uncertain foot. This is why it is the legs above all which, in our drawings, are the most agitated.

To come back to what escapes: we want to draw the instant. That instant which strikes between two instants, that instant which flies into bits under its own blow, which has neither length, nor duration, only its own shattering brilliance, the shock of the passage from night to light. Here, the instant is the height which this executioner's arm takes (a single double arm), grand high gesture, extremely fine and rapid line of extreme actuality. The instant is a drama without a stage.

I wanted to call this text: 'For the Instant,' or 'At the Instant,' but I changed my mind.

The instant, see how it's just fallen, between St John: the body is still living, but already the head is dead. It's this instant: the cut-off between life and death.

This is what we draw, tripping, because, instead of throbbing, we trace. We want to throw ourselves ahead and we go backwards. Do you see these footprints? We are advancing backwards.

How to draw speed?
Thinking about 'repentance' is extremely tiring. It's as though I were trying to think about the skin of thought with the skin of thought. One must think faster than oneself.

Observing it from very very close up very very fast, thought doesn't go straight ahead, as we think, but in a frenetic movement, invisible to the naked-eye-of-thought, it goes straight ahead of itself like lightning and almost simultaneously returns backwards on its own streak to step on it and erase it and almost simultaneously shoots forward like a rocket – if only I could draw *one* thought! – if I could photograph it – then we would see that thought is not a sentence at all, but, after several explosions, a fallout in words,

or else take the photograph of a dream!

I want to draw the present, say da Vinci? Picasso, Rembrandt, the fools for truth. How to make the portrait of lightning? At what speed draw speed? We have all cried out stop! to the instant. We who are the immoderate, through our slowness rapidity passes, through our narrow head the lightning of a thought passes.

The truth is approaching.

Arrives the Vision that neither we, nor even the saint, can predict. Be careful! It's coming . . .! Salvation! What agony! We fall like a dead body.

We don't have salvation: it is dealt us like a blow, we faint. We awake with a start, quick a pencil, and take down the ultimate glimmer of illumination, however much we say: 'what's the difference, we've seen our vision already,' we never resign ourselves.

At a gallop, the snail! We scribble while crawling in the wake of God.

We live more quickly than ourselves, the pen doesn't follow. To paint the present which is passing us by, we stop the present.

One cannot after all write a book with only one stroke, of only one page, and yet we should.

But we are born for lateness.

Time, the body, are our slow vehicles, our chariots without wheels.

Look, I've just this instant 'seen' a book – now I'm going to need two years and two hundred pages in order to recount it with my hands, with my staggering feet, and my breath harnessed to my chest, and from forward to backward and inversely.

This is why we desire so often to die, when we write, in order to see everything in a flash, and at least once shatter the spine of time with only one pencil stroke. And with only one word draw God .

N.B. There is not one single sentence in this text which I didn't write twenty times – As soon as I said the word 'Repentance,' it jumped on to my page, it spread everywhere, however much I denied it. One says this word and that's it.

N.B. N.B. Because after all that which they call Repentance is no one other than the demon of writing.

N.B. And now, what to call this essay?

– 'Without End' – No. – 'The Executioner's Taking Off' – No. Rather: Oh no, enough already, it's time! No more repenting! Not another word!

'Sans Arrêt, non, Etat de Dessination, non, plutôt: Le Décollage du Bourreau' was first published in *Repentirs* (Réunion des musées nationaux, 1991): 55–64; this translation first appeared in *New Literary History* 24: 1 (Winter 1993): 90–103.

CHAPTER 5

Jacques Derrida, 'Aphorism Countertime'

How could it be possible to say anything at once new and yet pertinent about Shakespeare's *Romeo and Juliet*, the play whose name has for centuries been a by-word for young, doomed love? This is not a question asked in Derrida's 'Aphorism Countertime', but might provide a helpful way to think about it. Thematically, the piece focuses on *missing* in a double sense: on the ways in which Romeo and Juliet both yearn for one another, and fail to coincide with one another. Such non-coincidence, Derrida suggests, is the condition of all love and of all relationships, and at the same time of all reading and writing. We can only love, or read, because there is some gap or distance between us and our love- or text-objects. Here we see a thought that resonates across many of the texts in this *Anthology*: the idea that the risk of failure, of falling short, of non-coincidence is the very — abyssal — ground of an adequate relationship to a work of literature or art. And here we see too the flicker of an answer to our opening question. Derrida reads *Romeo and Juliet* lovingly, and inventively, by staging the ways in which he is out of synch with it. He discusses it in his own blent idiom — at times high metaphysical, at others coloured with a more colloquial pathos — and cleaves to it from the bias of his own interests: interests in naming, in presence, in the philosophy of Hegel and Husserl, in being, in time, and in love, and in being in love in time.

The piece is written as a series of thirty-nine aphorisms. Aphorism is a form that has been practised since ancient times, and indeed its pithy maxims strive to break free from time, and stand as truths. Yet their ostensible severance from time is never absolute, but functions — rather like quotation — as a dislocation and a relocation, a forming of new relationships.

The form is chosen for a reason: Derrida's disjointed series of aphorisms mimics the disjunctions that he sees at the heart of the tragedy of *Romeo and Juliet*. In 'Aphorism Countertime' we have, then, an example of writing which – through its form – creatively addresses what is essential about the text it reads, without simply mirroring that text's own form.

This provides the provocation. Identify what seems to you the structuring tension or drama, the crux, in a text or image. What form is best suited to address or render this? Write a piece in which your chosen form bears some critical relation to what you take as the very heart of the text you are analysing.

Jacques Derrida, 'Aphorism Countertime' (1986), trans. Nicholas Royle, in *Acts of Literature*, ed. Derek Attridge (London: Routledge, 1992), pp. 414–33.

———

1. Aphorism is the name.

2. As its name indicates, aphorism separates, it marks dissociation (*apo*), it terminates, delimits, arrests (*horizō*). It brings to an end by separating, it separates in order to end – and to define [*finir – et definir*].

3. An aphorism is a name but every name can take on the figure of aphorism.

4. An aphorism is exposure to contretemps.[1] It exposes discourse – hands it over to contretemps. Literally – because it is abandoning a word [*une parole*] to its letter.

(Already this could be read as a series of aphorisms, the alea of an initial anachrony. In the beginning there was contretemps. In the beginning there is speed. Word and deed are *overtaken*. Aphorism outstrips.)

5. To abandon speech [*la parole*], to entrust the secret to letters – this is the stratagem of the third party, the mediator, the Friar, the matchmaker who, without any other desire but the desire of others, organizes the contretemps. He counts on the letters without taking account of them:

> In the meantime, against thou shalt awake,
> Shall Romeo by my letters know our drift,
> And hither shall he come. (IV, i, 113–15)[2]

6. Despite appearances, an aphorism never arrives by itself, it doesn't come all alone. It is part of a serial logic. As in Shakespeare's play, in the *trompe-l'oeil* depth of its paradigms, all the *Romeo and Juliet*s that came before it, there will be several series of aphorisms here.

7. Romeo and Juliet, the heroes of contretemps in our mythology, the positive heroes. They missed each other, how they missed each other! Did they miss each other? But they also survived, *both of them*, survived *one another*, in their name, through a studied effect of contretemps: an unfortunate crossing, by chance, of temporal and aphoristic series.[3]

8. Aphoristically, one must say that Romeo and Juliet will have lived, and lived on, through aphorism. *Romeo and Juliet* owes everything to aphorism. Aphorism can, of course, turn out to be a device of rhetoric, a sly calculation aiming at the greatest authority, an economy or strategy of mastery which knows very well how to potentialize meaning ('See how I formalize, in so few words I always say more than would appear'). But before letting itself be manipulated in this way, aphorism hands us over, defenseless, to the very experience of contretemps. Before every calculation but also across it, beyond the calculable itself.

9. The aphorism or discourse of dissociation: each sentence, each paragraph dedicates itself to separation, it shuts itself up, whether one likes it or not, in the solitude of its proper duration. Its encounter and its contact with the other are always given over to chance, to whatever may befall, good or ill. Nothing is absolutely assured, neither the linking nor the order. One aphorism in the series can come before or after the other, before *and* after the other, each can survive the other – and in the other series. Romeo and Juliet *are* aphorisms, in the first place in their name, which they are not (Juliet: ''Tis but thy name that is my enemy' . . . Romeo: 'My name, dear saint, is hateful to myself, / Because it is an enemy to thee. / Had I it written, I would tear the word' [II, ii, 38, 55–7]), for there is no aphorism without language, without nomination, without appellation, without a letter, even to be torn up.

10. Each aphorism, like Romeo and Juliet, each aphoristic series has its particular duration. Its temporal logic prevents it from sharing all its time with another place of discourse, with another discourse, with the discourse of the other. Impossible synchronization. I am speaking here of the discourse of time, of its marks, of its dates, of the course of time and of the essential digression which dislocates the time of desires and carries the step of those

who love one another off course. But that is not sufficient to characterize our aphorism, it is not sufficient that there be language or mark, nor that there be dissociation, dislocation, anachrony, in order for aphorism to take place. It still must have a determined form, a certain mode. Which? The bad aphorism, the *bad* of aphorism is sententious, but every aphorism cuts and delimits by virtue of its sententious character:[4] it says the truth in the form of the last judgment, and this truth carries [*porte*] death.[5] The death sentence [*l'arrêt de mort*], for Romeo and Juliet, is a contretemps which condemns them to death, both of them, but also a contretemps which arrests death, suspends its coming, secures for both of them the delay necessary in order to witness and survive the other's death.

11. Aphorism: that which hands over every rendezvous to chance. But desire does not lay itself open to aphorism by chance. There is no time for desire without aphorism. Desire has no place without aphorism. What Romeo and Juliet experience is the exemplary anachrony, the essential impossibility of any absolute synchronization. But *at the same time* they live – as we do – this disorder of the series. Disjunction, dislocation, separation of places, deployment or spacing of a story because of aphorism – would there be any theater without that? The survival of a theatrical work implies that, theatrically, it is saying something about theater itself, about its essential possibility. And that it does so, theatrically, then, through the play of uniqueness and repetition, by giving rise every time to the chance of an absolutely singular event as it does to the untranslatable idiom of a proper name, to its fatality (the 'enemy' that 'I hate'), to the fatality of a date and of a rendezvous. Dates, timetables, property registers, place-names, all the codes that we cast like nets over time and space – in order to reduce or master differences, to arrest them, determine them – these are also contretemps-traps. Intended to avoid contretemps, to be in harmony with our rhythms by bending them to objective measurement, they produce misunderstanding, they accumulate the opportunities for false steps or wrong moves, revealing and simultaneously increasing this anachrony of desires: *in the same time*. What is this time? There is no place for a question in aphorism.

12. Romeo *and* Juliet, the conjunction of two desires which are aphoristic but held together, maintained in the dislocated now of a love or a promise. A promise in their name, but across and beyond their given name, the promise of *another name*, its request rather: 'O be some other name . . .' (II, ii, 42). The *and* of this conjunction, the theater of this 'and,' has often

been presented, represented as the scene of fortuitous contretemps, of aleatory anachrony: the failed rendezvous, the unfortunate accident, the letter which does not arrive at its destination, the time of the detour prolonged for a *purloined letter*,[6] the remedy which transforms itself into poison when the stratagem of a third party, a brother, Friar Laurence, proposes simultaneously the remedy and the letter ('And if thou dar'st, I'll give thee remedy . . . In the meantime, against thou shalt awake, / Shall Romeo by my letters know our drift, / And hither shall he come . . .' [IV, i, 76, 113–15]). This representation is not false. But if this drama has thus been imprinted, superimprinted on the memory of Europe, text upon text, this is because the anachronous accident comes to illustrate an essential possibility. It confounds a philosophical logic which would like accidents to remain what they are, accidental. This logic, at the same time, throws out into the unthinkable an anachrony of structure, the absolute interruption of history as deployment of a temporality, of a single and organized temporality. What happens to Romeo and Juliet, and which remains in effect an accident whose aleatory and unforeseeable appearance cannot be effaced, at the crossing of several series and beyond common sense, can only be what it is, accidental, insofar as it has *already* happened, in essence, before it happens. The desire of Romeo and Juliet did not encounter the poison, the contretemps or the detour of the letter by chance. In order for this encounter to take place, there must *already* have been instituted a system of marks (names, hours, maps of places, dates and supposedly 'objective' place-names) to thwart, as it were, the dispersion of interior and heterogeneous durations, to frame, organize, put in order, render possible a rendezvous: in other words to deny, while taking note of it, non–coincidence, the separation of monads, infinite distance, the disconnection of experiences, the multiplicity of worlds, everything that renders possible a contretemps or the irremediable detour of a letter. But the desire of Romeo and Juliet is born in the heart of this possibility. There would have been no love, the pledge would not have taken place, nor time, nor its theater, without discordance. The accidental contretemps comes to *remark* the essential contretemps. Which is as much as to say it is not accidental. It does not, for all that, have the signification of an essence or of a formal structure. This is not the abstract condition of possibility, a universal form of the relation to the other in general, a dialectic of desire or consciousnesses. Rather the singularity of an imminence whose 'cutting point' spurs desire at its birth – the very birth of desire. I love because the other is the other, because its time will never be mine. The living duration, the very presence of its love remains infinitely distant from mine, distant from itself in that which stretches it toward mine and even in what one might want to describe as amorous euphoria, ecstatic communion, mystical intuition. I can love the other only in the passion of this aphorism. Which does not happen, does not come about like misfortune, bad luck, or negativity. It has the form of the most loving affirmation – it is the chance of desire. And it not only cuts into the fabric of durations, it spaces. Contretemps says something about topology or the visible; it opens theater.

13. Conversely, no contretemps, no aphorism without the promise of a now in common, without the pledge, the vow of synchrony, the desired sharing of a living present. In order that the sharing may be desired, must it not first be given, glimpsed, apprehended? But this sharing is just another name for aphorism.[7]

14. This aphoristic series crosses over another one. Because it traces, aphorism *lives on*, it lives much longer than its present and it lives longer than life. Death sentence [*arrêt de mort*]. It gives and carries death, but in order to make a decision thus on a sentence [*arret*] of death, it suspends death, it stops it once more [*il l'arrête encore*].

15. There would not be any contretemps, nor any anachrony, if the separation between monads only disjoined interiorities. Contretemps is produced at the intersection between interior experience (the 'phenomenology of internal time-consciousness'[8] or space-consciousness) and its chronological or topographical marks, those which are said to be 'objective,' 'in the world.' There would not be any series otherwise, without the possibility of this marked spacing, with its social conventions and the history of its codes, with its fictions and its simulacra, with its dates. With so-called proper names.

16. The simulacrum raises the curtain, it reveals, thanks to the dissociation of series, the theater of the impossible: two people each outlive the other. The absolute certainty which rules over the *duel* (*Romeo and Juliet* is the *mise-en-scène* of all duels) is that one must die before the other. One of them must see the other die. To no matter whom, I must be able to say: since we are two, we know in an absolutely ineluctable way that one of us will die before the other. One of us will see the other die, one of us will live on, even if only for an instant. One of us, only one of us, will carry the death of the other – and the mourning. It is impossible that we should each survive the other. That's the duel, the axiomatic of every duel, the scene

which is the most common and the least spoken of – or the most prohibited – concerning our relation to the other. Yet *the impossible happens – not* in 'objective reality,' which has no say here, but in the experience of Romeo and Juliet. And under the law of the pledge, which commands every given word. They live *in turn* the death of the other, for a time, the contretemps of their death. Both are in mourning – and both watch over the death of the other, attend to the death of the other. Double death sentence. Romeo dies before Juliet, whom he has seen dead. They both live, outlive the death of the other.

17. The impossible – this theater of double survival – also tells, like every aphorism, the truth. Right from the pledge which binds together two desires, each is already in mourning for the other, entrusts death to the other as well: if you die before me, I will keep you, if I die before you, you will carry me in yourself, one will keep the other, will already have kept the other from the first declaration. This double interiorization would be possible neither in monadic interiority nor in the logic of 'objective' time and space. It takes places nevertheless every time I love. Everything then begins with this survival. Each time that I love or each time that I hate, each time that a law *engages* me to the death of the other. And it is the same law, the same double law. A pledge which keeps (off) death can always invert itself.[9]

18. A given series of aphorisms crosses over into another one, the same under different names, under the name of the name. Romeo and Juliet love each other across their name, despite their name, they die on account of their name, they live on in their name. Since there is neither desire nor pledge nor sacred bond (*sacramentum*) without aphoristic separation, the greatest love springs from the greatest force of dissociation, here what opposes and divides the two families in their name. Romeo and Juliet bear these names. They bear them, support them even if they do not wish to assume them. From this name which separates them but which will at the same time have tightened their desire with all its aphoristic force, they would like to separate themselves. But the most vibrant declaration of their love still calls for the name that it denounces. One might be tempted to distinguish here, another aphorism, between the proper forename and the family name which would only be a proper name in a general way or according to genealogical classification. One might be tempted to distinguish Romeo from Montague and Juliet from Capulet. Perhaps they are, both of them, tempted to do it. But they don't do it, and one should notice

that in the denunciation of the name (Act II, scene ii), they also attack their forenames, or at least that of Romeo, which seems to form part of the family name. The forename still bears the name of the father, it recalls the law of genealogy. Romeo *himself*, the bearer of the name is not the name, it is *Romeo*, the name which he bears. And is it necessary to call the bearer by the name which he bears? She calls him by it in order to tell him: I love you, free us from your name, Romeo, don't bear it any longer, Romeo, the name of Romeo:

> JULIET.
> O Romeo, Romeo, wherefore art thou Romeo?
> Deny thy father and refuse thy name.
> Or if thou wilt not, be but sworn my love
> And I'll no longer be a Capulet. (II, ii, 33–6)

She is speaking, here, in the night, and there is nothing to assure her that she is addressing Romeo himself, present in person. In order to ask Romeo to refuse his name, she can only, in his absence, address his name or his shadow. Romeo – himself – is in the shadow and he wonders if it is time to take her at her word or if he should wait a little. Taking her at her word will mean committing himself to disowning his name, a little later on. For the moment, he decides to wait and to carry on listening:

> ROMEO [*aside*].
> Shall I hear more, or shall I speak at this?

> JULIET.
> 'Tis but thy name that is my enemy:
> Thou art thyself, though not a Montague.
> What's Montague? It is nor hand nor foot
> Nor arm nor face nor any other part
> Belonging to a man. O be some other name.
> What's in a name? That which we call a rose
> By any other word would smell as sweet;
> So Romeo would, were he not Romeo call'd,
> Retain that dear perfection which he owes
> Without that title. Romeo, doff thy name.
> And for thy name, which is no part of thee,
> Take all myself.

ROMEO.
                              I take thee at thy word.
Call me but love, and I'll be new baptis'd:
Henceforth I never will be Romeo.

JULIET.
What man art thou that thus bescreen'd in night
So stumblest on my counsel?

ROMEO.
                              By a name
I know not how to tell thee who I am:
My name, dear saint, is hateful to myself
Because it is an enemy to thee.
Had I it written, I would tear the word.

JULIET.
My ears have yet not drunk a hundred words
Of thy tongue's uttering, yet I know the sound,
Art thou not Romeo, and a Montague?

ROMEO.
Neither, fair maid, if either thee dislike.

                                        (II, ii, 37–61)

19. When she addresses Romeo in the night, when she asks him 'O Romeo, Romeo, wherefore art thou Romeo. / Deny thy father and refuse thy name,' she seems to be addressing *him*, *himself*, Romeo bearer of the name Romeo, the one who is not Romeo since he has been asked to disown his father and his name. She seems, then, to call him beyond his name. He is not present, she is not certain that he is there, *himself*, beyond his name, it is night and this night screens the lack of distinction between the name and the bearer of the name. It is in his name that she continues to call him, and that she calls on him not to call himself Romeo any longer, and that she asks him, Romeo, to renounce his name. But it is, whatever she may say or deny, he whom she loves. Who, him? Romeo. The one who calls himself Romeo, the bearer of the name, who calls himself Romeo although he is not only the one who bears this name and although he exists, without being visible or present in the night, outside his name.

20. Night. Everything that happens at night, for Romeo and Juliet, is decided rather in the penumbra, between night and day. The indecision between Romeo and the bearer of this name, between 'Romeo,' the name of Romeo and Romeo himself. Theater, we say, is visibility, the stage [*la scène*]. This drama belongs to the night because it stages what is not seen, the name; it stages what one calls because one cannot see or because one is not certain of seeing what one calls. Theater of the name, theater of night. The name calls beyond presence, phenomenon, light, beyond the day, beyond the theater. It keeps – whence the mourning and survival – what is no longer present, the invisible: what from now on will no longer see the light of day.

21. She wants the death of Romeo. She will have it. The death of his name (''Tis but thy name that is my enemy'), certainly, the death of 'Romeo,' but they will not be able to get free from their name, they know this without knowing it [*sans le savoir*]. She declares war on 'Romeo,' on his name, in his name, she will win this war only on the death of Romeo himself. Himself? Who? Romeo. But 'Romeo' is not Romeo. Precisely. She wants the death of 'Romeo.' Romeo dies, 'Romeo' lives on. She keeps him dead in his name. Who? Juliet, Romeo.

22. Aphorism: separation in language and, in it, through the name which closes the horizon. Aphorism is at once necessary and impossible. Romeo is radically separated from his name. He, his living self, living and singular desire, he is not 'Romeo,' but the separation, the aphorism of the name remains impossible. He dies without his name but he dies also because he has not been able to set himself free from his name, or from his father, even less to renounce him, to respond to Juliet's request ('Deny thy father and refuse thy name').

23. When she says to him: my enemy is only your name, she does not think 'my' enemy. Juliet, herself, has nothing against the name of Romeo. It is the name which she bears (Juliet and Capulet) that finds itself at war with the name of Romeo. The war takes place between the names. And when she says it, she is not sure, in the night, that she is making contact with Romeo himself. She speaks to him, she supposes him to be distinct from his name since she addresses him in order to say to him: 'You are yourself, not a Montague.' But he is not there. At least she cannot be sure of his presence. It is within herself, deep down inside, that she is addressing him in the night, but still him in his name, and in the most exclamatory form

of apostrophe: 'O Romeo, Romeo, wherefore art thou Romeo?' She does not say to him: why are you called Romeo, why do you bear this name (like an article of clothing, an ornament, a detachable sign)? She says to him: why *are you* Romeo? She knows it: detachable and dissociable, aphoristic though it be, his name is his essence. Inseparable from his being. And in asking him to abandon his name, she is no doubt asking him to live at last, and to live his love (for in order to live oneself truly, it is necessary to elude the law of the name, the familial law made for survival and constantly recalling me to death), but she is *just as much* asking him to die, since his life *is* his name. He exists in his name: 'wherefore art thou Romeo?' 'O Romeo, Romeo.' Romeo is Romeo, and Romeo is not Romeo. He is himself only in abandoning his name, he is himself only in his name. Romeo can (be) call(ed) himself only if he abandons his name, he calls himself only *from* his name. Sentence of death and of survival: twice rather than once.

24. Speaking to the one she loves within herself and outside herself, in the half-light, Juliet murmurs the most implacable analysis of the name. Of the name and the proper name. Implacable: she expresses the judgment, the death sentence [*l'arrêt de mort*], the fatal truth of the name. Pitilessly she analyzes, element by element. What's Montague? Nothing of yourself, you are yourself and not Montague, she tells him. Not only does this name say nothing about you as a totality but it doesn't say anything, it doesn't even name a part of you, neither your hand, nor your foot, neither your arm, nor your face, nothing that is human! This analysis is implacable for it announces or denounces the inhumanity or the ahumanity of the name. A proper name does not name anything which is human, which belongs to a human body, a human spirit, an essence of man. And yet this relation to the inhuman only befalls man, for him, to him, in the name of man. He alone gives himself this inhuman name. And Romeo would not be what he is, a stranger to his name, without this name. Juliet, then, pursues her analysis: the names of things do not belong to the things any more than the names of men belong to men, and yet they are quite differently separable. The example of the rose, once more. A rose remains what it is without its name, Romeo is no longer what he is without his name. But, for a while, Juliet makes out as if Romeo would lose nothing in losing his name: like the rose. But like a rose, she says to him in short, and without genealogy, 'without why.' (Supposing that the rose, all the roses of thought, of litera-ture, of mysticism, this 'formidable anthology,' absent from every bouquet . . .)

25. She does not tell him to lose all names, rather just to change names: 'O be some other name.' But that can mean two things: take another proper name (a human name, this inhuman thing which belongs only to man); *or*: take another kind of name, a name which is not that of a man, take the name of a thing then, a common name which, like the name of the rose, does not have that inhumanity which consists in affecting the very being of the one who bears it even though it names nothing of himself. And, after the colon, there is the question:

> O be some other name:
> What's in a name? That which we call a rose
> By any other word would smell as sweet;
> So Romeo would, were he not Romeo call'd
> Retain that dear perfection which he owes
> Without that title.[10]

26. The name would only be a 'title,' and the title is not the thing which it names, any more than a title of nobility participates in the very thing, the family, the work, to which it is said to belong. *Romeo and Juliet* also remains the – surviving – title of an entire family of plays. We must apply what goes on in these plays also to the plays themselves, to their genealogy, their idiom, their singularity, their survival.

27. Juliet offers Romeo an infinite deal, what is apparently the most dis-symmetrical of contracts: you can gain all without losing anything, it is just a matter of a name. In renouncing your name, you renounce nothing, nothing of you, of yourself, nor anything human. In exchange, and without losing anything, you gain me, and not just a part of me, but the whole of myself: 'Romeo, doff thy name, / And for thy name, which is no part of thee, / Take all myself.' He will have gained everything, he will have lost everything: name and life, and Juliet.

28. The circle of all these names in *o: words, Romeo, rose, love.* He has accepted the deal, he *takes her at her word* ('I take thee at thy word') at the moment where she proposes that he *take* her in her entirety ('Take all myself'). Play of idiom: in taking you at your word, in taking up the challenge, in agreeing to this incredible, priceless exchange, I take the whole of you. And in exchange for nothing, for a word, my name, which is nothing, nothing human, nothing of myself, or else nothing for myself. I give nothing in taking you at your word, I abandon nothing and take

absolutely all of you. In truth, and they both know the truth of aphorism, he will lose everything. They will lose everything in this aporia, this double aporia of the proper name. And for having agreed to exchange the proper name of Romeo for a common name: not that of *rose*, but of *love*. For Romeo does not renounce all of his name, only the name of his father, that is to say his proper name, if one can still say that: 'I take thee at thy word. / Call me but love, and I'll be new baptis'd: / Henceforth I never will be Romeo.' He simultaneously gains himself and loses himself not only in the common name, but also in the common law of love: Call *me love*. Call me your love.

29. The dissymmetry remains infinite. It also hangs on this: Romeo does not make the same demand of her. He does not request that this woman who is secretly to be his wife renounce her name or disown her father. As if that were obvious and there was no call for any such rift [*déchirement*] (he will speak in a moment of tearing [*déchirer*] his name, the writing or the letter of his name, that is if he had written it himself, which is just what is in principle and originarily excluded). Paradox, irony, reversal of the common law? Or a repetition which on the contrary confirms the truth of this law? Usually, in our cultures, the husband keeps his name, that of his father, and the wife renounces hers. When the husband gives his name to his wife, it is not, as here, in order to lose it, or to change it, but to impose it by keeping it. Here it is she who asks him to renounce his father and to change his name. But this inversion confirms the law: the name of the father should be kept by the son, it is from him that there is some sense in tearing it away, and not at all from the daughter who has never been put in charge of it. The terrible lucidity of Juliet. She knows the two bonds of the law, the *double bind*, which ties a son to the name of his father. He can only live if he asserts himself in a singular fashion, without his inherited name. But the writing of this name, which he has not written himself ('Had I it written, I would tear the word'), constitutes him in his very being, without naming anything of him, and by denying it he can only wipe himself out. In sum, at the very most he can deny it, renounce it, he can neither efface it nor tear it up. He is therefore lost in any case and she knows it. And she knows it because she loves him and she loves him because she knows it. And she demands his death from him by demanding that he hold onto his life because she loves him, because she knows, and because she knows that death will not come to him by accident. He is doomed [*voué*] to death, and she with him, by the double law of the name.

30. There would be no contretemps without the double law of the name. The contretemps presupposes this inhuman, too human, inadequation which always dislocates a proper name. The secret marriage, the pledge (*sacramentum*), the double survival which it involves, its constitutive anachrony, all of this obeys the same law. This law, the law of contretemps, is double since it is divided; it carries aphorism within itself, as its truth. Aphorism is the law.

31. Even if he wanted to, Romeo could not renounce his name and his father *of his own accord*. He cannot want to do so of his own accord, even though this emancipation is nevertheless being presented to him as the chance of at last being himself, beyond the name – the chance of at last living, for he carries the name as his death. He could not want it himself, in himself, because *he is not without* his name. He can only desire it from the call of the other, in the name of the other. Moreover he only hates his name starting from the moment Juliet, as it were, demands it from him:

> My name, dear saint, is hateful to myself
> Because it is an enemy to thee.
> Had I it written, I would tear the word.

32. When she thinks she recognizes him in the shadow, by moonlight, the drama of the name is consummated (Juliet: 'My ears have yet not drunk a hundred words / Of thy tongue's uttering, yet I know the sound. / Art thou not Romeo, and a Montague?' Romeo: 'Neither, fair maid, if either thee dislike'). She recognizes him and calls him by his name (Are you not Romeo and a Montague?), she *identifies* him on the one hand by the timbre of his voice, that is to say by the words she hears without being able to see, and on the other hand at the moment when he has, obeying the injunction, renounced his name and his father. Survival and death are at work, in other words the moon. But this power of death which appears by moonlight is called Juliet, and the sun which she comes to figure all of a sudden carries life *and* death *in the name of the father*. She kills the moon. What does Romeo say at the opening of the scene (which is not a scene since the name destines it to invisibility, but which is a theater since its light is artificial and figurative)? 'But soft, what light through yonder window breaks? / It is the east, and Juliet is the sun! / Arise fair sun and kill the envious moon, / Who is already sick and pale with grief' (II, ii, 2–5).

33. The lunar face of this shadow play, a certain coldness of *Romeo and Juliet*. Not all is of ice or glass, but the ice on it does not come only from

death, from the marble to which everything seems doomed (*the tomb, the monument, the grave, the flowers on the lady's grave*), in this sepulchrally statuesque fate which entwines and separates these two lovers, starting from the fact of their names. No, the coldness which little by little takes over the body of the play and, as if in advance, cadaverizes it, is perhaps irony, the figure or rhetoric of irony, the contretemps of ironic consciousness. It always places itself disproportionately between finitude and infinitude, it makes use of inadequation, of aphorism, it analyzes and analyzes, it analyzes the law of misidentification, the implacable necessity, the machine of the proper name that obliges me to live through precisely that, in other words my name, of which I am dying.

34. Irony of the proper name, as analyzed by Juliet. Sentence of truth which carries death, aphorism separates, and in the first place separates me from my name. I am not my name. One might as well say that I should be able to survive it. But firstly it is destined to survive me. In this way it announces my death. Non-coincidence and contretemps between my name and me, between the experience according to which I am named or hear myself named and my 'living present.' Rendezvous with my name. *Untimely*, bad timing, at the wrong moment.

35. Changing names: the dance, the substitution, the masks, the simulacrum, the rendezvous with death. *Untimely. Never on time.*

36. Speaking ironically, that is to say in the rhetorical sense of the figure of irony: conveying the opposite of what one says. Here, the *impossible* then: 1) two lovers both outlive each other, each seeing the other die; 2) the name constitutes them but without being anything of themselves, condemning them to be what, beneath the mask, they are not, to being merged with the mask; 3) the two are united by that which separates them, etc. And they state this clearly, they formalize it as even a philosopher would not have dared to do. A vein, through the sharp tip of this analysis, receives the distilled potion. It does not wait, it does not allow any time, not even that of the drama, it comes at once to turn to ice the heart of their pledges. This potion would be the true poison, the poisoned truth of this drama.

37. Irony of the aphorism. In the *Aesthetics*, Hegel pokes fun at those who, quick to heap praises on ironists, show themselves not even capable of analyzing the analytical irony of *Romeo and Juliet*. He has a go at Tieck: 'But when one thinks one has found the perfect opportunity to show what irony

is, for example in *Romeo and Juliet*, one is disappointed, for it is no longer a question of irony.'[11]

38. Another series, which cuts across all the others: the name, the law, the genealogy, the double survival, the contretemps, in short the aphorism of *Romeo and Juliet*. Not of Romeo and of Juliet but of *Romeo and Juliet*, Shakespeare's play of that title. It belongs to a series, to the still-living palimpsest, to the open theater of narratives which bear this name. It survives them, but they also survive thanks to it. Would such a double survival have been possible 'without that title,' as Juliet put it? And would the names of Matteo Bandello or Luigi da Porto survive without that of Shakespeare, who survived them?[12] And without the innumerable repetitions, each staked in its particular way, under the same name? Without the grafting of names? And of other plays? 'O be some other name . . .'

39. The absolute aphorism: a proper name. Without genealogy, without the least copula. End of drama. Curtain. Tableau (*The Two Lovers United in Death* by Angelo dall'Oca Bianca). Tourism, December sun in Verona ('Verona by that name is known' [V, iii, 299]). A true sun, the other ('The sun for sorrow will not show his head' [V, iii, 305]).

NOTES

The notes below were supplied by Nicholas Royle (NR), this piece's translator, and by Derek Attridge (DA), the editor of *Acts of Literature*, the volume in which this translation first appeared.

1. NR The word *contretemps* signifies, in English as well as French, 'an inopportune occurrence; an untoward accident; an unexpected mishap or hitch' (*OED*), but in French it also refers to being 'out of time' or 'off-beat' in the musical sense, to a sense of 'bad or wrong time,' 'counter-time.'
2. NR References to Shakespeare's *Romeo and Juliet* are to the Arden text, ed. Brian Gibbons (New York: Methuen, 1980).
3. NR Derrida's text works with several senses of the verb *survivre*: 'to survive,' 'to survive beyond' or 'survive through,' 'to live on,' and so forth. For a fuller account of 'living on?' and the related double-notion of 'death sentence' and 'arrest of death' [*l'arrêt de mort*], see Derrida's 'Living On/Borderlines.'
4. NR The French phrase here is *caractère de sentence*, which can also mean 'quality of judgment'; '*sentence*' carries the sense of 'moral saying' as well as 'judgment.'
5. NR 'Aphorism Countertime' contains – or carries – a certain play on the verb *porter*, corresponding in some ways to the English verb 'to bear' ('to carry' as well as 'to wear [clothes]'). *Porter* is the verb used to designate, for example, being called by,

having, or bearing a name [*porter le nom*], as well as being in mourning [*porter le deuil*]. Derrida treats the idea of the name as bearing death within it – and as being structurally conditioned to survive its bearer – in several of his works: among others, *Signéponge / Signsponge*, 'Otobiographies,' and *Mémoires*.

6. NR English in original. This is an allusion to Derrida's 'Le facteur de la verité,' a text concerned with Edgar Allan Poe's short story 'The Purloined Letter,' and Jacques Lacan's 'Seminar on "The Purloined Letter"' (the latter partly translated in *Yale French Studies* 48 [1973]: 38–72). 'Aphorism Countertime' follows Shakespeare's text in focusing on the (tragic, comic, ironic, and above all *necessary*) possibility that a letter can always *not* reach its destination.

7. DA *Partage*, the usual word for 'sharing,' also signifies 'division.'

8. NR The reference is to Husserl. See, for example, *The Phenomenology of Internal Time-Consciousness*, trans. James S. Churchill (Bloomington: Indiana University Press, 1964). See also Derrida's *Edmund Husserl's 'Origin of Geometry': An Introduction*, p. 57, and chapter 5 ('Signs and the Blink of an Eye') of his *Speech and Phenomena*.

9. NR The French text reads: *Un gage peut toujours s'inverser qui garde de la mort*. This double bind of what keeps off death and at the same time keeps it might be further elucidated by way of Derrida's *Mémoires*, where for example he explores the notion that '*already* you are *in memory of* your own death; and your friends as well, and all the others, both of your own death and already of their own through yours' (p. 87 n. 2).

10. NR I have followed the text of Derrida's quotation here, thus preserving the colon at the end of the first line. The Arden version, already cited, gives a full stop; as Brian Gibbons points out (p. 129), there have been several variants and varying hypotheses regarding these lines of the play. Confusingly perhaps, *Q*2–4 and *F* in fact give: 'ô be some other name / Belonging to a man.'

11. NR See G. W. F. Hegel, *Aesthetics: Lectures on Fine Art*, trans. T. M. Knox, vol. 1 (Oxford: Clarendon Press, 1975), p. 69.

12. DA Bandello and da Porto were the authors of two of the many earlier versions of the Romeo and Juliet story.

CHAPTER 6

Geoff Dyer, from *Out of Sheer Rage: In the Shadow of D. H. Lawrence*

One of the really irksome things about much critical writing is how consciously and virtuously hard-working it is, as though diligent drudgery had to be on display for its products to be worthwhile. Much labour, reading, research and thought has clearly gone into Geoff Dyer's funny, angry, intelligent *Out of Sheer Rage*, but it's a labour of love, or at least of passion, rather than the pious and alienated toil of a po-faced protestant work ethic. Dyer's book is a first-person account of the author's *failure* to write a critical study of D. H. Lawrence. It is literate and well-informed, but avowedly unscholarly. Its wager is that – through its digressions, ostensibly autobiographical anecdotes, performative procrastination and asides – it will be truer to the spirit of Lawrence's writings than would a head-on and more sober-sided critical treatise. The passage excerpted here is at the heart of the book, and contains a scene in which Dyer burns a copy of the *Longman Critical Reader* on Lawrence. That volume, he argues, is an avatar of the kind of academic criticism that 'kills everything it touches'. But Dyer's pyrotechnics should not be taken as his last word. 'Except this is nonsense of course. Scholars live their work too,' he writes a page later, in one of the many moments in which we glimpse the *process* of a critical argument being made, rather than the delivery of a final pronouncement. These pages also include some of Dyer's more overtly 'literary-critical' analysis, alongside an account of the appetitive experience of reading Lawrence's letters, discussions of Rilke and Kundera, allusions to Keats, and much else besides. In sum, this extract offers both a brilliant performance and a celebration of criticism in which 'the distinction between imaginative and critical writing disappears'.

As with all the pieces in this *Anthology*, the only way truly to take inspiration from Dyer's writing is to let it permit you to do something entirely different yourself, responding to the exigencies of what you are reading, rather than slavishly following a model. Trying out an autobiographical voice – yours, not a version of Dyer's – might be a start. Write a first-person account of a text, image or piece of music, in which your own life story is somehow implicated.

Geoff Dyer, from *Out of Sheer Rage: In the Shadow of D. H. Lawrence* (London: Abacus, 1998), pp. 86–122.

I drove back to Cheltenham, glad of the motorways that had ruined the countryside, glad of the car that smudged the air, back to my parents' house on the semi-detached estate on the edge of town that had played its part in ruining the Cotswolds. I took a detour, past the house in Fairfield Walk where I was born, where my mother used to wait for me to return from school in that smoky room. Like Lawrence's mother, she was proud of the fact that we had an *end* terrace. There had been a simple hierarchy of domestic architecture then: terrace, semi-, detached. We moved into a semi-detached house, partly, I think to consolidate my status as a grammar-school boy. Most of the people at grammar school lived in semis. Now the cramped terraced house is worth more than the semi we moved into as part of our move up in the world. These days we aspire to terraced housing. A few doors along from our old house a place was for sale. I had half a mind to call the estate agent: perhaps there would be some doomed fulfilment in ending up in the same street where I was born.

I also thought of knocking on the door of our old house, explaining that I was born there, that I lived there until I was eleven, and wanted to look around. I abandoned the idea as soon as I'd thought of it. Houses have no loyalty. We can live in a place ten years and within a fortnight of moving out it is as if we have never been there. It may still bear the scars of our occupancy, of our botched attempts at DIY, but it vacates itself of our memory as soon as the new people move their stuff in. We want houses to reciprocate our feelings of loss but, like the rectangle of unfaded paint where a favourite mirror once hung, they give us nothing to reflect upon. Often in films someone goes to a house where he once spent happier times and, slowly, the screen is filled with laughing. This convention works so powerfully precisely because, in life, it is not like that. It testifies to the strength of our longing: we want houses to be haunted. They never are.

When I last saw him my father said he was glad to leave our old house because of the view from the front-room window which was actually a view of nothing except other houses. When we were selling the house someone came to see it and said, looking out the window: 'Not very pretty is it?' It wasn't. Better than the view from Walker Street as it now is, not a patch on the view Lawrence evoked – and nothing like the view from the window of Laura's apartment where I sat looking through the notes I had made in Eastwood, where I am actually sitting, months later, writing this. What could be more lovely? A jumble of fifteenth-century buildings so close together that – Calvino has suggested – a bird might think that these roofs were the surface of the world, that the streets and alleys were canyons, cracks in the red-tiled crust of the earth. Sheets hung out to dry, pairs of jeans running on thin air. Balconies overflowing with plants. Just visible in the distance, the dome of Saint Peter's. And over all of this, a sky of Camus-blue . . .

When Laura came back from her assignment we spent our afternoons under that sky, sunbathing on the roof, and our evenings hanging out at the Calisto. I had a few articles to write, simple things, but time-consuming enough to make me lose what little momentum I had built up on my study of Lawrence. It was because these articles were so simple, in fact, that I stalled on the Lawrence book. What was the point flogging my guts out writing a study of Lawrence that no one would want to read when I could bang out articles that paid extremely well and took only a fraction of the effort? Especially since Lawrence himself felt the same way: 'I feel I never want to write another book. What's the good! I can eke out a living on stories and little articles, that don't cost a tithe of the output a book costs. Why write novels any more!' He expressed similar sentiments on numerous occasions; at one point he reckoned he was losing his 'will to write altogether', meaning, on this occasion, that he no longer even felt like writing letters. I was so heartened by this that my interest in writing about Lawrence revived to the extent that I started in on Rilke's letters again. By now, I had persuaded myself, reading Rilke was part and parcel of working on my study of Lawrence. '*Il faut travailler, rien que travailler.*' It was a shame, Rilke thought, that we had so many seductive memories of idleness; if only we had 'work-memories' then perhaps, without recourse to compulsion or discipline, it would be possible to find 'natural contentment' in work, in 'that one thing which nothing else touches'. The worst thing, for Rilke, was that he had these two kinds of memory, both these impulses, in himself: a longing, on the one hand, to devote himself to art and, on the other, to set up a simple shop with 'no thought for the morrow'. Laura's version of this normal life was – and still is – to run a *pensione*. She had mentioned it in Taormina and several times since coming back she had talked about the pride she would take in keeping it clean. My version of this was to live in England and watch telly. The ideal situation for us both would have been to have watched a series about an Italian *pensione* on telly. Rilke did more or less the same thing, reconciling these impulses by making his vision of contentment the subject of a poem, 'Evening Meal'. More broadly, this tension between life and work remained one of the dominant preoccupations of his life – and work. 'Either happiness or art,' he declared, struggling to assimilate the example of Rodin. 'All the great men have let their lives get overgrown like an old path and have carried everything into their art. Their life is stunted like an organ they no longer use.' Yeats offered the same choice: perfection of the man or the work.

For some writers there has scarcely been any friction between the demands of the life and the demands of the work. John Updike arranged his circumstances to his liking fairly early on and then simply got on with his writing, book after book, day after day. At the opposite extreme there was John Berger who only managed such extreme changes in his writing by corresponding changes in how and where he lived. For Rilke, too, the real work was to organise his existence, to will himself a life that would create the ideal conditions in which to work. Allowing life to atrophy so that he might work was itself a way of enhancing his life – even though the demands this made on his life, on his life-capacity, were immense and unremitting. To make *things* he had constantly to re-make himself: '*Du mußt dein Leben ändern*' ('i.e. find a different princess to live off' was Larkin's sardonic gloss).

And to what end, this subordination of life to work? There may be an 'ancient enmity between our daily life and the great work' but this relationship is more fluid, more complex, than the aphoristic formula from 'Requiem, for a Friend' allows. 'For one human being to love another human being: that', Rilke conceded, 'is perhaps the most difficult task that has been given to us, the ultimate final problem and proof, the work for which all other work is merely preparation.' Lawrence was untroubled by any of this. All the work of his maturity was built on his relationship with Frieda. 'Fidelity to oneself means fidelity single and unchanging, to one other one.' His adult life begins with the unalterable fact of his marriage. As for work, he wrote when he felt like it, didn't when he didn't. Idleness seems to have held no attraction for him as a seductive ideal: the division between work and rest seems to have been as natural as that between sleeping and waking. Writing the novels took an enormous toll, obviously, but to Lawrence, the miner's son who had grown up amidst the ravages of gruelling physical labour, living by his pen was not such a bad option. He spent no time agonising over the rival claims of work and life because the two were inextricably bound together. 'I don't sacrifice myself for anything but I do devote myself to something.' And to what did he devote himself? To writing? No. To living ('not the work I shall produce, but the real Me I shall achieve, that is the consideration'). To say this is to reiterate one of the most hackneyed aspects of the Lawrence myth but it is difficult to improve upon, or at least his own version of it is: 'I *don't* think that to work is to live. Work is all right in proportion: but one wants to have a certain richness and satisfaction in oneself, which is more than anything produced. One wants to *be*.'

That was all very well but I had no richness and satisfaction in myself, more like a poverty and dissatisfaction. I had made progress on my study, that is, I had made progress in my mental preparation but now I had stalled. My lassitude was irritating me a good deal and this meant that Rome irritated me a good deal too. There had been several mornings when the Caffè Farnese had not had the *cornetti integrali* that I depended on for my breakfast. Without these *integrali* – more accurately *with* the disappointment of not having had my *integrali* – I found it difficult to get started on my work. I sulked, I went on a tacit strike as a protest against the Farnese and its undependable supply of *integrali*. I picked up books and put them down, thought about doing some writing and then did the washing-up instead. I recognised all these signs of unfocused anxiety and began to wonder if it might not be a good idea to move somewhere else to write my study of Lawrence. Laura's apartment should have been the perfect place to work but I couldn't get any work done there. I recognised *that* feeling too. Over the years I had come across several places that offered the ideal conditions to work. The room in Montepulciano, for example, with the lovely wooden bed and white sheets, the window gazing out over the Tuscan countryside, the terrace formed by what had once been a little bridge connecting our building to the one next door. Or the house in Lauzun with the room overlooking a field of wheat, facing west so that in the evenings the paper on the desk was bathed red. Or my apartment on Rue Popincourt with the floor-to-ceiling window from which you could see right down Rue de la Roquette, as far as the Bastille almost.

What they all had in common, these ideal places for working, was that I never got any work done in them. I would sit down at my desk and think to myself *What perfect conditions for working*, then I would look out at the sun smouldering over the wheat, or at the trees gathering the Tuscan light around themselves, or at the Parisians walking through the twilight and traffic of Rue de la Roquette, and I would write a few lines like 'If I look up from my desk I can see the sun smouldering over the wheat'; or 'Through my window: crowded twilight on the Rue de la Roquette'; and then, in order to make sure that what I was writing was capturing exactly the moment and mood, I would look up again at the sun smouldering over the flame-red wheat or the crowds moving through the neon twilight of Rue de la Roquette and add a few more words like 'flame-red' or 'neon', and then, in order to give myself over totally to the scene, would lay down my pen and simply gaze out at the scene, thinking that it was actually a waste to sit here writing when I could be looking and by looking – especially on Rue de la Roquette where the pedestrians hurrying home in the neon twilight would look up and see a figure at his desk, bathed in the yellow light of the anglepoise – actually become a part of the scene, whereas writing involved not an immersion in the actual scene but its opposite, a detachment from it. After a very short time I would grow bored by contemplating the scene, would leave my desk and go for a walk in the wheatfield sunset or leave my apartment and walk down to the Bastille so that I could become one of the people walking back through the neon twilight of the Rue de la Roquette, looking up at the empty desk, bathed in the light of the anglepoise . . .

When I thought of the ideal conditions for working, in other words, I looked at things from the perspective of someone not working, of someone on holiday, of a tourist in Taormina. I always had in mind the view that my desk would overlook, thereby overlooking the fact that the view from the desk is invisible when you are actually working, and forgetting that of the many genres of sentence I dislike there is none that I despise more than ones which proceed along the lines of 'If I look up from my desk . . .' The ideal conditions for working were actually the worst possible conditions for working.

And in any case maybe all this fuss about the conditions for working was irrelevant. After all, did it matter so much *where* you lived? The important thing, surely, was to find some little niche where you could work; to settle into a groove and get your work done. Logically, yes, but once, in north

London, I had found myself walking along the road where Julian Barnes lived. I didn't see him but I knew that in one of these large, comfortable houses Julian Barnes was sitting at his desk, working, as he did every day. It seemed an intolerable waste of a life, *of a writer's life especially*, to sit at a desk in this nice, dull street in north London. It seemed, curiously, a betrayal of the idea of the writer. It made me think of a picture of Lawrence, sitting by a tree in the blazing afternoon, surrounded by the sizzle of cicadas, note-book on his knees, writing: an image of the ideal condition of the writer.

Or so it had appeared in memory. When I actually dug it out it turned out that there was no notebook on his knees. Lawrence is not writing, he is just sitting there: which is why, presumably, it is such an idyllic image of the writer.

He is wearing a white shirt, sitting with his back to a tree. (What kind of tree? Had he been looking at a photograph of someone else sitting there, Lawrence would have been able to identify it immediately. He was one of those writers who knew the names of trees.) Everything is still, but, sculpted by the absent wind, the branches record its passing. A hot, hot day. Lawrence sitting by the tree, the fingers of both hands laced together over his left knee. Schiele fingers. Thin wrists, thick trousers. Freshly laundered, pressed, his white shirt is full of the sun in which it has dried. Like the shirt of the prisoner facing execution in Goya's *The Third of May 1808*, it is the bright focus of all the light – and there is a *lot* of light – in the photograph.

Lawrence's jacket is rolled up beside him on the grass. The sleeves of his shirt are rolled down, buttoned around his bony wrists, lending a formal quality to the picture. By the 1920s photographs no longer required the interminable exposure times of the Victorian era (when heads and limbs had to be clamped in place to prevent blurring), but they were nearer to that unwieldy stage of photographic culture than to the Instamatic images of the post-war era. In early portraits, as part of the preparation for having a photograph taken, people focused their lives 'in the moment rather than hurrying past it'. Here, too, there is a strong sense of Lawrence *sitting* for a photograph. As far as formality is concerned the final touch is provided by the way that Lawrence's shirt is buttoned up to the collar. Why does that collar hold not just Lawrence's shirt but the photograph itself together?

Because even here, in the midst of this audible heat, Lawrence has to be careful to keep warm. He feels the cold, has to be careful not to catch a chill (the thick jacket is close to hand). His mother's concern for the sickly child – years of being told to keep warm, to keep his jacket on – have been internalised. By now, in the heat, it is second nature to cover up his skinniness, to keep himself warm.

His feet are invisible, buried in the grass, creating the impression – emphasised by the way that his body was surrounded by the trunk of the tree ('the tree's life penetrates my life, and my life the tree's') – that Lawrence is growing out of the ground. 'Thank God I am not free,' he wrote from Taos in 1922, 'any more than a rooted tree is free.' This line caused Larkin some astonishment. 'It is hard to see how he could have been less encumbered in the affairs of life,' he wrote from Leicester almost thirty years later. 'Put him down in salaried employment or with a growing family or an ageing one – why, he didn't even own a house & furniture!'

This is not strictly true: Lawrence *did* own some furniture (Brodsky was right: there is 'no life without furniture') much of which he made himself. And while he may not have owned a house, the Lawrences' constant moving obliged them to keep *making* home. It is typical of Lawrence that, on the one hand, he became more and more anxious about finding a place to settle and, on the other, achieved the ideal condition of being at home anywhere: 'I feel a great stranger, but have got used to that feeling, and prefer it to feeling "homely". After all, one is a stranger, nowhere so hopelessly as at home.' That was from Taos in 1922; three years later the emphasis had changed: 'One can no longer say: I'm a stranger everywhere, only "everywhere I'm at home".'

He had found a home within himself and in what he did, in his *being*. Rilke had admired the same thing in Rodin who lived in a house that 'meant nothing to him' [Rodin] because 'deep within him he bore the darkness, peace and shelter of a house and he himself had become the sky above it and the wood around it and the distance and the great river that always flowed past'. Lawrence had likened himself to a rooted tree; sunk in himself, Rodin, according to Rilke, was 'fuller of sap than an old tree in autumn'. He had 'grown deep'. This idea, of being at home in yourself as a way of being at home in the world, was to receive its most exalted expression in the final lines of the last of the *Sonnets to Orpheus*:

Whisper to the silent earth: I'm flowing.
To the flashing water say: I am.

I'd torn the photo of Lawrence by the tree out of a biography published by the University of New Mexico Press. Before doing so I had tried to find where and when it was taken but there was no information. It was the only uncaptioned photo in the book. Had there been a caption I might have felt more reluctant about committing that small act of bibliographical vandalism. As it was, there had been no text to anchor the photo to the book, nothing to keep it in place. It seemed apposite that this, the only uncaptioned image in the book, was now free of the only context – the physical one of the book – available. If the bust made by Jo Davidson showed Lawrence what he would become in death, when – as suggested earlier – the loose pages of his life were bound and dated, then this picture showed Lawrence unbound, alive.

A photograph's meaning is bound up closely with its caption. As the photograph frames the subject, so the caption frames the photograph. Without a caption a photograph is not quite developed, its meaning not fixed. With a little research I could have found out – could still find out – where and when it was taken but I preferred, and prefer, not to: it seemed fitting that this photograph of Lawrence sitting there, 'happy as a cicada', should elude place and time. Like this it was a photo of Lawrence in the state evoked by Rilke in his sonnet; like this I *could* identify the tree: it is a photo of Lawrence sitting by a bho tree.

Buddha was sitting under a bho tree when he achieved enlightenment and in the spring of 1926 Lawrence told Brewster that he was 'convinced that every man needs a bho tree of some sort in his life. What ails us is, we have cut down all our bho trees . . . Still, here and there in the world a solitary bho tree must be standing . . . And I'm going to sit right down under one, to be American about it, when I come across one.'*

Another picture of Lawrence, the one I always hoped to come across in bookshops, the one that I had seen when I was seventeen, showed him – if I remember rightly – standing towards the edge of a vast horizontal landscape. Clouds streamed across the sky. I forget which book I saw it in all those years ago but I remember thinking that the caption – 'A fine wind is blowing the new direction of Time' – had been chosen so perfectly that the picture seemed less a photograph of Lawrence (a tiny figure in the corner, recognisable only by his beard) than an illustration of this line. At the time I did not know where it was from: a quotation from Lawrence, presumably, but beyond that I had no idea. I wanted to track that quotation down – or, to put it more passively and accurately, I hoped to come across it – and the

---

* What Lawrence intended to sit under, Rilke, in the first of the *Duino Elegies*, was content merely to glimpse and speculate upon: 'Perhaps there remains for us some tree on a hillside . . .'

prospect was intriguing precisely because there was nothing to go on. From the start, in other words, I read Lawrence in order to make sense of – to better understand – a photograph of him.

The urge to discover the source of this caption also explains my pleasure in reading Lawrence's letters in what might seem to be the ludicrously complete Cambridge edition. Or, to make the same point the opposite way, perhaps my pleasure in reading Lawrence's letters is the culmination of an urge, the first pulse of which was felt twenty years ago when I saw what I later discovered was a line from 'Song of a Man Who Has Come Through'. From that moment on, part of the incentive to read Lawrence was to discover the source of this line, to read it in the original, as it were, without quotation marks. I came across it in the Penguin *Selected Poems* (the edition that I still had with me in Rome, the one that I didn't take to Alonissos) but my satisfaction was qualified (or so it seems to me now) because everything in a 'Selected' format comes in tacit quotation marks: those provided by the editor's choice of material. When we read a 'selection' we are, so to speak, in the realm of massively extended quotation. When we read the author's work in definitive or collected editions, however, we are *there*: nothing comes between us and the writer (the often cumbersome editorial apparatus serves, paradoxically, to facilitate the intimacy between reader and writer). Like this I can read Lawrence *unquoted*.

'You mustn't look in my novel for that old stable ego of the character . . . the ordinary novel would trace the history of the diamond – but I say "diamond, what! This is carbon".' *Those* lines, even if we read them in the collected edition of Lawrence's letters, seem like a citation. Their true context is in a book about Lawrence – this one, for example! When we see them in Volume 2 of the *Collected Letters* it almost seems as if Lawrence lifted them from one of the hundreds of critical studies of him. And so much of my early reading of Lawrence came in quotation marks. At a very early stage 'doing' English became synonymous with reading criticism, most of it by academics. Go into any university bookshop and you will see stacks and stacks of books on Lawrence by academics. Such books form the basis of literary study in universities and none of them has anything to do with literature.

In my final year at university there was a great deal of fuss about course reform. Instead of ploughing through everything from *Beowulf* to Beckett, academics like Terry Eagleton were proposing a 'theory' option. I didn't know what theory was but it sounded radical and challenging. Within a few years 'theory', whatever it was, had achieved a position of dominance in English departments throughout Britain. Synoptic works of theory were pouring from the presses. Fifteen years down the line these texts still appear radical and challenging except in one or two details, namely that they are neither radical nor challenging. One Christmas when I was about ten my parents gave me a *Beryl the Peril* annual which included some of Beryl's answers to difficult exam questions. Asked to construct a sentence using the word 'discourse' she wrote, '"Discourse is too hard for me," said the golfer.' How quaint! Twenty years on she would probably have no trouble coming up with a whole paper on 'The Self and its Others'. In no time at all theory had become more of an orthodoxy than the style of study it sought to overthrow. Any lecturer worth his weight in corduroy was fluent in discoursese, could signify-and-signified till the cows came home.

Hearing that I was 'working on Lawrence', an acquaintance lent me a book he thought I might find interesting: A Longman Critical Reader on Lawrence, edited by Peter Widdowson. I glanced at the contents page: old Eagleton was there, of course, together with some other state-of-the-fart theorists: Lydia Blanchard on 'Lawrence, Foucault and the Language of Sexuality' (in the section on 'Gender, Sexuality, Feminism'), Daniel J. Schneider on 'Alternatives to Logocentrism in D. H. Lawrence' (in the section featuring 'Post-Structuralist Turns'). I could feel myself getting angry and then I flicked through the introductory essay on 'Radical Indeterminacy: a post-modern Lawrence' and became angrier still. How could it have happened? How could these people with no feeling for literature have ended up *teaching* it, writing about it? I should have stopped there, should have avoided looking at any more, but I didn't because telling myself to stop always has the effect of urging me on. Instead, I kept looking at this group of wankers huddled in a circle, backs turned to the world so that no one would see them pulling each other off. Oh, it was too much, it was too stupid. I threw the book across the room and then I tried to tear it up but it was too resilient. By now I was blazing mad. I thought about getting Widdowson's phone number and making threatening phone calls. Then I looked around for the means to destroy his vile, filthy book. In the end it took a whole box of matches and some risk of personal injury before I succeeded in deconstructing it.

I burned it in self-defence. It was the book or me because writing like that kills everything it touches. That is the hallmark of academic criticism: it kills everything it touches. Walk around a university campus and there is an almost palpable smell of death about the place because hundreds of academics are busy killing everything they touch. I recently met an academic who said that he taught German literature. I was aghast: to think, this man who had been in universities all his life was teaching Rilke. Rilke! Oh, it was too much to bear. You don't teach Rilke, I wanted to say, you kill Rilke! You turn him to dust and then you go off to conferences where dozens of other academic-morticians gather with the express intention of killing Rilke and turning him to dust, and then, as part of the cover-up, the conference papers are published, the dust is embalmed and before you know it literature is a vast graveyard of dust, a dustyard of graves. I was beside myself with indignation. I wanted to maim and harm this polite, well-meaning academic who, for all I knew, was a brilliant teacher who had turned on generations of students to the *Duino Elegies*. Still, I thought to myself the following morning when I had calmed down, the general point stands: how can you know anything about literature if all you've done is read books?

Now, criticism is an integral part of the literary tradition and academics can sometimes write excellent works of criticism but these are exceptional: the vast majority, the overwhelming majority of books by academics, especially books like that Longman Reader, are a *crime against literature*. If you want to see how literature lives then you turn to writers, and see what they've said about each other, either in essays, reviews, in letters or journals – and in the works themselves. 'The best readings of art are art,' said George Steiner (an academic!); the great books add up to a tacit 'syllabus of enacted criticism'. This becomes explicit when poets write a poem about some great work of art – Auden's 'Musée des Beaux Arts' – or about another poet: Auden's elegy for Yeats, Brodsky's elegy for Auden, Heaney's elegy for Brodsky (the cleverly titled 'Audenesque'). In such instances the distinction between imaginative and critical writing disappears.

When it comes to reviews and essays in which writers address other writers and other books, on the other hand, it would seem that they are engaged in something indistinguishable from academic criticism. But this formal narrowing of difference in kind enhances the difference in spirit. Brodsky has gone through certain poems of Auden's with the finest of combs; Nabokov has subjected Pushkin to forensic scrutiny. The difference is that these works of Pushkin's and Auden's were not just studied: they were lived through in a way that is anathema to the academic . . .

Except this is nonsense of course. Scholars live their work too. Leon Edel – to take one example from hundreds – embraced Henry James's life and work as perilously intimately as any writer ever has. I withdraw that claim, it's ludicrous, it won't stand up to any kind of scrutiny. I withdraw it unconditionally – but I also want to let it stand, conditionally. Scholarly work on the texts, on preparing lovely editions of Lawrence's letters is one thing but those critical studies that we read at university . . . Research! Research! The very word is like a bell, tolling the death and the imminent turning to dust of whichever poor sod is being researched. Spare me. Spare me the drudgery of systematic examinations and give me the lightning flashes of those wild books in which there is no attempt to cover the ground thoroughly or reasonably. While preparing to write *Etruscan Places* Lawrence thanked a friend for sending an authoritative book on the subject by Roland Fell who was

> very thorough in washing out once more the few rags of information we have concerning the Etruscans: but not a thing has he to say. It's really disheartening: I shall just have to start in and go ahead, and be damned to all authorities! There really is next to nothing to be said, *scientifically*, about the Etruscans. Must take the imaginative line.

That's why Lawrence is so exciting: he took the imaginative line in all his criticism, in the *Study of Thomas Hardy* or the *Studies in Classic American Literature*, or the 'Introduction to his Paintings'. Each of them is an electrical storm of ideas! Hit and miss, illuminating even when hopelessly wide of the mark ('the judgment may be all wrong: but this was the impression I got'). Bang! Crash! Lightning flash after lightning flash, searing, unpredictable, dangerous.

In truth I prefer these books to the novels which I have kept putting off re-reading. I re-read *The Rainbow* in Rome and I could have forced myself to re-read *Women in Love*, could have forced myself to sit down and peer at every page – or so I like to believe: who knows if, when it came to the crunch, I really had it in me? – but, I thought, why should I? Why should I re-read this book that I not only had no desire to re-read but which I actively wanted not to re-read? I had no desire to re-read *The Rainbow* but, unwilling to give myself the benefit of the doubt, sat down and re-read it, just to be on the safe side. I re-read the same copy that I had read first time around: part of the uniform Penguin editions of Lawrence with photographs on the cover (roosters or hens in this case) and, on the back, a sepia photo of Lawrence with beard (naturally) and centre parting. When I re-read *The Rainbow* I had thought I might discover, like a flower pressed between the pages, the dried remains of my younger self preserved within it. In the most literal sense I was there, the underlinings and annotations, made when we did the book at Oxford (i.e. when we read a load of dreary critical studies about it), were still there but in any kind of metaphorical sense – no, there was nothing, no traces of my earlier self, no memories released by the act of re-reading the same page that I had read years before one particular afternoon wherever and whenever that was.

My impressions of the book were more or less unaltered. It remained a book which I had no desire to re-read; as soon as I had finished re-reading *The Rainbow* it reverted to being what it was *before* I re-read it: a book which I had read and which I had no desire to re-re-read. It was a closed book: even when it was open and being re-read it was somehow still a closed book. As for *Women in Love*, I read it in my teens and, as far as I am concerned, it can stay read.

If we're being utterly frank, I don't want to re-read *any* novels by Lawrence. And not only do I not want to re-read some of Lawrence's books, I don't even want to *read* all of them. I want to keep some in reserve – I want to know that there are bits and pieces of Lawrence that are still out there, still fresh, waiting to be discovered (by me at least), waiting to be read for the first time.

In this respect I made a serious mistake in Rome, a mistake of such magnitude, in fact, as to jeopardise any chance of going on with – let alone completing – my study of Lawrence. From the start I'd known that I had to write my book as I went along. There are people who like to complete all the reading, all the research, and then, when they have read everything that there is to read, when they have attained complete mastery of the material, *then* and only then do they sit down and write it up. Not me. Once I know enough about a subject to begin writing about it I lose interest in it immediately. In the case of Lawrence I knew I'd have to make sure that I finished writing my book at exactly the moment that I had satisfied my curiosity, and to do this the writing had to lag fractionally behind the reading. Especially when it came to Lawrence's letters. The letters were Lawrence's life and I knew I had to ration my reading of them, not get too far ahead of myself. They were my main resource, a source so rich I knew I'd squander them if I just burrowed away at them from beginning to end. I knew that I could not be closer to Lawrence than I was while reading his letters for the first time. Ideally, if I were going to spend eighteen months writing my book about D. H. Lawrence I would be reading those letters for sixteen or even seventeen months, for a year at the very least.

But what did I do? I read them, all seven volumes, cover to cover, in two months. It's my parents' fault. When I was a child they rationed out my sweets too slowly and so I grew up to be a gobbler. That's what I did with Lawrence's letters: I gobbled them all down and in no time at all there were none left, the bag was empty. I couldn't stop myself, couldn't help it. I loved reading them too much. I read Volume 2, then 3, then 5, then 4, then 6, then 1 (which I had no real interest in, whizzing through it in a day and a half). That left Volume 7. Whatever you do, I said to myself, keep Volume 7 in reserve: under no circumstances read Volume 7 because then you will have nothing left to read. It should have been relatively easy because there were so many other books to read – I could have re-read *Women in Love* (which I couldn't face re-reading), or one of the numerous critical books on Lawrence (which I had decided were a waste of anyone's time to read) or the poems or plays but instead I kept *glancing at* Volume 7, touching it, holding it, opening a few pages, reading the introduction. Finally I thought I would read just the first few letters even though I knew that reading the first few was exactly what I had to avoid because I would not be able to stop after three or four letters. After three or four I would keep reading another one or two until I had read so many that it would be pointless to stop reading the book and before I knew it I would have read all the Lawrence letters. And so the important thing was to avoid even opening the book: I knew it would be easier to avoid starting to read the book than it would be to stop reading the book once I had started. I knew all this but I opened it anyway, thinking to myself that I would read the first few letters. Which I did. But since these letters were pretty insignificant in themselves, harmless, I read one or two more which were also pretty innocuous and I thought I would keep reading until I came to a significant letter and *then* stop. It went on like that until I realised with a shock that I was in danger of finishing all of Lawrence's letters. I read one after another and the more I read the less there were to read and although I knew part of the reason for reading the letters of Lawrence was to put off the moment when I had to write about him I also realised that by reading the letters like this, by failing to moderate my consumption of the letters, I was caught up in the gathering momentum of his death. I was running out of letters to read just as Lawrence was running out of life. The nearer I got to the end of the book the shorter and more insignificant the letters became, little gasps of anger where before there had been long, thousand-word rants, and so the pace of decline accelerated. Even insignificant communications – 'Blair has been kind as an angel to me. Here is £10 for housekeeping' – became something to cherish against the coming end.

And then, abruptly, there were no more letters. It was the end: oblivion.

There were no more letters. If only, I found myself thinking, if only there had been Volumes 8, 9, 10 or 11. I had read four thousand pages of letters by Lawrence and I wanted thousands of pages more . . . I wanted them not to end. And yet, at the same time that I was wishing they would not come to an end, I was hurrying through these books because however much you are enjoying a book, however much you want it never to end, you are always eager for it to end. However much you are enjoying a book you are always flicking to the end, counting to see how many pages are left, looking forward to the time when you can put the book down and have done with it. At the back of our minds, however much we are enjoying a book, we come to the end of it and some little voice is always saying, 'Thank Christ for that!'

Still, better reading than writing. One of the reasons I was enjoying reading the Lawrence letters so much, and the main reason I wished that there were more Lawrence letters to read, was because they were a perfect excuse for not writing my book about Lawrence. Whereas now I had no choice, no choice at all.

It was a terrible prospect since although I had read the Lawrence letters and was therefore obliged to begin writing about Lawrence I had also read his letters in such a way that I was actually in no state to begin writing about Lawrence. Not only had I read them too fast, I'd also read them out of sequence, as they became available at the British Council Library in Rome, so that all sense of chronology, of development had been lost. One moment Lawrence was in New Mexico, the next he was eighteen months younger, in Italy, putting off going to America. If I had done it properly I would have read them sequentially and paced it so that my reading of the letters kept pace with the writing but now a huge six-volume gap had opened between my reading and my writing. I was like an out-of-condition athlete in a race who had lost touch with the front runners and the group in the middle: it was too much of a haul to get back in touch, I was out of the race, finished. The only alternative to giving up was to keep plodding round the track for the sake of finishing, grinding it out, metre by metre, page by page.

Not only had I read the Lawrence letters too fast and out of sequence, I had also failed to take notes. I had intended doing so as I went along, transcribing any particularly important passages and keeping a careful record of where these passages occurred, but I had been in such a hurry to gobble down the letters that, except on a few occasions, I had not done so. Not only that, I realised as I glanced back through the volumes of letters that I had already read, but there were many that, in my eagerness and impatience to get through all seven volumes, I had taken no notice of. The more I looked, the more letters there were that I had no recollection of. I could read the letters again because I had read them so badly the first time around. In fact, I realised with a sinking heart, I was practically obliged to re-read the Lawrence letters which I had longed to go on reading but which, now that I *had* to go on reading them, I wished to God I was shot of.

In no time at all, though, I was back under their spell. There were actually hundreds of letters which I had not read at all, which I saw for the first time as I re-read them. Like this one from November 1916 when, in the course of a letter to Kot, Lawrence remembered a time when he had seen an adder curled up in the spring sunshine, asleep. The snake was not aware of Lawrence's presence until he was very close and then 'she lifted her head like a queen to look' and moved away. 'She often comes into my mind, and I think I see her asleep in the sun, like a Princess of the fairy world. It is queer, the intimation of other worlds, which one catches.'

Queer, too, the intimation of future works which one catches so often in the letters. In this case the writing of the famous poem 'Snake' was still several years distant but here we have, as it were, a first draft of the experience which will later form the basis of the poem. This is one of the pleasures of the letters: one has the very first touch of a poem. It is like watching a fire and seeing the first lick of flame along a log: you think it is about to catch but then it vanishes. You watch and wait for the flame to come back. It doesn't – and then, after you have stopped looking, the flame flickers back again and the log catches.

Lawrence began writing his greatest poem, 'The Ship of Death', in the autumn of 1929. According to Keith Sagar, the opening image of the poem –

Now it is autumn and the falling fruit
and the long journey towards oblivion

– was suggested by a visit to Rottach in late August when he noticed the 'apples on tall old apple-trees, dropping so suddenly'. But the first intimation of the poem actually comes as early as New Year's Eve, 1913, in a letter to Edward Garnett: 'it is just beginning to look a bit like autumn – acorns and olives falling, and vine leaves going yellow'. I *had* made a note of that, and of the occasion a few months later when I felt the rhythm of the image pulsing into life long, long before Lawrence began working on the poem: 'the apples blown down lie almost like green lights in the grass'. It was like a cadential draft of a poem that was nowhere near being written, and as I went through the letters for the second time I noticed more and more pre-echoes like this. As Sagar points out, the immediate source for the image of the ship of death was a 'little bronze' one he saw in Cerveteri in April 1927. Already by the summer of 1925, however, the opening image is redolent with the atmosphere of departure and journeying that will make up the poem's narrative: 'seems already a bit like autumn, and there is feeling of going away in the air'.

Who can say when a poem begins to stir, to germinate, in the soil of the writer's mind? There are certain experiences waiting to happen: like the snake at Lawrence's water trough, the poem is already there, waiting for him. The poem is waiting for circumstance to activate it, to occasion its being written.

As time goes by we drift away from the great texts, the finished works on which an author's reputation is built, towards the journals, diaries, letters, manuscripts, jottings. This is not simply because, as an author's stature grows posthumously, the fund of published texts becomes exhausted and we have to make do not only with previously unpublished or unfinished material but, increasingly, with matter that was never intended for publication. It is also because we want to get nearer to the man or woman who wrote these books, to his or her being. We crave an increasingly intimate relationship with the author, unmediated, in so far as possible, by the contrivances of art. A curious reversal takes place. The finished works serve as prologue to the jottings; the published book becomes a stage to be passed through – a draft – en route to the definitive pleasure of the notes, the fleeting impressions, the sketches, in which it had its origin.

In the case of Lawrence this process coincides with the gravitational pull of his work, which is always – another reversal – away from the work, back towards the circumstances of its composition, towards the man and his sensations. As is so often the case, it is Frieda who best captured this: 'Since Lawrence died, all these donkeys years already, he has grown and grown for me . . . To me his relationship, his bond with everything in creation was so amazing, no preconceived ideas, just a meeting between him and a creature, a tree, a cloud, anything. I called it love, but it was something else – *Bejahung* in German, "saying yes".'

This saying 'yes' – like Larkin's saying 'no' – is heard most clearly in Lawrence's letters. It is audible in the novels, too, of course, but it becomes more pronounced, more exposed, as we descend the traditional hierarchy of genre. In the novels the meeting between Lawrence and the world is mediated, inevitably, by Gudrun and Ursula, by the authorial representatives, by the demands of novelisation. Always, in the major works, the primary meeting is between Lawrence and the novel form which he is trying to mould, to recast in his own needs. What we want now, 'all these donkeys years' later, is Lawrence in the midst of his sensations. 'Whoever reads me will be in the thick of the scrimmage,' he wrote in January 1925, 'and if he doesn't like it – if he wants a safe seat in the audience – let him read somebody else.' In the novels we are in the scrimmage of art which, however apparently artless, will always be less of a scrimmage than the life unfolding in the letters. It is there, in the letters, that the scrimmage – the essence of Lawrence's art – is most nakedly revealed. Nor does it matter, in Lawrence's case as it does with some writers, if the prose of the letters is less honed, more error-prone, than in his published writing. Lawrence was, in some ways, a relatively careless writer, indifferent, or so he claimed, to the appearance of his words on the page. 'What do I care if "e" is somewhere upside down, or "g" comes from the wrong fount? I really don't.' Needless to say, this easy-going attitude to matters typographical did not stop him lambasting publishers for failing to pick up on exactly these kind of mitsakes: without this capacity for energetic self-contradiction there would be no scrimmage.

It is for this reason, I think, not simply because of his fame, that Lawrence's manuscripts became so sought after. His writing urges us back to its source, to the experience in which it originates. Ideally – and I am here trying to suggest the *direction* of an urge not necessarily an actual wish – we would have *met* Lawrence (in a way that even his admirers, surely, have no desire to have met E. M. Forster). Failing that we want the experience of reading him to be as intimate as possible; for the collector – I imagine – this means unmediated even by typesetting. Frieda had as sharp a sense of the possible commercial value of the Lady Chatterley manuscripts as anyone but she also understood and expressed perfectly the special poignancy of this intimacy: 'I enjoy looking at them,' she said, 'and reading them in the raw as it were.'

Some of Lawrence's books would have benefited from thorough, careful revision but what was essential about Lawrence – the qualities that made his writing identifiably Lawrentian – is always present at a draft stage. The improvements that come from redrafting are of relatively minor importance compared to the shock of his first encounter with the subject or incident he is addressing. In the elegy written shortly after his death Rebecca

West explained how she felt unable to make the point that she wanted about Lawrence's work without recourse to her personal acquaintance with him (note again that familiar motion, from the work, back to the source, from the work to the man who made it). She met him, briefly, in Florence in the company of Norman Douglas who explained that it was Lawrence's habit to arrive in a place and immediately, before he was in any position to do so, to start banging out an article about it. Douglas and West knocked on the door of Lawrence's hotel room and there he was, fresh off the train, 'tapping out an article on the state of Florence at that moment without knowing enough about it to make his views of real value'. Later she realised that 'he was writing about the state of his own soul at that moment, which . . . he could render only in symbolic terms; and the city of Florence was as good a symbol as any other.'*

'I feel there is a curious grudge, or resentment against everything,' Lawrence observed, grudgingly, on arriving in New Mexico, 'almost in the very soil itself.'

Seven years earlier, in the autumn of 1915, Lawrence made a number of visits to Garsington Manor, the home of Ottoline Morrell. On 9 November, the day after his arrival, he wrote the first of several visionary accounts of his experiences there:

When I drive across this country, with the autumn falling and
rustling to pieces, I am so sad, for my country, for this great wave
of civilisation, 2000 years, which is now collapsing, that it is hard to
live. So much beauty and pathos of old things passing away and no
new things coming: this house of the Ottolines – It is England – my
God, it breaks my soul – this England, these shafted windows, the
elm trees, the blue distance – the past, the great past, crumbling
down, breaking down, not under the force of the coming buds but
under the weight of many exhausted, lovely yellow leaves, that drift
over the lawn and over the pond, like the soldiers, passing away, into
winter and the darkness of winter – no, I can't bear it. For the winter
stretches ahead, where all vision is lost and all memory dies out . . . I
can't bear it: the past, the past, the falling, perishing crumbling past
so great, so magnificent.

---

*   Lawrence himself said more or less the same thing in *Kangaroo*. The autobiographical figure Richard Lovat Somers 'wearied himself to death struggling with the problem of himself and calling it Australia'.

As soon as he returned to London he wrote to tell Ottoline how that visit would 'always be a sort of last vision of England to me, the beauty of England, the wonder of this terrible autumn: when we set the irises above the pond, in the stillness and the wetness'. By the end of the month he was back at Garsington again and from there he wrote another, related letter to his hostess:

So vivid a vision, everything so visually poignant, it is like that concentrated moment when a drowning man sees all his past crystallised into one jewel of recollection.

The slow, reluctant, pallid morning, unwillingly releasing its tarnished embellishment of gold, far off there, outside, beyond the shafted windows, beyond, over the forgotten, unseen country, that lies sunken in gloom below, whilst the dawn sluggishly bestirs itself, far off, beyond the window-shafts of stone, dark pillars, like bars, dark and unfathomed, set near me, before the reluctance of the far-off dawn:

the window-shafts, like pillars, like bars, the shallow Tudor arch looping over between them, looping the darkness in a pure edge, in front of the far-off reluctance of the dawn:

Shafted, looped windows between the without and the within, the old house, the perfect old intervention of fitted stone, fitted perfectly about a silent soul, the soul that in drowning under this last wave of time looks out clear through the shafted windows to see the dawn of all dawns taking place, the England of all recollection rousing into being:

the wet lawn drizzled with brown sodden leaves; the feathery heap of the ilex tree; the garden-seat all wet and reminiscent:

between the ilex tree and the bare, purplish elms, a gleaming segment of all England, the dark plough-land and wan grass, and the blue, hazy heap of the distance, under the accomplished morning.

So the day has taken place, all the visionary business of the day. The young cattle stand in the straw of the stack yard, the sun gleams on their white fleece, the eye of Io, and the man with side-whiskers carries more yellow straw into the compound. The sun comes in all down one side, and above, in the sky, all the gables and the grey stone chimney-stacks are floating in pure dreams.

There is threshed wheat smouldering in the great barn, the fire of life; and the sound of the threshing machine, running, drumming . . .

It is an extraordinary letter, an extraordinary vision – or series of visions – of England: a synthesis in prose of Blake, Constable and Turner. Part of Lawrence's intention was to show his aristocratic friend how full of writing he was but there is also a sense of the words welling up in him unbidden. Each paragraph pulses into life from the seed of the preceding one; each paragraph offers an amended version of the same material; each version enters more deeply into the experience and, at the same time, advances it incrementally. It is like hearing alternate takes of a piece of music but, as these different versions unfold, so a narrative emerges: the narrative of his attempts to fix an experience that is vast, shifting, apocalyptic.

In the earlier letters England was lodged precisely within the confines of the aristocratic house. There is no acknowledgement of Eastwood – of his own experience and history – being a part of this essential England. In the last letter, however, the world 'beyond', 'that lies sunken in gloom' is acknowledged, distantly. At this stage in the letter the house is evoked in terms of the architecture of its own soul ('the perfect old intervention of fitted stone' etc.); the spirit of the house is talking but, as we move through successive variations, this 'vision of a drowning man' becomes Lawrence's own vision 'of all that I am, all I have become, and ceased to be. It is me, generations and generations of me, every complex, gleaming fibre of me, every lucid pang of my coming into being. And oh, my God, I cannot bear it.' Effectively, Lawrence imaginatively claims the house as his own. He fuses absolutely with the house and the surrounding landscape so that what is really coming to an end here – or what is coming to consummation – is Lawrence the *English* writer. It is not only the most vivid example imaginable of West's point, it also shows us – at a moment of supreme tension in Lawrence's life – the process at work, as it is happening. Notes flare into writing, writing smoulders into notes, resulting in one of the most intense and revelatory passages Lawrence ever wrote.

If this book *aspires* to the condition of notes that is because, for me, Lawrence's prose is at its best when it comes closest to notes.

In *Sea and Sardinia*, for example, Lawrence *made* no notes during the ten-day trip but dashed off a book in a few weeks shortly afterwards. The lack of notes, in other words, accounts for the book's note-like immediacy. Notes taken at the time, on the move, and referred to later – as I referred later to the notes I had made in Eastwood – would have come between the experience and the writing. As it is, everything is written – rather than noted and then written – as experienced. The experience is created in the writing rather than re-created from notes. Reading it, you are drenched in a spray of ideas that never lets up. Impressions are experienced as ideas, ideas are glimpsed like fields through a train window, one after another. Opinions erupt into ideas, argument is conveyed as sensation, sensations are felt as argument. This immediacy is inscribed in the writing of the book. The transformation from 'notes' to 'prose' often takes place within the course of a sentence. We have to wait a long time for the pronoun that transforms the writing from diary-like jottings to finished prose. Sometimes it doesn't happen at all. Experience and sensation are rarely reined into shape until the last possible moment.

Would it be too silly – would it destroy any vestige of critical credibility this study might have – to claim that *Sea and Sardinia* is Lawrence's best book? Well it's my favourite at any rate ('the judgment may be all wrong: but this was the impression I got'), with *Studies in Classic American Literature*, *Twilight in Italy* and – if they count as a book – the posthumously published 'Last Poems' coming close behind. Best of all, though, are the letters: they show Lawrence at his most modern, his least dated. Unlike the thunderhead prose of the Garsington letters, Lawrence's later style of note-writing is unelaborated, spare. It is seen at its most minimal – so to speak – in the stunned letters dashed off soon after he arrived in Australia, a country he considered 'not so much new as non-existent':

> The land is here: sky high and blue and new, as if no one had ever
> taken a breath from it; and the air is new, strong, fresh as silver;
> and the land is terribly big and empty, still uninhabited . . . it is *too*
> new, you see: too vast. It needs hundreds of years yet before it can
> live. This is the land where the unborn souls, strange and not to be
> known, which shall be born in 500 years, live. A grey foreign spirit.
> And the people who are here, are not really here: only like ducks
> that swim on the surface of the pond: but the land has a 'fourth
> dimension' and the white people swim like shadows over the surface
> of it.

Bruce Chatwin doesn't even get *near* to that kind of responsiveness and suggestiveness in the three hundred pages of *The Songlines*.

'Have you noticed how often a writer's letters are superior to the rest of his work?' wonders Comtesse d'Arpajon in *Remembrance of Things Past*. She had in mind Flaubert (though his name escaped her at the time). I tend not only to agree but to wonder if this remark might not be prophetic. Could my own preference for writers' – not just Lawrence's – notes and letters be part of a general, historical drift away from the novel? For Lawrence the novel was 'the one bright book of life', 'the highest form of human expression so far attained'. Nowadays most novels are copies of other novels but, for Lawrence, the novel still contained these massive potentialities. Marguerite Yourcenar offers an important qualification to this idea when, in her notes on the composition of *Memoirs of Hadrian* (a text of far greater interest, to me, than the novel to which it is appended), she writes that 'In our time the novel devours all other forms; one is almost forced to use it as a medium of expression.' No more. Increasingly, the process of novelisation goes hand in hand with a strait-jacketing of the material's expressive potential. One gets so weary watching authors' sensations and thoughts get novelised, set into the concrete of fiction, that perhaps it is best to avoid the novel as a medium of expression.

Of course good, even great, novels continue to be written but – as someone remarks every twenty years or so – the moment of the form's historical urgency has passed. Part of the excitement of reading Lawrence comes from our sense of how the potentialities of the form are being expanded, forced forwards. That feeling is now almost wholly absent from our reading of contemporary novels. If the form advances at all it is by increments, not by the great surges of the heyday of modernism.

Milan Kundera's faith in the novel is the equal of Lawrence's but the logic of his *apologia* for the form actually carries him beyond it. Kundera takes inspiration from the unhindered exuberance of Rabelais and Sterne, before the compulsive realism of the nineteenth century. 'Their freedom of composition' set the young Kundera dreaming of 'creating a work in which the bridges and the filler have no reason to be and in which the novelist would never be forced – for the sake of form and its dictates – to stray by even a single line from what he cares about, what fascinates him'. Kundera duly achieved this in his own fictions, the famous novels 'in the form of variations'. In his 'Notes Inspired by *The Sleepwalkers*', meanwhile, Kundera paid tribute to Broch who demonstrated the need for 'a new art of the *specifically novelistic essay*'. Novels like *Immortality* are full of 'inquiring, hypothetical' or aphoristic essays like this but compared with these, my favourite passages, I found myself indifferent to Kundera's characters. After reading *Immortality* what I wanted from Kundera was a novel composed entirely of essays, stripped of the last rind of novelisation. Kundera duly obliged. His next book, *Testaments Betrayed*, provided all the pleasures – i.e. all the distractions – of his novels with, so to speak, none of the distractions of character and situation. By Kundera's own logic this 'essay in nine parts' – more accurately, a series of variations in the form of an essay – which has dispensed entirely with the trappings of novelisation, actually represents the most refined, the most extreme, version yet of Kundera's idea of the novel.

'A book which is not a copy of other books has its own construction,' warned Lawrence and the kind of novels I like are ones which bear no traces of *being* novels. Which is why the novelists I like best are, with the exception of the last-named, not novelists at all: Nietzsche, the Goncourt brothers, Barthes, Fernando Pessoa, Ryszard Kapuscinski, Thomas Bernhard . . .

NOTES

Abbreviations of principal editions used

Letters, vols 1–7, refers to the Cambridge University Press edition of Lawrence's Letters, respectively:

Volume 1: September 1901–May 1913, ed. James T. Boulton, 1979.
Volume 2: June 1913–October 1916, ed. George J. Zytaruk and James T. Boulton, 1981.
Volume 3: October 1916–June 1921, ed. James T. Boulton and Andrew Robertson, 1984.
Volume 4: June 1921–March 1924, ed. Warren Roberts, James T. Boulton and Elizabeth Mansfield, 1987.
Volume 5: March 1924–March 1927, ed. James T. Boulton and Lindeth Vasey, 1989.
Volume 6: March 1927–November 1928, ed. James T. Boulton, Margaret H. Boulton and Gerald M. Lacy, 1991.
Volume 7: November 1928–February 1930, ed. Keith Sagar and James T. Boulton, 1993.

Phoenix: The Posthumous Papers (1936), ed. Edward D. McDonald (Harmondsworth: Penguin, 1978).
Phoenix II: Uncollected, Unpublished, and Other Prose Works, ed. Warren Roberts and Harry T. Moore (Harmondsworth: Penguin, 1978).
Poems: The Complete Poems, ed. Vivian De Sola Pinto and F. Warren Roberts (Harmondsworth: Penguin, 1977).
Thomas Hardy: Study of Thomas Hardy and Other Essays, ed. Bruce Steele (Cambridge: Cambridge University Press, 1985).

Place of publication for the following is London unless otherwise stated:
p. 135 'I feel I . . .': *Letters*, vol. 6, p. 182.
p. 135 'will to write . . .': *Letters*, vol. 5, p. 621.
p. 136 'that one thing . . .': Rainer Maria Rilke, *Selected Letters 1902–1926*, trans. R. F. C. Hull (Quartet Books, 1988), p. 143.

p. 136 'Either happiness or . . .': ibid. p. 10.

p. 136 '*Du mußt dein* . . .': from 'Archaic Torso of Apollo', *The Selected Poetry of Rainer Maria Rilke*, ed. and trans. Stephen Mitchell (New York: Vintage International, 1989), p. 6.

p. 136 'i.e. find a different . . .': *Selected Letters*, ed. Anthony Thwaite (Faber, 1992), p. 315.

p. 136 'ancient enmity between . . .': *Selected Poetry*, p. 87.

p. 136 'For one human . . .': ibid. p. 306.

p. 136 'Fidelity to oneself . . .': *Letters*, vol. 4, p. 308.

p. 137 'I don't sacrifice . . .': *Letters*, vol. 5, p. 75.

p. 137 'not the work . . .': *Thomas Hardy*, p. 12.

p. 137 'I *don't* think . . .': *Letters*, vol. 3, p. 215.

p. 139 'in the moment . . .': Walter Benjamin, 'A Small History of Photography', in *One Way Street* (Verso, 1979), p. 245.

p. 140 'the tree's life . . .': 'Pan in America', in *Phoenix*, p. 25.

p. 140 'Thank God I . . .': *Letters*, vol. 4, p. 307.

p. 140 'It is hard . . .' *Selected Letters*, p. 157.

p. 140 'no life without . . .': from 'Lullaby of Cape Cod', *A Part of Speech* (Oxford: Oxford University Press, 1980), p. 113.

p. 140 'I feel a . . .': *Letters*, vol. 4, p. 301.

p. 140 'One can no . . .': *Letters*, vol. 5, p. 266.

p. 140 'meant nothing to . . .': Rilke, *Selected Letters*, p. 30.

p. 140 'Whisper to the . . .': *Selected Poetry*, p. 255.

p. 141 'happy as a . . .': Vincent Van Gogh, *The Letters*, selected and edited by Ronald De Leeuw (Allen Lane, 1996), p. 361.

p. 141 'convinced that every . . .': *Letters*, vol. 5, p. 436.

p. 141 'Perhaps there remains . . .': *Selected Poetry*, p. 151.

p. 141 'A fine wind . . .': *Poems*, p. 29.

p. 142 'You mustn't look . . .': *Letters*, vol. 5, p. 473.

p. 144 'The best readings . . .': *Real Presences* (Faber, 1989), p. 17.

p. 144 'syllabus of enacted . . .': ibid. p. 20.

p. 145 'very thorough in . . .': *Letters*, vol. 5, p. 473.

p. 145 'the judgment may . . .': *Sea and Sardinia* (Harmondsworth: Penguin, 1944), p. 131.

p. 147 'Blair has been . . .': *Letters*, vol. 7, p. 641.

p. 149 'she lifted her . . .': *Letters*, vol. 3, p. 40.

p. 149 'Now it is . . .': *Poems*, p. 716.

p. 149 'apples on tall . . .': *Letters*, vol. 7, p. 455, discussed by Sagar in *D. H. Lawrence: Life into Art* (Harmondsworth: Penguin, 1985), p. 341.

p. 149 'it is just . . .': *Letters*, vol. 2, p. 692.

p. 149 'the apples blown . . .': *Letters*, vol. 3, p. 216.

p. 150 'seems already a . . .': *Letters*, vol. 5, p. 201.

p. 150 'Since Lawrence died . . .': quoted by Janet Byrne in *A Genius for Living* (Bloomsbury, 1995), p. 376.

p. 151 'Whoever reads me . . .': *Letters*, vol. 5, p. 201.

p. 151 'What do I . . .': *Phoenix*, p. 232.

p. 151 'I enjoy looking . . .': quoted by Janet Byrne, p. 376.

p. 152 'tapping out an . . .': 'Elegy: D. H. Lawrence', in *The Essential Rebecca West* (Harmondsworth: Penguin, 1983), p. 392.

p. 152 'wearied himself to . . .': Harmondsworth: Penguin, 1950, p. 33.

p. 152 'I feel there . . .': *Letters*, vol. 4, p. 304.

p. 152 'When I drive . . .': *Letters*, vol. 2, p. 432.

p. 153 'always be a . . .': ibid. p. 434.

p. 154 ' So vivid a . . .': ibid. pp. 459–60.

p. 155 'not so much . . .': *Letters*, vol. 4, p. 235.

p. 155 'The land is . . .': ibid. p. 238.

p. 155 'Have you noticed . . .': vol. 2 (Harmondsworth: Penguin), p. 508.

p. 156 'the one bright . . .': 'Why the Novel Matters', in *Phoenix*, p. 535.

p. 156 'the highest form . . .': 'The Novel', in *Phoenix II*, p. 416.

p. 156 'In our time . . .': op. cit. p. 383.

p. 156 'Their freedom of . . .': *Testaments Betrayed* (Faber, 1995), p. 160.

p. 156 'a new art . . .': *The Art of the Novel* (Faber, 1988), p. 65.

p. 157 'A book which . . .': *Letters*, vol. 2, p. 479.

CHAPTER 7

Benjamin Friedlander, 'Gertrude Stein: A Retrospective Criticism'

Two opposing truisms of critical writing are examined in Benjamin Friedlander's 'Gertrude Stein: A Retrospective Criticism'. The first is that critical writing should be original, not plagiarised; the second, that in order to acknowledge traditions and forebears, such writing requires a degree of dutiful ventriloquy. The delicate balance, not to say potential paradox, of such assumptions is played out by Friedlander after the manner of conceptual art. Deference to precedent is taken to its logical conclusion in the copying, almost wholesale, of a pre-existent piece of criticism, in this case Edgar Allen Poe's 'Rufus Dawes: A Retrospective Criticism'. Friedlander takes out the relevant parts of his source material and replaces them with references to his chosen subject, Gertrude Stein. The result is a piece of writing by Friedlander about Stein that is not by Friedlander and not about Stein. Or is it? Again, this is creative-critical writing as conceptual art. The creativity is in the execution of the idea and in the cool unsettling of conventions. Who is the writer? What is the meaning of this? Who is in charge here? Can I have a go?

The experiment is relatively easy to repeat, as tends to be the case with, and part of the point of, conceptualism. Take a piece of critical prose, your own or that of another, erase parts of it and fill the resulting gaps in the original with related words from elsewhere. Or perform a treatment of another kind on an existing piece of critical prose, whether by erasing or alphabetising or reordering or some such intervention. Alternatively, take a piece of creative writing and through a targeted act of cut and paste, draw out a critical edge. The key in each case is to think carefully about the choices, and also where possible to allow the process to run its own course free of your own tweakings. It is only by deferring to rule and process that we allow the exercise a chance of revealing the unexpected.

Benjamin Friedlander, 'Gertrude Stein: A Retrospective Criticism', from 'Poe's Poetics and Selected Essays', in *Simulcast: Four Experiments in Criticism* (Tuscaloosa: University of Alabama Press, 2004), pp. 145–58.

'When I was a student,' says Prof. Schmitz, 'no one taught Gertrude Stein. She was encountered in Hemingway, cited as an influence. She had no standing as a poet. We all led comfortable lives inside patriarchal poetry. The chairs were good, the rugs plush, the bookcases lined with Uniform Editions. The study of literature was the study of sure things.' The *sureness* of her standing now, however, is quite apparent; and, while to many it is matter for wonder, to those who have the interest of our Literature at heart, it is, more properly, a source of bemusement and surprise. That the author in question has long enjoyed what we term 'a *cultic* celebrity' cannot be denied. She is 'a poet's poet,' and in no manner is this point more strikingly evinced than in the choice of one of her lesser known works, by one of our most enterprising publishers, as the first volume of a series, the avowed object of which is the setting forth, in the best combination of page design, price, and pictorial embellishment, the elite of our most 'experimental' writers. Now this same publisher returns to Stein, in the forty-fourth volume of the same series. As an author of occasional portraits, and as a memoirist, she has long been before the public; always eliciting, from a great variety of sources, *unqualified* commendation. With the exception of a solitary demurral, adventured by Prof. Davenport, there has been no written dissent from the recent opinion in her favor – the recent *apparent* opinion. Ms Stein's past standing differs from her current, as the short polar day from its contrasting night. Prof. Schmitz's recollections are undoubtedly accurate. Nevertheless, the rapidly growing 'celebrity' of Ms Stein, begun already in her own lifetime, aided by the publication of her memoirs, was furthered by a curious set of lectures, delivered in America to large assemblies of bewildered but applauding curiosity seekers. Since her death in 1946, selections of Ms Stein's works have remained continuously in print. Important studies have appeared at regular intervals, beginning with Prof. Sutherland's *Gertrude Stein: A Biography of Her Work*. Yale University Press brought out several volumes of posthumous writings, capped by a single-volume selection edited by Richard Kostelanetz.

Other attempts at selection were made by Carl Van Vechten and Patricia Meyerowitz, and, more recently, by Judy Grahn and Ulla Dydo.

The cultic decision, so frequent and so canonical now, in regard to the poetical ability of Ms Stein, might be received as evidence of her actual merit (and by thousands it *is* so received) were it not too scandalously at variance with a species of criticism which *will not* be resisted with the perfectly simplest precepts of the very commonest common sense. The peculiarity of Prof. Schmitz's recollection has induced us to make inquiry into the true character of the volume to which we have before alluded, and which embraces, we believe, the most respected example of the published verse-compositions of its author.* This inquiry has but resulted in the confirmation of our previous opinion; and we now hesitate not to say that no poetry in America has been more shamefully overestimated than that which forms the subject of this article. We say shamefully; for, though a better day is now dawning upon our literary interests, and a laudation so indiscriminate will never be sanctioned again, the laudation in this instance, as it stands upon record, must be regarded as a laughable though bitter addendum to the general zeal, inaccuracy, and pomposity of poetic spirit which has recently pervaded and degraded the land.

In what we shall say we have no intention of being profound. Here is a case in which anything like analysis would be utterly thrown away. Our purpose (which is truth) will be more fully answered by an unvarnished exposition of fact. It appears to us, indeed, that in excessive *abstraction* lies one of the leading errors of a poetry celebrated by a critical literature so decadent as our own. As poets, we dither rather than decide; delighting more in an aimless motion of sounds than in their particular and methodical development. The wildest and most erratic effusions of the muse, not utterly worthless, will be found more or less indebted to *attention* for whatever of value they embody; and we shall discover, conversely, that in any analysis of even these wildest effusions, we labor without end, when the poets themselves have labored without attention.

Stanzas in Meditation is the title of the longest of Ms Stein's poems. It embraces some one hundred and sixty-three stanzas – the whole being a most servile parody of her own most notorious affectations. The outrageous absurdity of the systematic *digression* in Stein's memoirs and lectures was so managed as to form not a little portion of their infinite interest and

---

*   *Stanzas in Meditation*, Sun & Moon Classics No. 44 (Los Angeles: Sun & Moon Press, 1994).

humor; and the fine discrimination imposed by the desire to communicate the essence of her life and thought pointed out to her a limit beyond which she never ventured with this tantalizing species of drollery. *Stanzas in Meditation* may be regarded, however, as a simple embodiment of the whole soul of digression. It is a mere mass of irrelevancy, amid the mad farrago of which we detect with difficulty even the faintest vestige of a narrative, and where the continuous lapse from impertinence to impertinence is seldom justified by any shadow of appositeness or even of the commonest relation.

To afford the reader any semblance of a *story* or *argument* is of course impossible; we must content ourselves with textual history, and a mere outline of the poem's conduct. This we shall endeavor to give without indulgence in those feelings of risibility stirred up in us by the primitive perusal. We shall rigorously avoid every species of exaggeration, and confine ourselves, with perfect honesty, to the conveyance of a distinct image.

Part I of *Stanzas* opens, then, with some fifteen meditations, varying in length from nine lines to eighty-three. Of descriptive scenes, and characters, and ideas, only the vaguest outline is given, but within this outline, many a sylvan scene has been imagined. Thus, in Stanza VII, a 'place made' solely of language, Mr Robert Duncan has found his famous 'meadow,' a 'made place' folded in thought, guarded by 'hosts' who are themselves 'a disturbance of words within words.' We could, perhaps, render Ms Stein's poetical reputation no greater service than by giving a large portion of this stanza, keeping in mind its later use by Mr Duncan:

Make a place made where they need land
It is a curious spot that they are alike

. . . .

Or wilder than without having thought Frank Wilder was
  a name
They knew without a thought that they could tell not then
Not known they were known then that is to say although

. . . .

Everyone knowing this could know then of this pleased
She can be thought in when in which in mine a pleasure.
Now let me think when.

. . . .

It is easier to know better when they are quite young

. . . .

By the time that they can think to sing in mountains.
Or much of which or meadows or a sunset hush or rather
By this time they could which they could think as selfish.
No one can know one can now or able.
They may be thought to be with or to be without now.

Here is an air of quietude in good keeping with the announced aim of meditation; the repetitions of 'thought' and 'think,' 'knew' and 'know,' redeem this stanza from much exception otherwise; and perhaps we need say nothing about the suspicious-looking non sequitur 'Frank Wilder.' These lines are interpreted by Mr Duncan as an adoration or invocation of 'the Lady,' a woman 'whose secret we see in a children's game / of ring a round of roses told.' A rose is a rose is a rose indeed!

We now know that the name of Ms Stein's first lover, May Bookstaver, was excised from the manuscript under duress (that is, was changed at the angry demand of the author's companion, Ms Alice B. Toklas), with the word 'can' substituted for 'may' wherever possible. Notwithstanding this astonishing insight, Prof. Dydo avers that the *Stanzas* '*must* be read as word constructions, *not* as concealed pieces of autobiography'; that their purport is 'to achieve in their disembodied form an "exactitude of abstract thought."' At this juncture, a single stanza excerpted will aid the reader's conception of the queer tone of rhapsody with which the poem thereby teems. From Part II, consisting of nineteen meditations ranging in length from one line to seventy-four, we choose the following passage in Prof. Dydo's corrected version:

She may think the thought that they will wish
And they will hold that they will spell anguish
And they will not be thought perverse
If they angle and the will for which they wish as verse
And so may be they may be asked
That they will answer this. (Stanza XIX)

Soon, however, Ms Stein's May is forgotten – and anguish and perversity too – and after fifty-one lines we are told instead that:

One is not one but two
Two two three one and any one.
Why they out tired Byron.

The Byron referred to here is *not*, we presume, the British poet, but a Mexican dog received by the author from the painter Francis Picabia – a person who is himself mentioned in a later stanza. Unfortunately, this clarification of Byron, like the clarification of 'may,' is of little use in gaining an understanding of the author's otherwise 'disembodied' intentions – a fact which brings into very disagreeable suspicion the advertised 'exactitude' of expression. At this point we may refer, with similar frustration, to such abstractions as:

> It is not which they knew when they could tell
> Not all of it of which they would know more
> Not where they could be left to have it do
> Just what they liked as they might say
> The one that comes and says
> Who will have which she knew (Part II, Stanza X)

And:

> Come which they are alike
> For which they do consider her
> Make it that they will not belie
> For which they will call it all (Part II, Stanza XVI)

Now, no one is presupposed to be cognizant of what another person is thinking; to be ignorant of Ms Stein's thinking is no crime; to pretend a knowledge is beneath contempt; and the pretender will attempt in vain to utter or write two consecutive sentences of interpretation without betraying his deficiency to those who equate exactitude with articulation.

Part III consists of twenty-two meditations similar to those which came before. These range in length from one line to one hundred and two. In Stanza II (the first of a pair so numbered), there is some prospect of a disruption in the monotony. Here we are given a series of names which arouses our curiosity regarding the persons signified:

> I think very well of Susan but I do not know her name
> I think very well of Ellen but which is not her same
> I think very well of Paul I tell him not to do so
> I think very well of Francis Charles but do I do so
> I think very well of Thomas but I do not not do so

I think very well of not very well of William
I think very well of any very well of him
I think very well of him.
It is remarkable how quickly they learn
But if they learn and it is very remarkable how quickly they learn
It makes not only but by and by
And they can not only be not here
But not there
Which after all makes no difference
After all this does not make any does not make any difference
I add added it to it.

Although it is tempting to do so, to speak of the names that appear in this stanza as characters would be a gross mistake; their brief and quixotic appearance contributes not a whit to the poem's dramatic action. 'Susan,' 'Ellen,' 'Paul,' 'Francis Charles,' 'Thomas,' and 'William' are at best subjects in an experiment. All that we learn about them is that they are well thought of by the author, and that they all learn remarkably quickly. In Ms Stein's own reiterated words, their individual traits and achievements and foibles 'do not make any do not make any difference.' This indifference – which extends over the entire work in question, and over a sizable portion of the author's other works as well – is evidently a consequence of her training in experimental psychology, one result of which was a brief study of the process by which a mental or physical action (such as writing) becomes automatic, that is, becomes a matter of indifference.* Let us speak the truth: this brief study (Ms Stein's first published work) may be regarded through and through as a grotesque specimen of the genre 'Defense of Poetry,' and, to say nothing of its utter absurdity per se, is so ludicrous in its definition of 'writing' that we found it impossible to refrain, during its perusal, from a most unbecoming and uproarious guffaw. We will be pardoned for giving an abbreviated survey of this essay's argument.

I have attempted to examine the phenomena of normal autonomism
by a study of normal individuals, both in regard to the variations in
this capacity found in a large number of subjects, and also in regard
to the types of character which accompany a greater or less tendency

*   'Cultivated Motor Automatism: A Study of Character in Its Relation to Attention,' *Psychological Review* 5: 3 (May 1898): 295–306.

to automatic action. Incidental to this main question have arisen the further questions of comparison between male and female subjects, and the variations of the female subjects in fatigue . . .

There was a great deal of variation in the ability to learn movements and write spontaneously. The subjects who did the best writing fall into two large groups very different both in characteristics and methods of response. Let us call them Type I. and Type II.

Type I. This consists mostly of girls who are found naturally in literature courses and men who are going in for law. The type is nervous, high-strung, very imaginative, has the capacity to be easily roused and intensely interested. Their attention is strongly and easily held by something which interests them, even to the extent quite commonly expressed of being oblivious to everything else. But, on the other hand, they find it hard to concentrate on anything that does not catch the attention and hold the interest . . . I could never get them to write well unless I got them distracted by talking to them or making them talk to me. The more interested and excited they got the more their hands would write . . .

Type II. is very different from Type I., is more varied, and gives more interesting results. In general, the individuals, often blonde and pale, are distinctly phlegmatic. If emotional, decidedly of a weakish sentimental order. They may be either large, healthy, rather heavy and lacking in vigor, or they may be what we call anaemic and phlegmatic. Their power of concentrated attention is very small. They describe themselves as never being held by their work; they say that their minds wander easily; that they work on after they are tired and just keep pegging away . . . They are often fatalistic in their ideas. They indulge in daydreams, but not those of a very stirring nature. As a rule they don't seem to have *bad* tempers – are rather sullen. Many of them are hopelessly self-conscious and rather morbid.

A sequence of case histories follows. For example:

TYPE II., . . . CASE III. Male, pale type. No automatic sleep habits, rather nervous and absent-minded. He has a tendency to forget his ideas just as he is expressing them. He has a worrying nature, gets very much interested in his work. He has difficulty in formulating his ideas and has to work them out with an effort, and is always uncertain as to exactly what is wanted of him. He is very conscientious and has had a nervous breakdown. During his writing he frequently got a nervous shiver.

RESPONSE. He wrote vigorously in rather a nervous fashion and was never conscious of any change in his movements. He commented upon his being uncertain as to whether he could stop his hand. He spoke of an indescribable impulse to go on, the effect of an outside dragging. He had a good deal of spontaneous movement that went on constantly and rapidly.

From these experiments Ms Stein learned, unhappily, that a careful consideration of one's words is debilitating to the goal of unimpeded writing:

In the subjects that I had think steadily of a word I was surprised to find that the motor reaction was very slow and in some cases did not come at all . . . The subjects also were unable to judge of their performance. One case repeated meaningless curves over and over again, convinced that he was writing a word, and another when fatigued started in on certain curves and repeated them again and again, finally convinced that they meant something, although she could give no explanation of them.

If, in the passage cited above, we replace the word *word* with 'meaningful statement,' and replace *curves* with 'words,' we describe with admirable 'exactitude' just the sort of 'motor autonomism' which Ms Stein herself performs in passages like the following, from 'Patriarchal Poetry':

For before let it before to be before spell to be before to be before to have to be to be for before to be tell to be to having held to be to be for before to call to be for to be before to till until to be till before to be for before to be until to be for before to for to be for before will for before to be shall to be to be for to be for to be before still to be will before to be before for to be to be for before to be before such to be for to be much before to be for before will be for to be for before to be well to be well before to be before for before might well to be might before to be might well to be might before while to be might to be while before for might to be for before to for while to be while

for before while before to for which as for before had for before had
for before had for before to for to before.

This reading has been, with us at least, a matter of no little difficulty. We
believe, however, that Prof. Davenport hit the nail on the head when he
wrote of another, similar effusion: 'It is the very literate equivalent of children playing in a sandbox. They are happy, busy, purposeful in their own
way, but only angels know what they think they're doing.'

But to continue. Part IV consists of twenty-four meditations. These
range in length from one line to one hundred and forty-eight. We are
here introduced, if briefly, to the author's long-standing fascination with
nationality. Earlier, in Part III, our eyes have met the words 'English,'
'Cuba,' and 'Italian,' but these stray mentions are nothing compared to the
concentrated outburst of Stanza IV.

> Mama loves you best because you are Spanish
> Mama loves you best because you are Spanish
> Spanish or which or a day.
> But whether or which or is languish
> Which or which is not Spanish
> Which or which not a way
> They will be manage or Spanish
> They will be which or which manage
> Which will they or which to say
> That they will which which they manage
> They need they plead they will indeed
> Refer to which which they will need
> Which is which is not Spanish
> Fifty which vanish which which is not Spanish.

Though peculiar, Ms Stein's treatment of the Spanish has never been
occasion for objection, owing, perhaps, to her happy association with the
Spanish painter Picasso. As a general practice, however, her compulsion to
categorize individuals according to general type – evident in the psychological study cited above – is scarcely defensible. Even after Hitler's rise to
power, Ms Stein clung to her belief in inviolate national traits. In *Wars I
Have Seen*, written in France under German occupation, the author recalls
her California childhood thusly:

Well all this time I went to school and school in California meant knowing lots of nationalities. And if you went to school with them and knew about their hair and their ways and all you were bound later not to be surprised that Germans are as they are and French and Greeks and Chinamen and Japs. There is nothing afterward but confirmation confirmation of what you knew, because nobody changes, they may develop but they do not change and so if you went to school with them why should you not know them. Some one was just telling me that in German universities they had professors who studied the characteristics of races. Quite unnecessary if you went to school with them but naturally the Germans did not know that.

How delightful a picture we have here! The author – a famous Jew, a homosexual, a 'decadent artist' in the eyes of the occupying force – writing her private thoughts in a barren house in the French countryside, threatened at every moment by deportation to a concentration camp, protected by the favor of a friend in the Vichy government (a man later sentenced to hard labor for crimes against the French people), asserting in chiding tones the inferiority of German racial thinking, *not* because it is incorrect, but because it is too *obvious*. For any California schoolgirl, apparently, the varieties of racial experience were already common knowledge.

Part V is the last and longest section, eighty-five meditations ranging in length from one line to one hundred and twenty-six. Several short passages very nearly answer to the best criteria of poetry. For example:

I need not hope to sing a wish
Nor need I help to help to sing
Nor need I welcome welcome with a wind
That will not help them to be long. (Stanza LXVIII)

Had Ms Stein always written even nearly so well, we should have been spared today the painful task imposed upon us by a stern sense of our critical duty. Unfortunately, the last two lines of this excerpt are far more typical of the poem's conduct. Perceiving this failing, perhaps, the author asks us in Stanza V to 'Please believe that I remember just what to do'; in Stanza VII, she tells us, 'I do very much regret to keep you awake.' On the other hand, despite these expressions of remorse, we learn in Stanza LXVII that a 'Shove is a proof of love' – a maxim which goes far toward explaining, however unconvincingly, the author's commitment to provocation.

It is impossible to convey, in any such digest as we have given, a full idea of the *confusions* with which this volume abounds. Nor are these confusions specific to *Stanzas in Meditation*. In 'Before the Flowers of Friendship Faded Friendship Faded' we read:

There are a few here now and the rest can follow a cow,
The rest can follow now there are a few here now,
They are all here now the rest can follow a cow
And mushrooms on a hill and anything else until
They can see and sink and swim with now and then a brim,
A brim to a hat
What is that,
Anyway in the house they say
Anyway every day
Anyway outside as they may
Think and swim with hearing him,
Love and sing not any song a song is always then too long to
just sit there and sing
Sing song is a song
When sing and sung
Is just the same as now among
Among them,
They are very well placed to be seated and sought
They are very well placed to be cheated and bought
And a bouquet makes a woods
A hat makes a man
And any little more is better than
The one.
And so a boat a goat and wood
And so a loaf which is not said to be just bread
Who can be made to think and die
And any one can come and cry and sing.
Which made butter look yellow
And a hope be relived
By all of it in case
Of my name.
What is my name.

That is the game
Georges Hugnet
By Gertrude Stein.

This poem, a wayward translation from the French of Georges Hugnet, we have recently seen cited as a fine specimen of Ms Stein's own poetical powers. Her genius, no doubt, is herein made to cut a very remarkable figure, if only we piece the fragments of her narrative together. Let us, then, imagine her as her poem presents her, chasing a cow down a mushroom-studded hill, sinking and swimming in the woods (literally, singing in and out of tune) while wearing a widebrimmed hat, gathering a bouquet of flowers, thinking her thoughts, crying at the same time, and, in conclusion, taking out some goat cheese 'Which made butter look yellow' and spreading it out on a fresh loaf of bread, asking every passerby to take a bite and guess at the name of the true author of her song. But we have already wearied the reader with this abominable rigmarole. We say this in the very teeth of the magnificent assembly that listens every other year to a marathon reading of *The Making of Americans*. We shall leave the remainder of her poetry, without comment, to the decision of those who have the time and temper for its perusal, and conclude our extracts by a quotation, from 'Lifting Belly,' of the following very respectable extract.

Eat the little girl I say.
Listen to me. Did you expect it to go back. Why do you do to stop.
What do you do to stop.
What do you do to go on.
I do the same.
Yes wishes. Oh yes wishes.
What do you do to turn a corner.
What do you do to sing.
We don't mention singing.
What do you do to be reformed.
You know.
Yes wishes.
What do you do to measure.
I do it in such a way.
I hope to see them come.
Lifting belly go around.
I was sorry to be blistered.

We were such company.
Did she say jelly.
Jelly my jelly.
Lifting belly is so round.
Big Caesars.
Two Caesars.
Little seize her.
Too.
Did I do my duty.
Did I wet my knife,
No I don't mean whet.
Exactly four teeth.
Little belly is so kind.
What did you say about accepting.
Yes.
Lifting belly another lifting belly.
I question the weather.
It is not necessary.
Lifting belly oh lifting belly in time.

Whatever shall be hereafter the position of Ms Stein in the poetical world, she will be indebted for it altogether to her erotic compositions, some of which have the merit of tenderness; others of melody and force. What seems to be the popular opinion in respect to her more *disembodied* effusions has been brought about, in some measure, by a certain general tact, nearly amounting to taste, and more nearly the converse of talent. This tact has been especially displayed in the choice of not inelegant titles and other externals; in a peculiar original speciousness of manner, pervading the surface of her writings; and (here we have the anomaly of a positive benefit deduced from a radical defect) in an absolute deficiency in basis, in *stamen*, in matter, or pungency, which, if even slightly evinced, might have invited the reader to an intimate and understanding perusal, whose result would have been disgust. The majority of her writings have not been condemned, only because they have never been read. The glitter upon the surface has sufficed, with the average 'fan,' to justify his hyperboles of praise. Very few scholars, and fewer poets we feel assured, have had sufficient nerve to wade *through* the entire volume now in a question, except, as in our own case, with the single object of criticism in view. Ms Stein has also, let it be said, been aided to her high poetical reputation by the richly peculiar quality of her character as a woman. How efficient such causes have before been in producing such effects is a point but too thoroughly understood.

We have already spoken of the numerous *adherents* of the poet; and we shall not here insist upon the fact that *we* bear her no personal ill will. With those who know us, such a declaration would appear supererogatory; and by those who know us not, it would, doubtless, be received with incredulity. What we have said, however, is not in opposition to Ms Stein, nor even so much in opposition to the poems of Ms Stein, as in defense of the many true souls, which, in Ms Stein's apotheosis, are aggrieved. The laudation of the unworthy is to the worthy the most bitter of all wrongs. But it is unbecoming in those who merely demonstrate a truth to offer reason or apology for the demonstration.

NOTES

'Gertrude Stein: A Retrospective Criticism'; the source text is Poe's 'Rufus Dawes: A Retrospective Criticism'.

p. 161   *says Prof. Schmitz*
In 'The Difference of Her Likeness: Gertrude Stein's *Stanzas in* Meditation', in *Gertrude Stein and the Making of Literature*, ed. Shirley Neuman and Ira B. Nadel (Boston: Northeastern University Press, 1988), p. 148.

p. 161   *a solitary demurral, adventured by Prof. Davenport*
'Late Gertrude', in *The Hunter Gracchus and Other Papers on Literature and Art* (Washington, DC: Counterpoint, 1996), pp. 187–91.

p. 161   *several volumes of posthumous writings . . . Other attempts at selection*
The Yale Gertrude Stein consists of eight volumes published between 1951 and 1958. Richard Kostelanetz brought out his single-volume collection, *The Yale Gertrude Stein*, in 1980. The other Stein anthologies mentioned are *Selected Writings*, ed. Carl Van Vechten (New York: Vintage, 1972); *Look at Me Now and Here I Am: Writing and Lectures 1909–45*, ed. Patricia Meyerowitz (Baltimore: Penguin Books, 1971); *Really Reading Gertrude Stein*, ed. Judy Grahn (Freedom, CA: Crossing Press, 1989); and *A Stein Reader*, ed. Ulla Dydo (Evanston: Northwestern University Press, 1993). Donald Sutherland's *Gertrude Stein: A Biography of Her Work* originally appeared from Yale in 1951.

p. 164   *These lines are interpreted by Mr Duncan*
In 'Often I Am Permitted to Return to a Meadow', in Robert Duncan, *The Opening of the Field* (New York: New Directions, 1960), p. 7.

p. 164   *Prof. Dydo avers*
In her *Stein Reader*, p. 569.

p. 168 *'Patriarchal Poetry'*
Gertrude Stein, *Writings 1903–1932* (New York: Library of America, 1998), p. 567.

p. 169 *Prof. Davenport hit the nail on the head*
Davenport, 'Late Gertrude', p. 191.

p. 169 *Ms Stein clung to her belief in inviolate national traits*
Gertrude Stein, *Wars I Have Seen* (New York: Random House, 1945), p. 8.

p. 171 *'Before the Flowers of Friendship Faded Friendship Faded'*
Stein, *Look at Me Now and Here I Am*, pp. 286–7.

p. 172 *'Lifting Belly'*
Stein, *Writings*, pp. 427–8.

CHAPTER 8

Peter Gizzi, 'Correspondences of the Book'

'Correspondences of the Book' is a hard piece to gloss, not least because the work of glossing and critical commentary is one of its fundamental concerns. (For other creative-critical explorations of the age-old scholarly practice of commentary, see the online journal *Glossator: Practice and Theory of the Commentary*.) Best to start with its most evident trait – the apparent disproportion here between quotation and commentary. Quotations are supposed to give the measure of a work; and commentary on those quotations to register that measure. But to quote is also to cut, to displace, and to lose proportion. Gizzi's piece catches us in the binds that occur whenever we weave quotations into our commentary; and ups the ante insofar as his chosen quotations themselves speak of the relation between part and whole, continuity and discontinuity. How, here, to make the statement 'the true test of poetry is in its ability to endure and cohere in time' cohere with 'do not try to make it all cohere?' Do we follow the logic of the first comment, and try to, or the second, and not? This trap isn't tricksy. It makes us feel from the inside our own complicated involvement in one of the central problems Gizzi stages and explores: that of the critic's relationship with the words on which she comments, and of all our words with the world. Is there a world in which John Ruskin and Emily Dickinson can cohere? Do they even correspond? They both seem to agree on a principle of *incongruity* – but to say that is to posit a congruence, and so to risk treachery in the very enaction of our ostensibly faithful commentary. We find ourselves in a hall of mirrors – and the mirror is one of several motifs stitched through this text, setting up a different, perhaps more musical, set of correspondences.

'Fill this space with writing,' Gizzi concludes. So: cull some quotations from three or more texts, and try to find the best way 1) to stage the question of their relationship and 2) to register in your commentary what is at stake in the act of quoting from your, very particular, texts. Quoting from the tissue of quotations that is Eliot's *The Waste Land*, for example, will raise different issues than quoting from a detective story, where the flourishing of details as clues and as evidence forms part of the work of the narrative.

Peter Gizzi, 'Correspondences of the Book', in *A Poetics of Criticism*, ed. Juliana Spahr, Mark Wallace, Kristin Prevallet and Pam Rehm (Buffalo: Leave Books, 1994), pp. 179–86.

Correspondences of the Book
for Susan Howe

She dealt her pretty words like Blades –
How glittering they shone –
And every One unbared Nerve
Or wantoned with a bone
— Emily Dickinson, 479

Unbare, to lay bare as in reveal or flay.
Attentive grace to a violent gesture.
The surface of meaning wears a mask, and it is only with long attention that the actual face of the poet comes through the mask of lines.

In thought a fine human brow is like the east when troubled
with the morning.
— Herman Melville, *Moby Dick*

A child would, I suppose, receive a religious lesson from a flower
more willingly than from a print of one; and might be taught to
understand the nineteenth psalm, on a starry night, better than by
diagrams of the constellations.
— John Ruskin, *Modern Painters*

Worlds – and the objects they contain – are not only unbared by the poet but vibrate independently in their own language. If words are signs then the poem is a universe, a complex of memory and emotion put into action or into a state of active listening, listing the catalogue of things (nouns) and actions (verbs) combined to re/create an event (language) in the mind, that is a body.

The revealed world is itself a matrix of distance and desire.

In a world in which everything teaches – everything emits some note – every body is a singer and the Atom and the Lion, the Robin and the Reader, are of one house and one story.

Our language is a web or net to recover and translate this dialogue of forms.

I dreaded that first Robin, so,
But he is mastered, now

> – Dickinson, 348

——

Psalm 19
1. The heavens declare the glory of God; and the firmament sheweth his handywork.
2. Day unto day uttereth speech, and night unto night sheweth knowledge.
3. There is no speech nor language, where their voice is not heard.

The poem of a singer to a master contains and calls forth a dialogue of earth and ether.

We don't control this commerce but transmit its irreducible message.

One may appear as a 'master' or as a robin 'mastered.'

One is a figure in a landscape whose horizon is time.

——

All true landscape, whether simple or exalted, depends primarily for its interest on connection with humanity, or with spiritual powers. Banish your heroes and nymphs from the classical landscape – its laurel shades will move you no more.

> – Ruskin, *Modern Painters*

A landscape. A connection.

Dickinson's landscape is at once haunted and human because it is inhabited simultaneously with persons from her immediate world and those transmitted from language – her relation with books and in letters.

Jack Spicer says, '*Things do not connect; they correspond*' (34).

All correspondences are inseparable.

This infinite universe is unfathomable, inconceivable, in its
whole; every human creature must slowly spell out, and long
contemplate, such part of it as may be possible for [her] to
reach; . . . extricating it from infinity, as one gathers a violet
out of grass; one does not improve either violet or grass in
gathering it, but one makes the flower visible.

– Ruskin, *Stones of Venice*

'*To make things visible rather than to make pictures of them (phantasia non imaginari)*' (Spicer 34). The true test of poetry is in its ability to endure and cohere in time. In other words/worlds. This moment of extrication and illumination is the commerce of the real with the world. Ruskin rescues the violet out of infinity. '*The imagination pictures the real*' (Spicer 33).

—————

I heard a Fly buzz – when I died –

– Dickinson, 465

Do not be afraid of incongruities – do not think of unities of
effect.

– Ruskin, *The Lamp of Beauty*

Do not be afraid of the absurd. Do not try to make it all cohere.

Interruption, line break, is the stitch of a single death in a series of deaths on the way to absence.

Interruption, the fly, admits the sublime that is both above and beneath the human order '*as the great extreme of dimension is sublime, so the last extreme of littleness is in some measure sublime likewise*' (Burke 72).

Shelley, in *A Defence of Poetry*, says '. . . [poetry] *compels us to feel that which we perceive, and to imagine that which we know*' (49). Dickinson transforms her language to reveal her more subtle mind. Her ability is to make her language become her feeling mind. She places herself equally inside all the nouns in her lines. There is an inventiveness or insecurity at the beginning of this American identity, American landscape.

She never *presumes*. Never tells what she means. She shows what she feels and thinks. We always *perceive* what she *feels* and *know* what she imagines.

Charles Olson at the end of his life:

A big fat fly
lives in my house
and in the air
he goes about
as though in fact the house
were just as much his
as it is
mine
. . .

And I am,
suddenly only
a co-dweller here
where I had thought
until he seemed to fly
right out of the wall itself
I was
alone

(*Collected Poems* 642–3)

———

To love purely is to consent to distance, it is to adore the distance between ourselves and that which we love.
                                        – Simone Weil, *Gravity and Grace*

'Things do not connect; they correspond.'
'*There is no speech nor language where their voice is not heard*' (Psalms 19:4).

The poet is co-dweller, is an object in the field of the poem or the page, the way the writer is the reader. Making poems is an act of transmission.

A life composed of language is made into object.

The object is transmitted to breath.

Solids become air, air combined with desire to communicate thingness becomes a conflagration of the inanimate with the living.

This blaze becomes an action or an act of writing, which returns us to active listening.

One thing reading another thing becomes this new thing. This is the nature of things.

The act of writing is the enactment of desire.

Each poem fails to capture or fulfill the double bind of self and other.

The poem is an artifact of this difficult relationship, never the fulfillment of this love.

Her song wounds as it delights, questions the very order of our commitment to self, to other, in the world. The genius of Dickinson is in her almost supernatural ease of simplicity, shot through with contrapuntal complexity.

_____

> I cannot live with You –
> It would be Life –
> And Life is over there –
>
>   – Dickinson, 640

The image – which is always also the image of the face – our own and those of our masters – remains broken and separate from ourselves, yet intact through time.

> Not change. So far as we live, the image is still there; defiled,
> if you will; broken, if you will; all but effaced, if you will,
> by the death and the shadow of it. But not changed.
>   – Ruskin, *Modern Painters*

The power of the image of the face contains the history of Medusa, of Narcissus, of Christ, and of Jehovah. In it we see our sacred and profane others and ourselves unbared – to the brink of blindness.

_____

Because You saturated Sight –
And I had no more Eyes

                             – Dickinson, 640

Here the real or the face of the other – like the sun – is too much to bear. It must first be refracted inwardly to be recorded or translated into a site of writing in order to be seen or witnessed in time.

It is the body (the physical eyes) that is in danger for it is the body which is the instrument to construct a transmission of the real into the future (eternity).

the soul of man is still a mirror, wherein may be seen,
darkly, the image of the mind of God.

                             – Ruskin, *Modern Painters*

Nor could I rise – with You –
Because Your Face
Would put out Jesus' –
That New Grace

Glow plain – and foreign
On my homesick Eye –

                             – Dickinson, 640

————

A mirror, dark, distorted, broken, use what blameful words
you please of its state; yet in the main, a true mirror, out of
which alone, and by which alone, we can know anything of
God at all

                             – Ruskin, *Modern Painters*

A text is also the *beloved*, and is awaited and must be cared for.

Not in the World to see his face –
Sounds long – until I read the place
Where this – is said to be
But just the Primer – to a life –

Unopened – rare – Upon the Shelf –
Clasped yet – to Him – and me

– Dickinson, 418

Emily Dickinson's dark mirror is the god of her poems.

Her dark mirror is contrary.

She is capable of rending multiple meaning from the words in her lexicon.

She never comes to rest or resolve.

What Melville writes to Hawthorne in a letter in 1851 is true of Dickinson – '*take God out of the dictionary and you would have Him in the street*' (125).

Her ability to do this in almost every instance is astounding.

She invents America by democratizing her nouns.

She empties the dictionary into her Real.

Scatter the dictionaries, they dont
Tell the truth yet, I mix up words with truth
And abstraction with presence . . .

– Bernadette Mayer, *Mutual Aid*

Look into the mirror, and you will see. Out of your own heart,
you may know what love is.

– Ruskin, *Modern Painters*

———

'But the poor miserable Me! Is this, then, all the book I have
got to read about God in?' Yes, truly so. No other book, nor
fragment of book than that, will you ever find; no velvet-
bound missal, nor frankincensed manuscript;– nothing hi-
eroglyphic nor cuneiform; papyrus and pyramid are alike
silent on this matter; – nothing in the clouds above, nor in the
earth beneath. The flesh-bound volume is the only revelation
that is, that was, or that can be.

– Ruskin, *Modern Painters*

The book as strange object to discover ourselves.
The flesh-bound volume is also the reader, and is wounded.

Through the glass, darkly. But, except through the glass, in
nowise.

> – Ruskin, *Modern Painters*

We want to see ourselves: this is the distance the poem traverses. '*Over
near somewhere else there is the problem of the difficulty*' (Ashbery 91). To
displace an object in art is to see through to our first light when we *were*
the things themselves and *were* equal and are now equal therefore in this
action, of writing, this physical activity, we are whole, healed, consoled for
an instant.

> We keep coming back and coming back
> To the real . . . We seek
> The poem of pure reality, untouched
> By trope or deviation, straight to the word
> Straight to the transfixing object, to the object
>
> At the exactest point at which it is itself,
> Transfixing by being purely what it is . . .
> > – Wallace Stevens, 'An Ordinary Evening in New Haven'

For an instant the mirror becomes window, and we are translated into
the world, then '*I heard a Fly buzz – when I died.*'

> And then the Windows failed – and then
> I could not see to see –
>
> > – Dickinson, 465

> All the words and sounds ever uttered, all the revelations of
> cloud, or flame, or crystal, are utterly powerless. They
> cannot tell you, in the smallest point, what love means.
> Only the broken mirror can.
> > – Ruskin, *Modern Painters*

Distance is the arena.
Place embodies desire to fill that space with self to be part of every living
form. Connect the void of self and other with the actual lines of a poem.
Fill this space with writing.

WORKS CITED

Ashbery, John, *As We Know* (New York: Viking, 1979).

Burke, Edmond, *A Philosophical Enquiry into the Origin of our Ideas of the Sublime and the Beautiful*, ed. J. T. Boulton (London: Routledge, 1958).

Dickinson, Emily, *Complete Poems of Emily Dickinson*, ed. Thomas H. Johnson (Boston: Little Brown, 1960).

Mayer, Bernadette, *Mutual Aid* (New York: Mademoiselle de la Mole, 1985).

Melville, Herman, *Letters of HHerman Melville*, ed. Merrell R. David and William H. Gilman (New Haven: Yale University Press, 1960).

Melville, Herman, *Moby Dick* (New York: Modern Library, 1982).

Olson, Charles, *Collected Poems*, ed. George Butterick (Berkeley: University of California Press, 1987).

Ruskin, John, *Complete Works*, 39 vols (London: George Allen, 1903–12).

Shelley, Percy Bysshe, *A Defence of Poetry* (1840) (London: Porcupine Press, 1948).

Spicer, Jack, *Collected Books of Jack Spicer*, ed. Robin Blaser (Los Angeles: Black Sparrow, 1975).

Stevens, Wallace, *Collected Poems* (New York: Knopf, 1954).

Weil, Simone, *Gravity and Grace* (London: Routledge, 1952).

CHAPTER 9

Kevin Kopelson, 'Music Lessons'

The question of how to speak of things loved, of influence as affection, sounds variously through the pieces gathered here, nowhere more provokingly than in the fondly bitchy tone of Kevin Kopelson's 'Music Lessons'. Kopelson, a self-confessed 'Barthesian', writes a love letter to the scene of teaching, making clear that pedagogical matters of method, obedience, performance and mastery are at stake similarly in any act of criticism. Rather than repress all such desires and anxieties, Kopelson unashamedly lays them bare via the semi-invented figure of the 'maiden piano teacher' as encountered in his own life and in the lives of literature and film, using as model Wallace Stevens's thirteen ways of looking. Adequacy is once again invoked – is this 'A fragmentary *tour de force*' or 'A miniature fiasco'? – as is the elusive matter of tone. Kopelson's camp, off-hand performance is deceptively light (and genuinely funny), written in a tone of which teacher might well not approve. If the tone is calculated to play up the guilty pleasures of instruction and learning it knows too that tone is nothing less than a way of seeing, hence of making. And the author is well aware that naughtiness is sometimes required. Kopelson's tone is not altogether '*nice*', and we can hear the influence of various significant others, including Wayne Koestenbaum (*The Queen's Throat; Hotel Theory; Humiliation*), and two of our own anthology guests: Eve Kosofsky Sedgwick and Roland Barthes.

In order to make something of the lessons on display in this piece we need to be ready to perform, and to accept the risks of performance, in particular, the risk of appearing otherwise, both to ourselves and to others. The possibility is that in performing we gain valuable first-hand experience of the workings of voice in writing – all writing – and of performance as a rule of the game rather than the exception. So, pick an object – an artwork; a character, a figure; an idea – and a set of relatively identifiable ways of speaking, including, for example, a style, an attitude, a methodology, a rhetorical term, or the mode of a particular author or character. Think about the relations that might be established between each of the ways of speaking, and between these ways and the cherished object. Kopelson's exercise is as much a matter of arranging a recital as it is of raiding the dressing-up box. Risk a fiasco.

Kevin Kopelson, 'Music Lessons', in *Beethoven's Kiss: Pianism, Perversion, and the Mastery of Desire* (Stanford: Stanford University Press, 1996), pp. 117–36.

———

I know noble accents
And lucid, inescapable rhythms;
But I know, too,
That the blackbird is involved
In what I know.
      Wallace Stevens, 'Thirteen Ways of Looking at a Blackbird'

There aren't many women in this book, and most of the ones I do include are teachers. Well, why *don't* I write about female amateurs? Why, for example, do I trivialize Carol Turchin? And why don't I write about female virtuosos? (Koestenbaum does, more or less. He plays 'like someone who studied with someone who studied with Myra Hess' ['Piano Life' l. 142].) Why, for example, don't I write about Martha Argerich, who's sexier than Horowitz and whose Tchaikovsky Concerto is the best on record?

    Yes, I'm phallocentric. I prefer men – in bed. And yes, I'm phallogocentric. I prefer to argue – in print. But does that make me misogynistic? Do I dislike women just because I dislike *écriture féminine* – or bad *écriture féminine*? After all, many of my favorite colleagues write like Mary Daly, something I'll attempt as well. Do I dislike women just because – or despite the fact that – I dislike feminine stereotypes, and in particular the stereotype 'maiden piano teacher'? I don't *think* so. After all, 'some of my best friends,' including my former teacher Arlene Portney, are women. On the other hand, I'm not very fond of Kathrine Parker.

I know I *should* be fond of her. In fact, I'd *love* to be fond of her. But how can I learn to appreciate this problematic Other – Parker in particular, the 'maiden piano teacher' in general? What's my methodology? I can't exactly remember her as 'nice' and at any rate am too cynical to be seduced by niceness. (*Niceness*, it's so – high school.) I can't look her up and have her speak 'for herself.' She wouldn't know what to say or, more to the point, what I need to hear. (Even I don't know what I need – yet.) My methodology, as usual, is one *Parker* taught me. I'll try to understand her by acting like a typical student – and typical teacher, and typical writer. I'll *perform* comprehension, and try to please and impress the teacher – the student, the reader. Only now that I teach cultural studies (now that I'm no longer learning concert études), I'll do so by using the tools, the critical techniques, of my latest trade. Why use them? Because the techniques do access Others who can't, or whom we can't have, express themselves. How will I use them? Nonparodically. Parody, here, would signal disbelief I'd rather suspend and insecurity I'd rather transcend. (The insecurity: that I haven't really mastered techniques I'm willing to take seriously.) And unscientifically. I'm Barthesian, not Althusserian. I approach the Other from *within* our mythic relationship and intersubjectivity. After all, she's 'involved in what I [want to] know.' And I myself am now a maiden piano teacher – a supposed celibate who proffers critical, as opposed to musical, capital to bourgeois kids who, by and large, aren't very interested in it. And so, 'Thirteen Ways of Looking at a Maiden Piano Teacher.' A fragmentary *tour de force*? A miniature fiasco?[1]

LYRICAL

Wayne Koestenbaum begins 'Piano Life' with a work Horowitz mastered and an equivocation I find suggestive:

Today I sightread the last
Schubert sonata: he wanders between keys: evasive

and elementary, his melodies
meander. Tipsy Schubert,

if I were to return to 1974 for a piano lesson,
would my teacher say, 'You've ruined your life,'

or would she just say 'hello,'
and with her faraway 'hello'

would possibilities cluster around my feet like clouds
    above the Andes?

(lines 1–9)

I, too, would lyricize the maiden piano teacher. (Contrary to popular belief, poetry can be critical. So can camp.) I, too, would provide oblique answers to nostalgic questions.

If *I* were to return to 1974 for a piano lesson, would Miss Parker say, 'You've ruined your life,' or would she just say 'hello'? She'd *never* say, 'You've ruined your life.' She'd probably say, 'You've *saved* your life – by not becoming a concert pianist (you don't have what it takes), by not becoming a piano teacher (you wouldn't like it), and by being an amateur (nothing wrong with that).' Why, then, the intimation of disgrace? Why did these women terrorize us? Because their teachers terrorized them? (Kathrine Parker as Rosina Lhevinne: VOT IS ALL DIS BANGING!!?' – only without the Russian accent.) Because their mothers did? Their fathers? Terror, in fact, isn't a very efficient learning device. (Children need cheerleaders, not drill sergeants.) And teachers shouldn't act like parents, or like abusive parents, even though it can be hard not to. Especially when you care for the kid.

She'd just say, 'hello,' and with that 'hello' possibilities *would* cluster like clouds above the Andes. The possibility that other adults (adults not paid to) will have found me special and have tried to cultivate me. (The piano teacher is the primal mentor.) The possibility that I will have learned to do the impossible – play Chopin, play Liszt. The possibility that I will have found pleasure in the passé. (Regressive pleasure? Transgressive?) But the hello would be so 'faraway.' Why? Because she'd rather be somewhere else? Or someone else? Or *with* someone else? And if so, once again, why?

CAMPY

Jeffrey Swann's been on the rag since 1977, when she dropped her fire baton and lost the Miss Universe pageant. Came in third, to be precise – after Steven De Groote (of South Africa) and Alexander Toradze (of the former Soviet Union). First there were the tacky comments about Lili Kraus, who judged the competition. Then there were the rumors about

Youri Egorov, who didn't even make the finals.[2] Now she's letting Diana Graa have it: '[Young American pianists are] dominated by older women, many of whom have unfulfilled relationships with their [husbands and] encourage an undirected sexuality. This may be one reason . . . there are an awful lot of homosexual pianists' (Horowitz 137n).

Nurse, give Miss Swann some Pamprin. And while you're at it, give some to Miss Horowitz (Miss *Joseph* Horowitz), who calls this a 'provocative' analysis of pianistic 'pathology' and an 'illustrative' look at pedagogical 'castration.' *Unfulfilled* relationships? An *awful* lot of homosexual pianists? How would *they* know how much sex these women are having? (Maybe they do find their husbands fulfilling. Maybe they have affairs. Maybe they masturbate.) How would they know whether these women 'castrate' us? (Maybe we're just born this way.) Or whether they *want* to castrate us. (Maybe they have other things on their mind, consciously or not.) And even if they do castrate us, why *blame* them? I, for one, enjoy being a girl. (I'm simply *fabulous*, Mrs Graa. Thank you *so* much.) Anyway, you'd think a pianist who finds heterosexuality and homosexuality equally undesirable ('unfulfilled' and 'awful') would rather be 'undirected' – whatever that may mean.

SENTIMENTAL

Diana, it's me. Albert. I hear you're not doing too well. You're teaching again, but don't have many students. (Well, you *are* a little scary.) You're socializing again, but don't have many friends. (You never did, but you had *me*.) And that Kopelson kid is ruining your reputation. I wish he could see you through my eyes. He'd see a beautiful young woman who could have had anyone, but married an elderly invalid, and a gifted pianist who could have concertized, but taught in order to support him. I do love you, Diana. I love your playing, your kindness, your devotion, your generosity. I even love you enough to wish you'd remarried, because you'd have been so much happier. More money, more room, more comfort. More company. (Really, Diana, all those cats!) Or has the memory of our marriage sufficed? It has for me. I've been thinking of you, for the most part, and barely recall the life I led before we met. (Do you remember the beach? The cast-off kitten you made me take home?) I've been waiting for you, too.

What was the name of that piece you used to play? It's quite slow. It's in minor. I think it's by Scriabin. I hear it whenever I think of you, and am filled with sadness and longing.

TROPOLOGICAL

Metaphor: conceptual displacement. Metonymy: conceptual contiguity. Synecdoche: conceptual partiality. Knowledge, we know, is fundamentally figurative and therefore problematic.

The *metaphor* of the maiden piano teacher. Felisberto Hernández (1902–64) opens 'The Stray Horse,' one of his *Piano Stories*, with a description of Celina's studio:

> First you saw only white: the large slipcovers on the piano and the sofa and the smaller ones on the chairs and armchairs. And underneath was the furniture, which you knew was black because of the legs sticking out from under the white skirts.
>
> Once when I was alone in the room, I raised a chair's skirt and found that although the wood was black the seat was a silky green. (5)

Celina, it turns out, is the teacher the narrator had when he was ten, and a woman who bears a striking resemblance to her furniture:

> Once when my hands were reaching out for the skirt of a chair they were stopped short by the loud noise of the hallway door as Celina hurried in from the street. I barely had time to pull the hands back when she came up in her usual way and kissed me. (The habit was ruthlessly suppressed as we parted one afternoon and she told my mother something in the order of, 'This young gentleman is growing up and from now on we'll have to shake hands.') She was in black, her tall, slim figure bound tight in her heavy wool dress, as if she had run her hands many times down the curves formed by the corset to smooth out every wrinkle and then up to choke her neck in the high collar that reached to her ears. Topping it all was her very white face with very black eyes, a very white forehead and very black hair done up in a bun like that of a queen I had seen on some coins: it reminded me of a burned pudding.
>
> I was just beginning to digest the surprise of Celina's noisy

entrance and her kiss when she reappeared in the room. But now, over the stern black dress, she wore white: a starched smock of lightweight material that had short flared sleeves with ruffles. (10–11)

Presumably, Celina's seat is 'silky green' as well. But what's a woman's 'seat'? Her lap? Her soul? And what would it mean for it to be silky green?

The *metonymy* of the maiden piano teacher. We hear Celina play, and expect triumphant self-expression. We're disappointed.

My mother or my grandmother has asked her to play and she sits down at the piano. My grandmother must be thinking, 'The teacher is going to play'; my mother: 'Celina is going to play'; and I '*She* is going to play' . . . Celina says she is not sure she remembers the piece. She is nervous, and on her way to the piano she trips over a chair, which must make a noise – but we are not supposed to notice. She has gathered enough speed that the impulse carries her past the chair and the accident is immediately forgotten. She sits down at the piano: we are hoping nothing unpleasant happens to her. Before she begins, we have just enough time to imagine she will play something impressive which will make us recommend her to our acquaintances. She is so nervous, and so aware of being the teacher, that my grandmother and my mother both try to advance her a bit of success, willing their favorable expectations on her and anxiously awaiting the performance that will allow them to match their expectations with reality . . .

When Celina performed for us that time I took in everything that reached my eyes and ears. Before that, I had been letting things become too familiar, until they had almost stopped surprising me and I no longer really appreciated what she did.

My mother and grandmother seemed to be halfway into a sigh from which they hung suspended, as if afraid that at the supreme moment, just when their effort to understand was supposed to take off, their wings would carry them about as far as useless hens' wings.

I was probably very bored, after a while. (26–8)

The *synecdoche* of the maiden piano teacher. We now know how little we know about Celina.

When the child's eyes seize a part of something, they think it is the whole thing. (And the child cares no more than a dream does whether his images are complete or similar to those of real life: he simply proceeds as if they were.) When the child looked at Celina's bare arm he felt the whole of her was in that arm. The eyes I have now want to capture Celina's mouth, but they can't define the shape of her lips in relation to the rest of her face; they want to grasp a single feature and are left with none. The parts have lost their mysterious relationship to each other, they have lost their balance and natural proportion and seem disconnected, as if a clumsy hand had drawn them. If the hand tries to get the lips to articulate a word, their movements are as forced as those of a wind-up doll. (29–30)

NARRATOLOGICAL

What if Celina had been silent and hadn't played at all? This is a question to which we know the gnomic answer: 'Those who can, do; those who can't, teach.' [*Gnomic*: aphoristic; 'made in a collective and anonymous voice originating in traditional human experience' (Barthes, *S/Z*, 18).]

Louise Bogan (1897–1970) invokes this answer in writing autobiographically of a teacher she used to love.

> Miss Cooper lived in my mind at a continual point of perfection; she was like a picture: she existed, but not in any degree did she live or change. She existed beyond simple human needs, beyond hunger and thirst, beyond loneliness, weariness, below the heights of joy and despair. (Limmer 41–2)

The crystallization ends, however, when, having questioned Miss Cooper's competence (the woman never demonstrates the skills she's paid to impart), Bogan sees her for what she is. [*Crystallization*: the process by which lovers succumb to 'patterns of exquisite illusion' (Stendhal 128).]

> One afternoon she came out of the kitchen and stood behind me. She had something in her hand that crackled like paper, and when she spoke she mumbled as if her mouth were full. I turned and looked at her; she was standing with a greasy paper bag in one hand and a half-eaten doughnut in the other. Her hair was still beautifully arranged;

she still wore the silver and fire-opal ring on the little finger of her right hand. But in that moment she and the room died for me. She . . . had betrayed me. She . . . had let me down; she had appeared as she was: a tired old woman who fed herself for comfort. (42)

Who is speaking here? No one in particular, of course. But Bogan as well. Bogan in particular. Bogan, who *discredits* the gnomic answer:

A tired old woman who fed herself for comfort. With perfect ruthlessness I rejected her utterly. And for weeks, at night, in the bedroom of the frame house in Harold Street, I shed tears that rose from anger as much as disappointment, from disillusion and from dismay. I can't remember that for one moment I entertained pity for her. It was for myself that I kept that tender and cleansing emotion. Yes, it was for myself and for dignity and gentility soiled and broken that I shed those tears. At fifteen and for a long time thereafter, it is a monstrous thing, the heart. (42–3)

Pity? It's a pity autobiography isn't dialogical. Bogan does interrogate the gnomic answer, but she can't impersonate another position. She can't, for example, impersonate Miss Cooper, who may have antignomic, or paradoxical, questions of her own. Questions like: Need love be illusory? ('Couldn't you love me as I am? Couldn't you love me as a friend?') Need teachers be masterful? ('There is an age at which we teach what we know. Then comes an age at which we teach what we do not know. [Now] comes the age of unlearning, of yielding seeable change which forgetting imposes on the [knowledge] we have traversed' [Barthes, 'Inaugural Lecture,' 478].) And is pity all that tender and cleansing? ('Don't cry for me, Louise. I'm a doughty old woman who happens to like doughnuts, not a tired old woman who feeds herself for comfort.')

MARIOLOGICAL

The maiden teacher is a virgin mother. The maiden teacher of a child prodigy, *theotokos*. The maiden teacher of a child who forsakes her, *mater dolorosa*.

Madame Sousatzka (Shirley MacLaine) nurtures Manek Sen (Navin Chowdry), a brilliant fifteen-year-old, and can't let him go.[3] It's a pattern.

Madame Sousatzka mothers all her gifted boys (abusively, as did her own mother). In fact, she infantalizes them. They 'stay babies' even though she'd have them 'become men.' And she grieves when they finally leave the nest. 'Of course I was in love with you,' she tells one tearfully. 'Isn't every mother in love with the son she creates?' Why do they leave? She's not *that* bad – just a *little* abusive. ('You're a failure,' she yells at Manek, but only when he has one foot out the door.) She's not that bizarre – just a little batty. They leave Madame Sousatzka (her mother's maiden name) for other men. They leave her for the all-male world of the virtuoso. For male mentors and cohorts. (God the Father, John the Baptist, the apostles.) They also leave her for women. Manek loses his virginity to maudlin Jenny (Twiggy) [Mary Magdalene] the night he decides to study with Leo Milev.

Is it worth it? Is raising children who go on to greater glory worth the trouble? Mary joins Jesus in heaven. Madame Sousatzka stays where she is: munching cookies ('Maman's recipe') in a seedy apartment, bullying boys who'll break her heart, sneaking into concerts given by former students, enjoying the vicarious thrill of hearing them play well in public (but is it really enjoyable, or so very thrilling?), and knowing they're *somewhat* grateful.

MARY–DALY–OLOGICAL

Who is Madame Sousatzka? Beldame Sousatzka is a Virgin who revels in be-ing Alone, a Virago who avoids the Comatose State of matrimony. She's an Unsubdued Survivor, a Spinster who twirls the thread of Life on her own axis and lives beyond the pale of patriarchy.

Is she ever sad? Not at all. Beldame Sousatzka is a Howling Hag who frightens fools. She's a Raving Lunatic who laughs out loud, and in laughing shatters the hierarchs' house of mirrors, defusing their power of deluding Others.

So she IS *batty.* Yes, but batty in the way Bette Davis was batty – Self-directed, Uncanny, Eccentric.

Who, then, is Manek Sen? Manek Sen is a fool. He's a phallic fool who resists Beldame Sousatzka's Archimagical charms (*Arch-Image*: Mary: vestige of the Goddess symbol preserved in christianity as a hook for Heathen masses; tamed Goddess symbol intended to conceal the Background Memory of the Arch-Image, but that functions to evoke Archaic Active Potency in women). He's a wantwit who'd rather join a gynocidal cockocracy (yahweh & son, steinway & sons) than belong to a bevy of Wild Women (Gertrude Stein & Daughters) and who'd rather conceive of The Incarnation (sublimated sexual fantasy promulgated as sublime christian dogma; mythic super-rape of the Virgin Mother) than comprehend an a-mazing musical dis-covery.[4]

PSYCHOANALYTIC

Isabelle Vengerova (1877–1955), the piano teacher who, according to Curtis Institute lore, inspired the film *Madame Sousatzka*, was both abusive and idealistic. One student, Harry Neal, reports that lessons would begin with helpful instruction ('Let not the tiniest flaw slip from underneath your fingers' [94]) and end with hurtful interrogation ('Are you lazy or conceited – or just stupid?' [93]). Other students predicate her in similar terms:

> 'Autocratic, didactic, unsympathetic, impatient, destructive' . . . 'A perfectionist, a terrible taskmaster (who expected more from her students than they were capable of)' . . . 'Sincere, strict, a perfectionist' . . . 'Intolerant (yet, underneath it all, warmhearted and compassionate)' . . . 'Very thorough, very demanding' . . . 'Strong-willed, authoritative (sometimes to the point of "destroying" a student)' . . . 'Profound, stoic, majestic, indomitable' . . . 'Inspiring, unreasonable, dogmatic, dynamic' . . . 'Tyrannical, relentless, awesome, authoritarian, uncompromising, overpowering' . . . 'Inflexible, impersonal' . . . 'Ominous, hypersensitive, erratic, "Russian-paranoid," devoted, loving, strong' . . . 'Blunt, undiplomatic, impolite (but capable of curing pianistic diseases with a high degree of skill)' . . . 'Dedicated, imperious, intransigent, demanding, totally devoid of personal vanity, a true idealist' . . . 'Intimidating, egotistical, sadistic, cold and cruel' . . . 'Overperfectionist' (Rezits 21–2)

Many Vengerova students – Leonard Bernstein, Gary Graffman, Gilbert Kalish, Jacob Lateiner – seem to have risen, or to want to rise, to the challenge. (Neal, 'long after her death, [is] still trying to win [his] way back into her favor' [90].) Others do seem to have been 'destroyed' (Vengerova, who could be 'withering', tied little Betty Benthin up in 'knots' [Rezits 22]).

But *why* did Vengerova involve them 'in an unending search for perfection' and refuse to 'let them settle into . . . mediocrity' (Neal 75, 86)? Why did she have to ruin – and then renovate – their self-esteem? ('What do you want of me? That I should pamper your little ego? No! For you my studio is a jungle, and in it you must fight for your life. Stand up like a man and I'll goad you, and I'll drive you, and I'll torment you until you grow into more than you know!' [Neal 101].) Because the ego ideal Vengerova introjected doesn't appear to have been impossible. She was a Theodor Leschetizky protégé who measured up to, and probably surpassed, his exacting standards. She *knew* she was a great teacher, moreover, and didn't credit the conventional wisdom that figures pedagogues as would-be performers. She had no desire to be Rudolf Serkin (the head of the Curtis piano department), even though she never played in public and so might have seen herself as a 'failed concert artist,' and even though she was a woman and so might have seen herself as a 'failed man' – nearly irresistible constructions that happen to reinforce one another. Hence her 'strength.'

We can all learn from Madame Vengerova. Barthes, for example, would have been a lot happier had he wanted to be literary critic Raymond Picard, and not André Gide or Marcel Proust. Then again, we'd never know the pleasure of this self-critical writer's 'writerly' criticism.

SEMIOTIC

Nicolas Slonimsky studied with Vengerova – who was, as it happens, his aunt – soon after she left Leschetizky. She wasn't yet a perfectionist – not with a young relative, at any rate.

> [My first concert] went off well. I tried to forget the few wrong notes
> I played, and my aunt did not mention these mistakes. She . . . was
> pleased with my 'expression.' (Slonimsky 3)

Barthes, too, studied with a maiden aunt – Aunt Alice, the only piano teacher he ever had and a woman even less demanding than Slonimsky's Aunt Isabelle. Or so we gather from Barthes's own attitude toward the instrument:

> If I play badly – aside from the lack of velocity, which is a purely
> muscular problem – it is because I fail to abide by the written
> fingering: I improvise, each time I play, the position of my fingers,

and therefore I can never play anything without making mistakes. The reason for this is obviously that I want an immediate pleasure and reject the tedium of training, for training hampers pleasure – for the sake of a greater ulterior pleasure, as they say (we tell the pianist what the gods said to Orpheus: Don't turn back *prematurely* on the effects of your action). So that the piece, in the perfection attributed to it but never really attained, functions as a bit of a hallucination: I gladly give myself up to the watchword of a fantasy: '*Immediately!*' even at the cost of a considerable loss of reality. (*Roland Barthes* 70)

Like Barthes, Aunt Alice knows there's no such thing as a transcendental signifier. No rehearsal is flawless. No performance is perfect. So why listen to, or degrade, yourself? Simply *imagine* yourself playing better than you do. And like Isabelle, but for an unrelated reason, Alice was a happy pianist. Thanks to her proto-deconstructive insight, she didn't measure herself against an impossible musical standard and never tried to satisfy an unrealistic musical demand.

The insight Alice shared with her nephew is *pseudo*deconstructive as well. Even though they don't believe in transcendental signifiers, they do believe in transcendental *signifieds*. They believe in make-believe perfection, in hallucinatory virtuosity. If only Barthes had fantasized having *written* wonderfully. ('Listen to this, Aunt Alice. Don't I sound like Racine?')

MATERIALIST

Miss Eckhart, the impoverished piano teacher in Eudora Welty's 'June Recital,' keeps her metronome locked in a safe. It's the only thing she keeps in there, and she keeps it there long after she's lost her last student. Miss Eckhart sees the metronome as her pedagogic essence. ('The old woman held her possession [and] stood looking at the three people fixedly, as if she showed them her insides, her live heart' [85].) Jinny, a selfish student, sees it as a worthless fetish. Cassie, a devoted one, sees it as a bit of both:

Miss Eckhart worshiped her metronome. She kept it, like the most precious secret in the teaching of music, in a wall safe. Jinny Love Stark, who was only seven or eight years old but had her tongue, did suggest that this was the only thing Miss Eckhart owned of the correct size to lock up there . . .

Cassie, out of nice feeling, looked the other way when it was time for the . . . opening of the safe. It seemed awful, and yet imminent, that . . . she, Cassie Morrison, might be the one to call logical attention to the absurdity of a safe in which there were no jewels, in which there was the very opposite of a jewel. (45–6)

However, male characters – Cassie's brother Loch, Old Man Moody, and Mr Fatty Bowles – see it a bit differently. They see the metronome as a bomb.

If only it were. Miss Eckhart is imprisoned within a system that pays women poorly for the few skills it lets them learn. She's also asked to believe in the system: to find her poverty appropriate and to see the relatively useless service she provides as worthwhile. In reality, Miss Eckhart's metronome is neither essence nor fetish. It's a device that thinks rhythm for her – just as price thinks value and ideology thinks (feminine) subjectivity Miss Eckhart, who doesn't count (socially), doesn't *have* to count (musically) – nor can she account for either incapacity. Too bad she can't take her timepiece and blow it all up. Too bad she doesn't have the wherewithal – material as well as mental – to explode the exploitative world we find her in. Although Miss Eckhart, now reduced to agricultural labor, does set fire to the studio apartment she's been forced to leave, she does so not out of feminist rage and class resentment, but to protest her dispossession from an abject situation she can only see as a classy vocation.

EROTIC

'Love's Litany,' Wilde's name for the discursive basis of that many-splendored thing which makes the world go round, can be wonderful – divine, heroic, enchanting, providential, transcendental.[5] But it can be dreary as well – violent, combative, poisonous, enthralling, tyrannical, sacrificial. Devoted mothers, for example, are abandoned by grown children. Devoted 'crystallizers' are disillusioned by imperfect love objects. Witty playwrights are betrayed by litigious paramours. And, thanks to Goethe, Wertheresque lovers – sad, solitary, suicidal – have an especially doleful part to play.

Welty's maiden piano teacher is Wertheresque. Cassie Morrison may love Miss Eckhart, but Miss Eckhart loves Virgie Rainey, a prodigy who doesn't love her back. Can brilliance alone account for the teacher's feelings? Miss Eckhart loves the girl's brutality too ('There was a little weak place in her, vulnerable, and Virgie Rainey found it and showed it to people' [45]), even though she finds the cathexis indiscriminate ('For Miss Eckhart love was just as arbitrary and one-sided as music teaching' [65]) and useless ('Her love never did anybody any good' [65]) and even though she finds herself alone ('She had nobody at all' [66]). She's grateful, in fact, but her pretentious refrain, 'Virgie Rainey, *danke schoen*,' leaves us wondering which is the icing and which the cake – brilliance or brutality. According to Cassie, it's the brutality the teacher craves: 'It was as though Miss Eckhart, at the last, were grateful to you for *anything*' (73).

Why is Virgie brutal? At first, she resents the way Miss Eckhart imagines her: as an up-and-coming virtuoso, as a gifted pianist who won't have failed. (It's hard to love people who expect too much.) In the end, though, she sees herself as Miss Eckhart: a gifted pianist who *did* fail. Miss Eckhart has already lost her studio. Miss Rainey is about to lose her job as 'the piano player at the picture show' (24), a prospect *both* of them should find horrifying. (What teacher wants to know her beloved student has come to naught? What student wants to fail a teacher?)

And yet, to hear Cassie tell it, when the two happen to meet after years of separation, 'They did not even horrify each other.'

> *Danke schoen* . . . That much was out in the open. Gratitude – like rescue – was simply no more. It was not only past; it was outworn and cast away. Both Miss Eckhart and Virgie Rainey were human beings terribly at large, roaming on the face of the earth. And there were others of them – human beings, roaming, like lost beasts. (96)

BARTHESIAN

Balzac, 'Sarrasine' (1830): Marianina de Lanty, a brilliant soprano, bids farewell to La Zambinella, a famous castrato, with an odd little flourish. '"Addio, addio," she said, with the prettiest inflection in her youthful voice. She added to the final syllable a marvelously well-executed trill, but in a soft voice, as if to give poetic expression to the emotion in her heart' (232–3). According to Barthes, the flourish predicates Marianina as 'musical.' But –

What would happen if one actually performed Marianina's '*addio*' as it is described in the discourse? Something incongruous, no doubt, extravagant, and not musical. More: is it really possible to perform the act described? This leads to two propositions. The first is that the discourse has no responsibility vis-à-vis the real: in the most realistic novel, the referent has no 'reality': suffice it to imagine the disorder the most orderly narrative would create were its descriptions taken at face value, converted into operative programs and simply executed. In short (this is the second proposition), what we call 'real' (in the theory of the realistic text) is never more than a code of representation (of signification): it is never a code of execution: *the novelistic real is not operable*. (Barthes, *S/Z*, 80)

Kate Chopin, *The Awakening* (1899): Mademoiselle Reisz, a stereotypically unpleasant piano teacher who plays Frédéric Chopin to perfection, does something incredible – and rather seductive – when Edna Pontellier, the lovelorn heroine, wants to hear an Impromptu.

Mademoiselle played a soft interlude. It was an improvisation. She sat low at the instrument, and the lines of her body settled into ungraceful curves and angles that gave it an appearance of deformity. Gradually and imperceptibly the interlude melted into the soft opening minor chords of the Chopin Impromptu.

Edna did not know when the Impromptu began or ended. She sat in the sofa corner reading Robert's letter by the fading light. Mademoiselle had glided from the Chopin into the quivering lovenotes of Isolde's song, and back again to the Impromptu with its soulful and poignant longing.

The shadows deepened in the little room. The music grew strange and fantastic – turbulent, insistent, plaintive, and soft with entreaty. The shadows grew deeper. The music filled the room. It floated out upon the night, over the housetops, the crescent of the river, losing itself in the silence of the upper air.

Edna was sobbing. (527)

There is no such Impromptu. The Chopin Impromptus are in major, and the Fantasie-Impromptu (C-sharp minor) opens with left-hand figuration. And even if the Impromptu did exist, what kind of musician would interpolate the *Liebestod*?

According to Mademoiselle Reisz, and quite possibly according to Kate: a *true* musician. 'The artist,' she tells Edna, 'must possess the courageous soul . . . [t]he soul that dares and defies' (527). Edna does dare and defy, but doesn't do so aesthetically – something she realizes just before she drowns herself: 'How Mademoiselle Reisz would have laughed, perhaps sneered, if she knew! "And you call yourself an artist! What pretensions, Madame!"' (527). ('The natural aversion for water,' moreover, is 'believed to accompany the artistic temperament' [518]. Who is speaking here? Kate? Edna? Anyone in particular?) Edna defies her husband, refusing to act the wife and mother. But she's both too timid to paint unconventionally (everything she does is 'lifelike': or tries to be [522]) and too timid to *live* unconventionally. In other words, she's too bourgeois to face the music. Mademoiselle Reisz, however, does face – and de-face – the music. She, like Barthes, throws caution to the wind, plays paradoxically (yet affectingly), and doesn't give a damn whether people 'like' her.[6]

The woman, after all, isn't very *nice*.

QUEER

Cassie Morrison knows about Miss Eckhart's metronome, but doesn't know what makes the woman tick. Edna Pontellier knows about her own desire, but not about anyone else's. Fortunately, Welty and Chopin – both Southern *belles lettristes* – may know more than Cassie and Edna. (Most Southern belles know more than they can say.) Where Cassie assumes Miss Eckhart loves Virgie Rainey's brutality, Welty seems to believe the teacher finds the student arousing: 'Those two . . . had been making a trip . . . the sailor [Virgie slept with] was only starting' (96). And where Edna assumes Mademoiselle Reisz has 'never been in love, and know[s] nothing about it' (536), Chopin seems to realize the teacher is in love with Edna. According to Edna, Mademoiselle Reisz finds 'queer' reasons to embrace her: 'For instance, when I left her to-day, she put her arms around me and felt my shoulder blades, to see if my wings were strong, she said' (537). (They weren't, making Edna a false Winged Victory.)

Is Kathrine Parker a lesbian? Is she bisexual? Was Rosina Lhevinne? (What *was* all that banging, anyway?) Rumor has it Myra Hess was a lesbian, and I, for one, believe it. Not because I find her playing, or anyone ever found her teaching, lesbianic, but because queer Wayne Koestenbaum claims to be a 'descendant' ('Piano Life,' line 123). And because when Hess first saw the true Winged Victory she was 'overwhelmed', spent several hours 'drinking it in' and 'let it have its way' with her (MacKail 13).

NOTES

1. See Trinh: 'In writing close to the other of the other, I can only choose to maintain a self-reflexively critical relationship toward the material, a relationship that defines both the subject written and the writing subject, undoing the I while asking "what do I want wanting to *know you* or me?"' (76).
2. These remarks are fictitious. Jeffrey Swann doesn't really defame pianists associated with the Van Cliburn Competition.
3. The references are to John Schlesinger's film *Madame Sousatzka* (1988).
4. These figures can be found in Daly's *Wickedary*.
5. As Wilde says: 'Do you wish to love? Use Love's Litany, and the words will create the yearning from which the world fancies that they spring' ('The Critic as Artist' 399).
6. 'I don't know whether I like you or not,' Edna tells Mademoiselle Reisz at their first tête-à-tête. It's a remark the teacher finds 'pleasing' (Chopin, *The Awakening*, 526).

WORKS CITED

Balzac, Honoré de, 'Sarrasine,' in Roland Barthes, *S/Z*, trans. Richard Miller (New York: Hill & Wang, 1977).

Barthes, Roland, 'Inaugural Lecture, Collège de France,' trans. Richard Miller, in *A Barthes Reader*, ed. Susan Sontag (New York: Hill & Wang, 1985).

Barthes, Roland, *Roland Barthes by Roland Barthes*, trans. Richard Howard (New York: Hill & Wang, 1977).

Barthes, Roland, *S/Z*, trans. Richard Miller (New York: Hill & Wang, 1977).

Chopin, Kate, *The Awakening* (1899), in *Contexts for Criticism*, ed. Donald Kesey (Mountain View, CA: Mayfield, 1994).

Daly, Mary, *Websters' First Intergalactic Wickedary of the English Language* (New York: HarperCollins, 1987).

Hernández, Felisberto, 'The Stray Horse,' in *Piano Stories*, trans. Luis Harss (New York: Marsilio, 1993).

Horowitz, Joseph, *The Ivory Trade: Piano Competitions and the Business of Music* (Boston: Northeastern University Press, 1990).

Koestenbaum, Wayne, 'The Answer is in the Garden,' in *Ode to Anna Moffo and Other Poems* (New York: Persea, 1990).

Koestenbaum, Wayne, 'Piano Life,' in *Rhapsodies of a Repeat Offender* (New York: Persea, 1994).

Limmer, Ruth, *Journey Around My Room: The Autobiography of Louise Bogan* (New York: Penguin, 1981).

MacKail, Clare, 'Early Days,' in *Myra Hess by Her Friends*, ed. Howard Ferguson (London: Hamish Hamilton, 1966).

Neal, Harry Lee, *Wave as You Pass* (Philadelphia: Lippincott, 1958).

Rezits, Joseph, 'The Teaching of Isabelle Vengerova,' *Piano Quarterly* 106 (Summer 1979): 16–23.

Slonimsky, Nicolas, '"Musique": Reminiscences of a Vanished World and a Great Teacher,' *The Piano Teacher* (September–October 1963): 2–4.

Stendhal, *Love*, trans. Gilbert and Susan Sale (Harmondsworth: Penguin, 1975).

Stevens, Wallace, 'Thirteen Ways of Looking at a Blackbird' (1917), in *The Palm at the End of the Mind*, ed. Holly Stevens (New York: Vintage, 1972).

Trinh T. Minh-ha, *Woman, Native, Other: Writing Post-coloniality and Feminism* (Bloomington: Indiana University Press, 1989).

Welty, Eudora, 'June Recital,' in *The Golden Apples* (1949) (New York: Harcourt Brace Jovanovich, 1977).

Wilde, Oscar, 'The Critic as Artist,' in *The Artist as Critic: Critical Writings of Oscar Wilde*, ed. Richard Ellmann (Chicago: University of Chicago Press, 1968).

CHAPTER 10

Denise Riley, 'Lyric Selves'

'Lyric Selves', a chapter from Denise Riley's *The Words of Selves: Identification, Solidarity, Irony*, offers an exquisitely pitched account of an age-old subject, namely our inheritance of language and the senses of selfhood that arise from this inheritance. Riley, a poet-critic, uses a form of auto-commentary, a mixture of poetry and prose that works both to enact the comings and goings of voice and to give voice to the grass-roots politics, both limiting and liberating, that resides in this very movement. Lyric is important to Riley as a poet, and because it is in lyric, in the history of the idea as well as in the individual poems, that we find the most extraordinary repertoire of ways of saying and knowing our selves in language.

Auto-commentary is a standard mode for the assessment of creative writing in the academy, where it figures as a form of show-and-tell in which the telling frequently involves a scrambled invention of process and influence. Riley does away with this fiction; or rather, she does away with the 'sticky sanctity' that would divide the creative from the critical. Rather than lay claim to the received certainties of description and explanation, Riley uses her form to set in play a series of echoes, and to experiment with echo itself as a form in and with which to work through the workings of our lyric selves. And with echo comes Echo; and with Echo comes Narcissus. We inherit the stories by which we know ourselves, but that shouldn't be a cause for resignation. Our stories are there for the taking, as is our language.

To experiment after Riley we need first to think about the possibilities of auto-commentary. If you are a creative writer, try to write back to or into your own work in ways other than the straightforwardly expository. You might begin by resisting the lure of the fully controlling first person – that is, you might begin by accepting Riley's chief proposition. Write back to your work using a character, perhaps a character from a novel or a poem that bears some relation with your own writing. If you are not a creative writer, now might be the time to experiment. Select a piece of critical prose, one that does not have an obvious primary text. It can be yours or someone else's. Either have a stab at writing a poem or short fiction that can then be placed alongside the criticism, or see what happens when you select part of a piece of literature to serve the same purpose.

Riley's other strategy is to use Echo and Narcissus as a means to conceive and dramatise aspects of our life in language. Take a figure from myth or folk tale or some other cultural medium, and write a piece in which this figure is put to critical work. Either the figure will suggest the subject or vice versa; either way, the two are likely to become intertwined.

Denise Riley, 'Lyric Selves', in *The Words of Selves: Identification, Solidarity, Irony* (Stanford: Stanford University Press, 2000), pp. 93–112.

Filled with joy and pride, we come to believe we have
created what we have only heard.

LONGINUS[1]

Some speculations which run throughout [*The Words of Selves*] are put directly as prosaic verse here. It's doggerel, to flesh out questions of the self's presence to itself that might, in a more laboured way, be raised in critical prose; and it would be a sticky sanctity which, glamorising 'creative writing' as unassailable, insisted on an unbridgeable demarcation between the poetic and the analytic. My two exhibits here continue some of the suggestions already advanced. The first sifts through ideas of lyrical self-presentation as they emerge in some contemporary dilemmas and compulsions of style. The second separates Narcissus from his recent adhesions of 'narcissism' and returns him back to his roots in Ovid and to his roots as a dried bulb once used for healing 'affections of the ear', afflicted hearing. It also includes some special pleading for Echo, too, and it proposes her role, fleshed out in my last chapter, as an adjunct of irony.

The Castalian Spring, a first draught

I

A gush of water, welling from some cave, which slopped
Down to a stone trough squatting stout and chalky as a

Morning sky: I plumped myself on lizard-ridden stone to stare
Into its old truth square that struck me as perhaps another lie
So serious did it look while it promised me, oh, everything.
That honest look of water nursed in stone excited me. Under
The generous trees, tall splotchy planes and brittle ilex, their
Dark flopped down, sun-glare and dust spun through it.

1. The spring lies close to Delphi, on Mount Parnassus. Not that the reader can know this yet, but we're at the start of a fable of self-presentation; it's going to resemble an ancient book of conversations between species likely to undergo metamorphoses, although here it's a bestiary populated with only one beast. The question of the speaking 'I', and of its possible egotism, arises immediately here. Is the lyric 'I' an irretrievably outdated form, as some would argue, a poetic version of that overthrown omniscient narrator we used to hear such a lot about and shouldn't much like to meet? But you can also have an impersonal lyric 'I', not at all confessional or self-aggrandising. Lyrical self-presentation distils all these worries, which are old enough.[2] The less that the poetic work is taken to be only consciously generated by its author, and the more archaic and dubious aspirations to technical control begin to sound, then, paradoxically, the more important the actual figure of the poet may become. Presenting the self and its fine sensibilities reaches fever pitch within some contemporary poetics. Poetry can be heard to stagger under a weight of self-portrayal, having taken this as its sole and proper object. Today's lyric form, frequently a vehicle for innocuous display and confessionals, is at odds with its remoter history. What might transpire if this discontinuous legacy in self-telling became the topic of a poem itself? Attempting this, the 'I' above has adopted a chatty conversational tone, yet the listener suspects this is some imaginary scenario flanked with venerable stage props. All we know so far about this speaker is that she possesses an odd psychology, some fixed anxiety about truth and appearance.

2

I sipped that cold and leafy water tentatively, lost lipstick
Dabbing my mouth, gulped down a little slippery grit I hoped
Was not ferny mosquito larvae; then sat on, guidebook-learned
To get gorgeous and pneumatic in the throat, my bulk deflating
Slowly until the sunset, when the last coach parties slid away.

The heat of the day peeled off, the light got blurred and hummed,
Pounding dusk struck up then a strong swelling rose in my throat
Thick with significant utterance. So, shivery in my cool and newly
Warty skin, I raised this novel voice to honk and boom.

2. The narrator knows, because she's read her Blue Guide, that if she drinks some water from the Castalian Spring, she will automatically turn into a poet. In this poem, however, she also turns into a toad, though she's perhaps surprisingly unfazed by such a strange translation. But what justification can there be for the cod antiquarianism of this piece? 'The history of the imitation of ancient poetry, especially as practised in foreign countries, is among other things useful in permitting us to derive most easily and fully the important concepts of unconscious parody and passive wit,' observed Schlegel.[3] Unfortunately the writer of this piece, like its imagined narrator, can discover only an inverse ratio between knowingness and confidence. The matter of having the confidence to make a noise at all continues to vex her in the next stanzas.

3
I was small enough now, and stoical, to squat on the slabs of rock
Edging the trough, splashed with the spring that welled steadily into
    it
Shaking its stone-cupped water. I wear yet a precious jewel in my
    head,
I mused, this line of old rhetoric floating back through me, as quite
Unsurprised I settled to study the night, flexing my long damp
    thighs
Now as studded and ridged as the best dill pickles in Whitechapel.
Into the cooling air I gave tongue, my ears blurred with the lyre
Of my larynx, its vibrato reverberant into the struck-dumb dusk.

3. Lyric poetry was, originally, simply words accompanied by the music of the lyre. 'Dill pickles' are gherkins. This sanguine tourist-toad somehow recalls her school Shakespeare's lines from *As You Like It*, 'Sweet are the uses of adversity, / Which like the toad, ugly and venomous, / Wears yet a precious jewel in his head'. One inescapable and deeply disconcerting effect of writing is such unwanted intrusions. Your own automatic 'intertextuality', to give it a misleadingly dignified name from the lit-crit lexicon, drives you spare. Quotation as white noise can be maddening. But this is a

bookish amphibian, whose preoccupations are largely with what she can do with her new voice, so I let this one stay in.

'Picking up other people's ideas like dead birds'[4] can be replaced by an uncomfortable awareness that all writing is derivative: a truism in, say, the history of ideas, where an acknowledgement that you are at best going to manage a cut-and-paste job is the minimum you require to proceed at all. But if poetry is also an affair of high-speed autodictation and half-conscious gluing, then the concept of the poem as a protected reservation for the unique personal voice is torn apart. Catching my borrowed rhetoric at its work on the page, I suddenly realise what I've been up to, and my whole bag of tricks, once exposed to me, becomes unusable. I append my signature sheepishly because I know I am a sounding chamber in poetry, even more so than in prose, since more than the content of the poem is derived. Its style is also a set of mechanical effects which spring up, felicitously or miserably, as that inescapable unconscious of language. I'm left with a peculiar new status of my own, now not so much the author as the editor of my own work but an editor inevitably so conscious of the automata which have leapt into life without her active consent that she must become a sharp censor. When the work still fails (as it does fail), that marks a lapse of retrospective vigilance rather than some shortfall of authorial 'originality'.

4
What should I sing out on this gratuitous new instrument?
Not much liking minimalism, I tried out some Messiaen,
Found I was a natural as a bassoon, indeed the ondes martenot
Simply oozed out of me. Or should lyric well up less, be bonier?
So I fluted like HD's muse in spiky girlish hellenics, slimmed
My voice down to twig-size, so shooting out stiffly it quivered
In firework bursts of sharp flowers. Or had I a responsibility to
Speak to society: though how could it hear me? It lay in its hotels.

4. The she-toad rehearses some familiar debates using as analogies the sounds of particular instruments. She skips through simplified versions of some positions in contemporary poetics and, as will happen all the way through this poem, abandons each in turn. So here she wonders about how full-bodied and gorgeous a contemporary lyric writer can allow herself to be – or whether something bleaker and bonier is in order, especially if the writer is female, and here she invokes the precedent of the poet HD. Is the

very demanding labour to produce beautiful utterance enough in itself, or should she make some extra, violent effort to get through to some audience? What if it's asleep, or out having a perfectly good time somewhere else?

5
I spun out some long lines, let them loop in sound ribbons
Lassoed the high branches where they dangled and trailed
Landing like leathery bats in vacancy; alighted, they pleated,
Composed themselves flawlessly, as lifeless as gloves.
The silence that hung on these sounds made me sheepish.
I fished for my German, broke out into lieder, rhymed
Sieg with Krieg, so explaining our century; I was hooked
On my theory of militarism as stemming from lyricism.

5. She has a go at working with pure line, and so she runs straight into the problem of the apparent self-sufficiency of the aesthetic object, here of decorative sound and its strange excluding quality of finishedness, when what you have made stares back at you like an angry adolescent. The insistent theme of 'social responsibility' can never be held at bay for very long, though, and she is briefly entranced with her idea that some common rhymes that a particular language generates might have a powerful effect on ways of writing and of thinking in that country. 'Sieg' is German for victory, and 'Krieg', for war. This isn't far from the way that the wild French linguist, Jean-Pierre Brisset, reasoned. (He's appeared in the previous chapter [of *The Words of Selves*].) He also held that humans were descended from frogs, and this historical fact partly explains the amphibious nature of my narrator here. Another German rhyme, 'Herz', meaning heart, with 'Schmerz', meaning pain, facilitates the concept that love lies very close to sorrow in the lyric tradition, as it so often lies in life. Once you could have had that same rhyme and meaning in British English, too: 'heart' with 'smart'. But in modern British English, 'smart' now means well turned out or flashily dressed, while in American English it means acute, clever; although this usage, originally from early English, is drifting back again across the Atlantic. The older sense of a 'smart' as a burning pain is now lost. Still, you could invent the argument that cleverness and elegance are stalked by feelings of apartness or loneliness, and so you've caught a shadow of that original meaning of a stinging pain, preserved forever in amber at the heart of hipness.

6

I'd crouched close by a cemetery; at twilight its keeper
Lit oil lamps in shrines on the pale marble graves, each
Brandishing silver-framed photographs; fresh flowers
For the well-furnished dead shone out amiably, while
The scops owl in residence served up its decorous gulps.
Lights burned on steadfastly in this town of the dead,
Each soul in for a long night, their curtains undrawn.
My monotone croaking rang crude in such company.

6. Graveyards in Greece are often tenderly kept, and at dusk, once the little
oil lamps on the tombstones are illuminated, they take on the aspect of a
glowing village. In the face of this company of the dead, the speaker forgets
her theories of poetics for a while in the face of grave matters, and must
recognise that she is coarse and inelegant of expression. She's tacitly feeling
a serious lack, that of any useful contemporary notion of Rhetoric – which
is, arguably, desperately needed for understanding how languages work.
Meanwhile, no way of rising to the elegiac occasion is open to her since
there is now no available tradition of civic song to which she has access, so
now she feels herself small. Which indeed she is.

7

Black plane trees bent over me, crouched in the night breeze.
For hours I called out on a sonorous roll, growing somewhat self-
Conscious I'd nothing to do but to sound: yet sound was so stirring
And beauty of utterance was surely enough, I thought I had read
     this.
A wind rose as I tore out my ravishing tenor, or sank down to throb
On my pitted hindquarters while my neck with its primrose
     striations
Pulsated and gleamed. Then beauty sobbed back to me, shocking,
Its counterpoint catching my harmonies; I had heard a fresh voice.

7. Here she temporarily abandons her worries about the social responsibility of the performing artist and the vacuum that her cemetery experience
has just painfully revealed, and instead simply sings out alone, still wondering whether a purely aesthetic approach to lyric noise is adequate and
if 'purity' is the best she can realistically manage; and then wouldn't that
be a lot to achieve, anyway? Yet she's feeling cut off until, as in an ancient

device, out of the darkness emerges another voice, miraculously in tune with her own.

She is seized briefly by the romantic solution to the problem of how she should speak, because her conviction of the arrival of that sole addressee who will completely understand her words has temporarily put paid to her earlier anxieties of audience. This dazzling immediacy has for the moment stilled her problem of knowing that to speak is to settle to be heard under some designation. Speaking as a literary social subject carries a consent to be it: someone appraised for marketing purposes as 'a Yorkshire writer' knows, when he too takes up this designation, that he's doing something beyond letting his home town of Bradford, or a sepia dream of the West Riding, sell his novels. Under his breath he has said to himself, Right, from now on, this is what I'll be. This personal agreement could conceal many undertones, perhaps an angry determination, a satirical concession, or a gracefully ironical resignation. But I cannot peaceably and quiescently inhabit a literary social category, any more than I can be an original author, and for analogous reasons. I am prey to whatever noisy inscriptions have run in advance of me. If the notion of 'integrity' conveys an originary wholeness, then writing, quintessentially derivative, must find some quite other basis for its truth. I might try to substitute the resigned compromise of collage for the impossible integrity of originality so that, for any assembly of fragments, it is those acts of selecting, pasting and reshaping which bestow virtue on my effort. Yet even this thinned-down 'integrity' of the collagist remains a disappointingly slight notion.

8

No longer alone, not espousing Narcissus, I answered each peal
In a drum of delirium, recalling with shame the dry white thighs
Of frogs like baked chicken wishbones, sorely in need of a sauce.
Our calls clasped in common, as heavy as love, and convulsively
Thickened by love – until ashamed of such ordinariness, I wailed
In sheer vowels. Aaghoooh, I sloughed off raark, aaarrgh noises,
Deliberately degenerate; exuded ooeeehaargh-I-oohyuuuh; then
Randomly honked 'darkling blue of Dimitrios': I had dreamed that.

8. Here the toad, having on the instant fallen for the call of a creature who sounds just like her, a common enough provocation for falling in love, suffers from memories of having, in her human shape, eaten a dish of baked frogs in a restaurant. Guilt fires her embarrassment at finding herself in the

supremely ordinary predicament of being so captivated, yet having nothing original to say or write on the subject. Her fruitless search for originality leads her to zip through a few current theories in poetics; so she tries to use pure noise like some contemporary sound poets may do, sometimes to get rid of the supposed imperfections and corruptions of signifying language by jettisoning semantic meaning. Next she goes for big, random sounds. Then finally, harking back to earlier surrealist experiments, she has a go at incorporating verbatim into her song work a fragment from one of her dreams.

Common hesitations shadow her closely related uncertainties of writing and of self-description. Both share a frustrated longing for resolution through an ideal of integrity, which itself sits close to that of originality. While I may have my doubts about the virtues of either ideal, nevertheless I can't fail to realise that while I can't be original, I nevertheless need to discover some helpful way of understanding the nature of my failure. The author who acknowledges herself a plagiarist – that, however much she strives for originality, she's merely parroting the accumulated insights of others – is she relying on a sickly charm to get her through, the old 'frank admission'? Every time I open my mouth, I'm insinuating myself into some conversation which pre-exists me and to which my contribution is only a rustle of echoes – on paper, which is where we all must live. Nevertheless, writing moves through its own simulacrum of originality; for even if its 'creativity' is conceived as really a matter of endless refashioning and involuntary plagiarising, it still retains, in the lonely fact of the signature, its final flourish of individuation. Then it's a question of how one takes on responsibility for the text in all its weaknesses, while in the same breath avoiding the gorgeous mantle of 'being a writer'.

9
The voice hears itself as it sings to its fellows – must
Thrum in its own ears, like any noise thumping down
Anywhere airwaves must equably fall. I was not that
Narcissus who stared stunned by his handsomeness;
Or I was, but not culpably, since as I sang, so I loved.
In that instant of calling hope out I embodied it, got
Solemn and swollen ushering in my own utterance.
I rang florid yet grave in my ears, as I had to.

9. Noticing the workings which accompany overhearing yourself write can produce effects on the page that you may need to distinguish from an undesirable self-attention or conceit. The toad has an optimistic line here on thought as echoing in the ear of its originator, although it's treated somewhat ironically. Distinguishing blind self-regard from that devotion to another which must always aim for the clearest address, she attempts a tranquil reflexivity. Yet she totters on the brink of being jarred by noticing herself doing so.

10

Did I need to account for myself as noise-maker?
I had stared in the windows of Clerkenwell clock shops
At dusty brand oils for the watchmakers' trade, made for
Easing the wound spring – some horo-prefixed, and so close
To my horror of time ticking by – brown bottles of clock oil
Labelled Horolene, Horotech. Should I wind up my own time,
Chant, 'I was dropped on the Borders, a poor scraplet of
Langholm, illegit. and state's burden, lone mother of three'?

10. Clerkenwell is a district in inner London where all the watchmakers had their shops; many hang on to this day, although their windows are dusty and funereal, some still full of bottles of the oil labelled for 'easing the wound spring' of the clockwork mechanisms. It's almost impossible not to pronounce this piece of the innards of a clock to yourself as 'woond' spring, with the sound of a wound as a hurt rather than what it means, a mechanism to be wound. And then the Greek-derived prefix 'horo', meaning time, easily slides into 'horror' to become a compacted shorthand for the fear of time passing, of mortality. This is one of those inescapable echolalic effects that worry the lyric toad, because they crop up so forcefully in the act of writing, whether or not they are wanted, and are yet another instance of language speaking you. Then at the end of the stanza, there is a movement from thoughts about time slipping away, implicitly towards death, to thoughts about presenting a conclusive autobiography (a deathly preoccupation) and how, if at all, the modernist, let alone the postmodernist, creature can speak accurately about her life. A homely example of these troubles of presentation and self-presentation returns to her mind from a memory prior to her metamorphosis; bookshops' shelving policies groan under them. The best-intentioned classifications can result in obscurantism and comedy. The class, for instance, of 'woman writers' will swell for

just as long as this marketing device might work commercially without bursting, and meanwhile it forcibly embraces those who'd spin in their graves at being so designated, such as Edith Sitwell, boxed as a 'woman poet'. One side effect is that shops are lined with neutrally labelled 'poetry' shelves, yet these contain only the work of men poets as an unadmitted – and deeply uninteresting – category, since the generically captioned shelves are flanked by a smaller quantity of weeded-out and separately designated 'women's poetry'. If 'Black writers' and 'Asian writers' are by now bracketed with some attempts at a greater refinement, nevertheless, under these headings, Guyanese and Ghanaian sports journalists may rub shoulders awkwardly as 'Black', and Chinese and Indonesian novelists must coexist unhappily as 'Asian'. Meanwhile the yards of nonethnically designated shelves are, by implication, heavy with the work of nonblack or 'white' writers, who are never thus specified, thereby silently exposing the weakness of the catch-all category of 'Black'. Admittedly all such classifications must be approximate and nowhere near those of the library; the absurd end result of the demand for precise specification would be an individualised classification for each title. For finer and finer subdivisions will arise ad infinitum, yet always obscuring someone else beneath them. Granting this, the failure of categories to keep pace with their claimants can still result in dark humour. The label of 'Irish writers' may readily be affixed to London bookshelves yet will not always differentiate between those who'd make furious neighbours, whether as Ulster opponents of Stormont or devotees of the Red Hand, as Anglo-Irish golfers or as mystical Fenians, or as solitary modernists dreaming internationalism in Dublin.

The pretender to lyric worries with reason, then, about espousing self-presentation within the conventional categories, about tying herself up or winding up her story of her own case, subjecting herself to subjectification and loudly inhabiting her potential identities, including having been born in an area so long fought over between Scotland and England that it was designated only as the blurred 'Debatable Lands'. She senses that she nevertheless can't erect her minuscule tale into any consoling identity, not even into that pleasing identity of being 'debatable'. Is that apt matter for lyric poetry – the presentation of a self, within such received groupings, as pitiful or as proud? But much contemporary work does exactly this, and its defences and damages do need to be debated. In the next stanza, she goes on wondering about this, so revealing more of her webbed hand.

11

Could I try on that song of my sociologised self? Its
Long angry flounce, tuned to piping self-sorrow, flopped
Lax in my gullet – 'But we're all *bufo bufo*', I sobbed –
Suddenly charmed by community – 'all warty we are'.
Low booms from the blackness welled up like dark liquid
Of 'wart' Ich auf Dich'. One Love was pulsed out from our
Isolate throats, concertina'ed in common; 'Du mit Mir' was
A comforting wheeze of old buffers, all coupled, one breed.

11. This stanza lets rip sound echoes, for instance of 'buffer' with '*bufo*'
– the Latin name for the main toad genus. And there are more echoes
between 'warty' and 'wart' ich' – German for 'I wait', implicitly for
You. Anyone who works in a medium which uses quotation, in words or
paint or celluloid or sound, will be all too familiar with this phenomenon
of irrational associations arising spontaneously, crowding in, generating
a constant headache of self-editing. There's a characteristic excess in
working with lyric, that buzz of ramifications through sound-echoes and
not, in the first place, sense-echoes, and which resemble forms of speech
disturbance as described in the literature on aphasia or schizophrenia. You
need to process them into a controlled mania, but you exert such control
only after they have arrived; you may be able to cut through the blur of
sound associations, but only retrospectively, after you've detected them
swarming on your page. Do they stay or do they go? There's a feeling of
being seized by too much language or of being inscribed by language, as not
their meaning but the aural resonances of your words very often determine
what you'll say next, in an untidy vacillating process, after which you have
to dust yourself down, to realise 'what's really been going on here' only in
retrospect. But the experience of retrospective knowledge that floats up at
you from the surface of the freshly written page, when you suddenly see
something of what you've actually written, may be alarming.

Back to the content of this eleventh stanza, where happy song arises.
Lyrics of the 1960s espouse this cheerful communitarianism, although
some may suspect these echoes on the grounds that popular music is
rankest commerce, it cheapens the emotions, and so on. Still, the narrator's prejudice is solidly in favour of such lyrics on the grounds that if her
amphibian emotion is at once very powerful and very ordinary, popular
song can encapsulate the coincidence of both, which is reassuring. 'Du mit

Mir' just means 'you with me'. These words are kept in German, in part because that's the language of the early nineteenth-century song cycles, in which words and notes hang intimately together. By now the toad has given up on her string of self-pitying self-presentations and stumbles instead upon an ideal of social identification. It's a hymn of togetherness, not only the togetherness of the couples joined to each other in their affections but beyond that, for they are linked in a feeling of unification with every other member of their species, such as the old Coca-Cola television advertisements with people clasping hands to chorus about 'one world'. The myriad selves volunteer for a happy self-alienation, a merciful release from solitariness into unison. Her stanza is rude about this. There are more worrying undertones here because it's not yet possible to use the German language to talk about group emotion and identity without recalling, in Reich's contentious phrase, a mass psychology of fascism – even if there are now all too many contemporary claimants for this unhappy association.

12
But then I heard others, odd pockets of sound; why wouldn't these
Claim me to chant in their choir? As I grew lonelier, I got
   philosophical,
Piped up this line: 'Don't fall for paradox, to lie choked in its coils
While your years sidle by.' Some hooted reproachfully out of the
   dawn,
'Don't you stifle us with your egotist's narrative or go soft on
   "sameness",
We'll plait our own wildly elaborate patterns' – they bristled like
   movies
By Kurosawa. By then I'd reflated, abandoned my toadhood, had
   pulled on
My usual skin like old nylons. I drifted to Delphi, I'd a temple to
   see.

12. The she-toad, now restored to her original condition of being a tourist, goes off, surprisingly unshaken by her metamorphosis, to Delphi, the small town where the oracle-containing temple of Apollo lies. There's a reference to the Japanese director Kurosawa in here, only because I happened to see a movie of his, *Ran*, based on the *King Lear* story which is so full of bristling arrows and lances and spears that the screen is frequently a mass of

spiky diagonals. This jump-cut brings up an etiquette of private allusion: Suppose you have odd associations which your audience aren't necessarily going to catch, do you cut these out in the interests of intelligibility or accessibility? Here I let Kurosawa and his bristling arrows stand, not because of their weight but because of their slightness in their context; it makes no difference if you miss them, and if you don't, they might entertain you by recalling the movie. The others who chorus in this final stanza are vexed with the speaker for having, during her phase of professing One Love, occupied a position which seemed to obliterate their real differences and had homogenised them into a mass. The speaker toad has had enough by now, as this writer felt that this doggerel was too slight to bear any more weight. So she becomes human again, and we abandon her at the point of resuming her tourism. The problem is how to end such an unresolved composition. Do you just give up on it, maybe wishing you'd somehow tried harder? Does it walk out on you – do you both somehow know when things are irretrievably over between you?

Affections of the Ear

I

Here's the original Narcissus story: The blue nymph Leiriope,
    called the lily-faced,
Clear blue as any Cretan iris, got the river-god, summer Cephissus,
    so on the boil
That lapped by his skeins of water, soused in them, spun round,
    twirled, interlaced
Until made pregnant, she had Narcissus. Stupefied well before he
    was pulped to oil
What future did he ever really have, with that slight azure mother of
    his embraced
By slippery Cephissus, insinuating himself everywhere to flatter,
    linger, and coil?
Leiriope chased Tiresias to set him his very first poser: would her
    boy be effaced
By a rapid death? The seer said No – just as long as he didn't know
    himself. Recoil
From the goal of self-knowledge! That maxim, chiselled in temple
    rock, gets erased
By the case of Narcissus who came to know himself to be loved
    water. Philosophy

Recommends a severe self-scrutiny to us, while a blithe self-
indifference is disgraced:
Yet for gorgeous Narcissus to know himself was sheer torment, and
his catastrophe.

II
He did know he was beautiful before he ever caught sight of himself
in the water.
One youth he didn't want died cursing 'Let him love, too, yet not
get what he'll love'.
(I should explain myself, I sound derivative? Because I am, I'm
Echo, your reporter.
I'll pick up any sound to flick it back if it's pitched louder than the
muttering of a dove.
I am mere derivation, and doomed by Mrs Zeus to hang out in this
Thespian backwater.)
He pushed into the surface of the lake; when push had come, as
come it will, to shove
Narcissus had to know. Then deathly recognition drew him, lamb-
like, to his slaughter.
His object was no wavering boy beneath the water, he was far more
than hand in glove
With what he saw. I know his problem, though at least I do have
Iynx my bird daughter.
To love himself was pain precisely when he came to understand that
truth, most bitterly.
I got hurt too, by ox-eyed Hera as they call her although I'd say cow,
recumbent above.
For me, Echo, to forcibly repeat others' words is my ear torment,
my own catastrophe.

III
I told stories so Zeus' lovers escaped, as under cover of my chatter
they'd slip past Hera.
I did things with words until she caught me, to rage 'False fluency,
your gossip's untrue
You've always wanted the last word – see what good it'll do you'. I
was right to fear her

For now I have got it. So exiled, I fell for Narcissus. I had no voice
    to plead so I'd pursue.
He called 'I'd die before I'd give myself to you!' I shrilled 'I'd give
    myself to you!' ran nearer.
If he'd cried 'I'd die before I'd fuck you', at least I could have echoed
    back that 'Fuck you'.
Sorry – I have to bounce back each last phrase. Half-petrified, I
    voice dead gorges. Dearer
My daughter Iynx, a wryneck, torticollis, twisted neck, barred and
    secretive as any cuckoo,
A writher in the woods – as a mother I am, and am merely,
    responsive; still, I keep near her.
My body goes rocky when I hang round Narcissus. Numbed to a
    trace of ruined articulacy
I mouth words I can't voice; half-turned to stone, am rigid with
    memory of what I could do.
So for lonely Narcissus fruitlessly knowing himself as his object was
    torture, a catastrophe.

IV
He saw truth in fluidity, was an offshoot of water; he dreamily
    propped himself prone
Beside his reflection; the image that shone yet broke at his touch he
    did not misconstrue.
He lay dumb in the daze of himself by the glaze of the lake with his
    face set like stone.
If your mother was blue and your father was water, then mightn't
    you try to be true?
'Only the thinnest liquid film parts us; which is why, unlike most
    lovers', I heard him groan,
'I long for more distance between us; only then could I start to get
    near him'. Narcissus knew.
In the end, he was not misled by vanity. He saw it was himself he
    loved, and not his clone:
In just that lay his torture. I've said that as a bulb he got pulped
    down to oil, mashed to a stew.
Narcissus oil's a narcotic, both stem from the same root *narcos*,
    numb; the bulb was known

As the botanical root to cure 'affections of the ear'. (I'll need that oil
on my tympanum, too,
If thought is truly a bone.) His becoming a herbal remedy concludes
Narcissus' biography.
Dying by water in knowing misery, he's recycled as unguent to drop
on the sounding tissue
Of sore ears to heal their affections. Affections of the ear, not of the
heart; familiar catastrophe.

v
'Ears are the only orifices that can't be closed' – though force may
get some others to succumb.
My inward ears will jam wide open to internal words that overlying
verbiage can't smother.
Boated over the Styx, Narcissus' shade peered in its black waters
just in case his image swum.
Numbed by affection of his heart, now dried he'll cure the ear
affections.
Son of his lily mother
His beauty drove me deeper into repetition as a sounding-board, a
ringing rock, a mere eardrum.
A rhyme rears up before me to insist on how I should repeat a
stanza's formal utterance – other
Than this I cannot do, unless my hearers find a way of speaking to
me so I don't stay semi-dumb
Or pirouette, a languid Sugarplum. Echo's a trope for lyric poetry's
endemic barely hidden bother:
As I am made to parrot others' words so I am forced to form ideas by
rhymes, the most humdrum.
All I may say is through constraint, dictation straight from sounds
doggedly at work in a strophe.
'To make yourself seen reflects back to you, but to make yourself
heard goes out towards another'.
That's all I, Echo, ever do. Occasionally diverting, it stays my
passive hell and small catastrophe.

All these details of the story of Narcissus and Echo are taken straight
from Ovid's *Metamorphoses*, book 3. It also incorporates Robert Graves's
claim that narcissus oil, crushed out of the bulb, was used as a cure for

'affections of the ears'.[5] The word 'affection' is an archaism for 'disease' (as an example, the *Oxford English Dictionary* says that to possess 'an affection of the heart' was, in 1853, to suffer from heart disease). These lines have resurrected Ovid's antihero, who perfectly came to realise his mistake of falling in love with his own reflection, and so they disinter the first Narcissus, aeons before our popular psychology of 'narcissism'. That original Narcissus, though, was not so short on self-knowledge as his later version implies. And self-knowledge need not, anyway, inevitably induce self-absorption. As Nietzsche remarked, 'A thing explained is a thing we have no further concerns with. What did that god mean who counselled: "Know thyself"? Does that perhaps mean "Have no further concern with thyself! Become objective!"'[6] 'Knowing oneself' can be a catastrophic undertaking – yes, but only if that Socratic injunction is taken in its modern deployment, to mean the introspection of individual self-consciousness. Then the risk of self-knowledge becomes that of complacency: 'How many people know how to observe something? Of the few who do, how many observe themselves? "Everybody is farthest away – from himself"; all who try the reins know this to their chagrin, and the maxim "know thyself!", addressed to human beings by a god, is almost malicious. That the case of self-observation is indeed as desperate as that is attested best of all by the manner in which almost everybody talks about the essence of moral actions – this quick, eager, convinced, and garrulous manner with its expression, its smile, and its obliging ardor!'[7] Classical writers, too, were often sardonic about the famous injunction. So Lucian's amiable cynic Menippus runs out of patience with the complaining shades of Croesus, Midas and Sardanapalus and lambasts them: 'You, for your part lament and weep and I will accompany you and occasionally join in with the refrain "Know thyself": for it would be quite a suitable accompaniment to such howling.'[8] But the injunction is saved if you agree with Hegel that self-knowledge implies a knowledge of Mind itself, rather than of the quirks of any individual idiosyncratic psychology.[9] Or that, as in Kierkegaard's gloss on Socrates, you should come to self-knowledge as an act of helpful differentiation and separation from yourself.[10] 'Knowing yourself is valuable, so that the self can be removed from the process', as Mark Rothko, a man sadly all too good at removing himself, observed.[11]

Although later he was compelled by Freud to undergo yet another metamorphosis into the emblem of his concept of narcissism, Narcissus' original mythological dilemma was profoundly different from that sketched in that familiar modern characterology. Narcissus suffered not error but horror. No ignorance through vanity tormented him at the last but rather his horrified and transfixing knowledge of the true nature of what he loved. If he had to endure his own impenetrability as he withers, Echo, his companion in Ovid's story, has to endure a passivity which, nonetheless, has its marked effects. Lacan offered the line, 'In the field of the unconscious the ears are the only orifice that cannot be closed', while his assertion that making oneself seen 'comes back towards the subject', but 'making oneself heard goes towards the other' repeated his own extension of Freud.[12] The verses above, however, wonder aloud about both these assertions and are not convinced by them. They suggest instead that Echo might be taken as a figure or a trope for the troubled nature of lyric poetry, driven on by rhyme, and condemned to hapless repetition of the cadences and sound associations in others' utterances. This piece also deploys such a long line itself that any listening ears will not catch its structure of rhymed alternating couplets. There seems to be a 'natural' length for the heard line, beyond which the ear cannot stretch, so that here an elaborate structure has turned out to be a workup for nothing. In that respect, it's in a rather worse position than poor Echo's enforced repetitions of others' endings. But in the final chapter, she'll make a more constructively passive appearance.

Yet how can I defend my flippant doggerel and its tongue-in-cheek exegesis here as having anything much to do with the serious question of how political subjects are consolidated? Only thus: Calling out, calling myself, and being called are all intimately related incarnations of the flesh of words. This materiality of language is packed through and through with its own historicity. Such a materiality isn't some antiquarian's decorative piecrust of orality or of etymology to garnish the real meat of what is being said, its meaning-content. The linguistic materiality lies rather in the reiteration, the echoes, the reflexivity, the cadences, the automatic self-parodies and the self-monumentalising which, constituting both being called and calling oneself, constitute the formation of categories of persons. There is nowhere beyond interpellation for us. Not so much because any speaker is also spoken by language and trapped, but rather because we do not and cannot have naming's full measure (indeed that 'we' is interpellation's measure of us) as it runs across and through us to go beyond itself. There is, in effect, a will to name. Often it pursues incalculable directions; it may run wild, or may look less anarchic altogether and appear to rein itself in or even make a display of its own historical sense. To attend to the inherently rhetorical nature of its calling, so often a latent political calling, wouldn't mean policing or cleaning off its rhetoricity but trying to track both its effect and its affect. (And this kind of attending isn't so far removed from the experience of writing lyric as might first seem.) The materiality of words isn't the secondary but the immediate stuff of the political, while what's assigned as rhetoric bleeds and seeps so steadily into ordinary language that its boundaries are of degree and convention, not of kind. Yet though being named and self-naming happen from the outside as well as within any speaker, as exteriority as well as interiority, this doesn't imply that their affective temporality is an undistinguishable blur between verbal outer and verbal inner which renders these always the same. (A claim that sameness does exist here – which is also a claim to that 'successful' interpellation which indeed never fails – is what defines the ideological.) It's exactly in the lack of such a homogenised linguistic temporality, and instead within naming's very differences and repetitions, that for good or ill the possibilities of politics constantly arise.

NOTES

1. Longinus, *On Sublimity*, no certain date but assumed to be the first century AD, trans. D. A. Russell (Oxford: Clarendon Press, 1965), p. 7.
2. See, for instance, *The Poet's I in Archaic Greek Lyric*, ed. S. R. Sling (Amsterdam: VU University Press, 1990).
3. Friedrich Schlegel, *Critical Fragments*, §39, in *Friedrich Schlegel's 'Lucinde' and the Fragments*, trans. Peter Firchow (Minneapolis: University of Minnesota Press, 1971), p. 147.
4. Remark attributed to the late Harold Brodkey.
5. Robert Graves, *The Greek Myths*, vol. 1 (Harmondsworth: Penguin Books, 1960), pp. 286–8.
6. Friedrich Nietzsche, *Beyond Good and Evil* (1886), trans. R. J. Hollingdale (Harmondsworth: Penguin Books, 1981), p. 74.
7. Friedrich Nietzsche, *The Gay Science*, §335, trans. Walter Kaufmann (New York: Vintage Books, 1974), p. 263.
8. Lucian, *Dialogues of the Dead II, Lucian's Dialogues*, trans. with notes by Howard Williams (London: George Bell and Sons, 1888), p. 91. Williams comments here that 'Menander, the first of the New Comedy dramatists, parodies this well-worn adage and holds that "Know Others" might be more useful' (p. 91).
9. G. W. F. Hegel, *The Encyclopaedia Logic*, Part 1 of the *Encyclopaedia of Philosophical Sciences*, trans. T. F. Geraets, W. A. Suchting and H. S. Harris (Indianapolis: Hackett, 1991), p. 212.
10. Søren Kierkegaard, *The Concept of Irony: With Constant Reference to Socrates*, trans. and historical introduction by Lee M. Capel (London: Collins, 1966), p. 202.

11. Dore Ashton recalls the painter's assertions that to aim at self-expression is erroneous in art, since the point is to be drawn well outside oneself. She discusses his enthusiasm for Nietzsche here in her *About Rothko* (New York: Oxford University Press, 1983), p. 120.

12. Jacques Lacan, 'From Love to the Libido', in *The Four Fundamental Concepts of Psycho-analysis*, ed. Jacques-Alain Miller, trans. Alan Sheridan (Harmondsworth: Penguin Books, 1977), p. 195.

CHAPTER II

Eve Kosofsky Sedgwick, 'Jane Austen and the Masturbating Girl'

'Jane Austen and the Masturbating Girl' would definitely win first prize in any Most Startling Title competition. But Sedgwick's chutzpah in linking 'this common form of isometric exercise' with an author whose novels are a by-word for decorum is only one reason for the essay's inclusion here. Less overtly outrageous, but at least as remarkable, is Sedgwick's treatment of historical evidence, of literary theory, and of the act of reading itself. Sedgwick reads passages from *Sense and Sensibility* (1811) representing the desirous and fidgety Marianne Dashwood, alongside extracts from a late-nineteenth-century medical case study of female onanism, but this is not a 'straight', historical or historicist study. For a start, the texts she reads are hardly contemporaneous; and, as she points out, 'masturbation' is a practice which leaves few legible traces, and rarely coalesces into an identity. The desirousness of historicising itself is at issue here. Drawing attention to the ways in which a disciplinary, anti-masturbatory language is to be heard too in twentieth-century readings of Austen's novel, Sedgwick also flaunts the self-gratifying sexiness of her own readings of it. But this isn't just a one-woman show. Her essay draws with gusto on literary theory of the last four decades, in particular the work of Michel Foucault. It does this, not to 'apply' theory, or to process 'Jane Austen' through a machinery of received terms and concepts, but rather in a two-way movement, in which theory is transformed and criticised, even as it opens up hitherto unacknowledged possibilities in literature. If her essay reaches back into the literature of the past, it does so to find resources for the present in which she writes, offering an intervention at once into queer politics and Austen scholarship. We invite you to find your own singular pleasures, however perverse, in this fiercely intelligent, often funny, sometimes wayward, and always provocative meditation on 'the highly relational but, in practical terms, solitary pleasure and adventure of writing itself'.

And then embark on your own adventure. Write a piece which takes the most shocking line you can imagine on a single work of art or literature. The scandal you are looking to provoke absolutely needn't be to do with sex of course. It could be a question of making something extremely unusual into your 'theme', or making palpable a telling silence in your work, or eliciting an odd obsession in the critical literature already written on it.

Eve Kosofsky Sedgwick, 'Jane Austen and the Masturbating Girl', *Critical Inquiry* 17 (1991): 818–37.

I

The phrase itself is already evidence. Roger Kimball in *Tenured Radicals* – a treatise on educational 'corruption' that must have gone to press before the offending paper was so much as written – cites the title 'Jane Austen and the Masturbating Girl' from an MLA convention program quite as if he were Perry Mason, the six words a smoking gun:[1] the warm gun that, for the journalists who have adopted the phrase as an index of depravity in academe, is happiness – offering the squibby pop (fulmination? prurience? funniness?) that lets absolutely anyone, in the righteously exciting vicinity of the masturbating girl, feel a very pundit.[2]

There seems to be something self-evident – irresistibly so, to judge from its gleeful propagation – about use of the phrase, 'Jane Austen and the Masturbating Girl,' as the QED of phobic narratives about the degeneracy of academic discourse in the humanities. But what? The narrative link between masturbation itself and degeneracy, though a staple of pre-1920s medical and racial science, no longer has any respectable currency. To the contrary: modern views of masturbation tend to place it firmly in the framework of optimistic, hygienic narratives of all-too-normative individual development. When Jane E. Brody, in a recent 'Personal Health' column in the *New York Times*, reassures her readers that, according to experts, it is actually entirely possible for people to be healthy *without* masturbating; 'that the practice is not essential to normal development and that no one who thinks it is wrong or sinful should feel he or she must try it'; and that even 'those who have not masturbated . . . can have perfectly normal sex lives as adults,' the all but perfectly normal Victorianist may be forgiven for feeling just a little – out of breath.[3] In this altered context, the self-evidence of a polemical link between autoeroticism and narratives of wholesale degeneracy (or, in one journalist's historically redolent term, 'idiocy')[4] draws on a very widely discredited body of psychiatric and eugenic expertise whose only direct historical continuity with late-twentieth-century thought has been routed straight through the rhetoric and practice of fascism. But it does so under the more acceptable gloss of the modern trivializing, hygienic developmental discourse, according to which autoeroticism not only is funny – any sexuality of any power is likely to hover near the threshold of hilarity – but must be relegated to the inarticulable space of (a barely superseded) infantility.

'Jane Austen and the Masturbating Girl' – the paper, not the phrase – began as a contribution to a Modern Language Association session that the three of us who proposed it entitled 'The Muse of Masturbation.' In spite of the half-century-long normalizing rehabilitation of this common form of isometric exercise, the proposal to begin an exploration of literary aspects of autoeroticism seemed to leave many people gasping. That could hardly be because literary pleasure, critical self-scrutiny, and autoeroticism have nothing in common. What seems likelier, indeed, is that the literal-minded and censorious metaphor that labels any criticism one doesn't like, or doesn't understand, with the would-be-damning epithet 'mental masturbation' actually refers to a much vaster, indeed foundational open secret about how hard it is to circumscribe the vibrations of the highly relational but, in practical terms, solitary pleasure and adventure of writing itself.

As the historicization of sexuality, following the work of Foucault, becomes increasingly involved with issues of representation, different varieties of sexual experience and identity are being discovered both to possess a diachronic history – a history of significant change – and to be entangled in particularly indicative ways with aspects of epistemology and of literary creation and reception.[5] This is no less true of autoeroticism than of other forms of sexuality. For example, the Aesthetic in Kant is substantively indistinguishable from, but at the same time definitionally opposed against, autoerotic pleasure. Sensibility, too – even more tellingly for the example of Austen – named the locus of a similarly dangerous overlap. As John Mullan points out in *Sentiment and Sociability: The Language of Feeling in the Eighteenth Century*, the empathetic allo-identifications that were supposed to guarantee the sociable nature of sensibility could not finally be distinguished from an epistemological solipsism, a somatics of trembling self-absorption, and ultimately – in the durable medical code for autoeroticism and its supposed sequelae – 'neurasthenia.'[6] Similarly unstable dichotomies between art and masturbation have persisted, culminating in those recurrent indictments of self-reflexive art and critical theory themselves as forms of mental masturbation.

Masturbation itself, as we will see, like homosexuality and heterosexuality, is being demonstrated to have a complex history. Yet there are senses in which autoeroticism seems almost uniquely – or at least distinctively – to challenge the historicizing impulse. It is unlike heterosexuality, whose history is difficult to construct because it masquerades so readily as History itself; it is unlike homosexuality, for centuries the *crimen nefandum* or 'love that dare not speak its name,' the compilation of whose history requires acculturation in a rhetoric of the most pointed preterition. Because it escapes both the narrative of reproduction and (when practiced solo) even the creation of any interpersonal trace, it seems to have an affinity with amnesia, repetition or the repetition compulsion, and ahistorical or history-rupturing rhetorics of sublimity. Neil Hertz has pointed out how much of the disciplinary discourse around masturbation has been aimed at discovering or inventing proprietary traces to attach to a practice which, itself relatively traceless, may seem distinctively to threaten the orders of propriety and property.[7] And in the context of hierarchically oppressive relations between genders and between sexualities, masturbation can seem to offer – not least as an analogy to writing – a reservoir of potentially utopian metaphors and energies for independence, self-possession, and a rapture that may owe relatively little to political or interpersonal abjection.

The three participants in 'The Muse of Masturbation,' like most of the other scholars I know of who think and write about masturbation, have been active in lesbian and gay as well as in feminist studies. This makes sense because thinking about autoeroticism is beginning to seem a productive and necessary switch-point in thinking about the relations – historical as well as intrapsychic – between homo- and heteroeroticism: a project that has not seemed engaging or necessary to scholars who do not register the antiheterosexist pressure of gay and lesbian interrogation. Additionally, it is through gay and lesbian studies that the skills for a project of historicizing any sexuality have developed; along with a tradition of valuing nonprocreative forms of creativity and pleasure; a history of being suspicious of the tendentious functioning of open secrets; and a politically urgent tropism toward the gaily and, if necessary, the defiantly explicit.

At the same time, part of the great interest of autoeroticism for lesbian and gay thought is that it is a long-execrated form of sexuality, intimately and invaluably entangled with the physical, emotional, and intellectual adventures of many, many people, that today completely *fails* to constitute anything remotely like a minority identity. The history of masturbation phobia – the astonishing range of legitimate institutions that so recently surveilled, punished, jawboned, imprisoned, terrorized, shackled, diagnosed, purged, and physically mutilated so many people, to prevent a behavior that those same institutions now consider innocuity itself – has complex messages for sexual activism today. It seems to provide the most compelling possible exposure of the fraudulence of the scientistic claims of any discourse, *including medicine*, to say, in relation to human behavior, what constitutes disease. 'The mass of "self-defilement" literature,' as Vernon A. Rosario II rather mildly points out, can 'be read as a gross travesty of public health education.'[8] And queer people have recently needed every available tool of critical leverage, including travesty, against the crushing mass of legitimated discourses showing us to be moribund, mutant, pathetic, virulent, or impossible. Even as it demonstrates the absolutely discrediting inability of the 'human sciences' to offer any effectual resistance to the most grossly, punitively inflictive moralistic hijacking, however, the same history of masturbation phobia can also seem to offer the heartening spectacle of a terrible oppression based on 'fear' and 'ignorance' that, ultimately, withered away from sheer transparent absurdity. The danger of this view is that the encouragement it offers – an encouragement we can hardly forgo, so much need do we have of courage – depends on an Enlightenment narrative that can only relegitimate the same institutions of knowledge by which the crime was in the first place done.

Today there is no corpus of law or of medicine about masturbation; it sways no electoral politics; institutional violence and street violence do not surround it, nor does an epistemology of accusation; people who have masturbated who may contract illnesses are treated as people who are sick with specific disease organisms, rather than as revelatory embodiments of sexual fatality. Yet when so many confident jeremiads are spontaneously launched at the explicit invocation of the masturbator, it seems that her power to guarantee a Truth from which she is herself excluded has not lessened in two centuries. To have so powerful a form of *sexuality* run so fully athwart the precious and embattled sexual *identities* whose meaning and outlines we always insist on thinking we know, is only part of the revelatory power of the Muse of masturbation.

2

Bedroom scenes are not so commonplace in Jane Austen's novels that readers get jaded with the chiaroscuro of sleep and passion, wan light, damp linen, physical abandon, naked dependency, and the imperfectly clothed body. *Sense and Sensibility* has a particularly devastating bedroom scene, which begins:

> Before the house-maid had lit their fire the next day, or the
> sun gained any power over a cold, gloomy morning in January,
> Marianne, only half-dressed, was kneeling against one of the
> window-seats for the sake of all the little light she could command
> from it, and writing as fast as a continual flow of tears would permit
> her. In this situation, Elinor, roused from sleep by her agitation and
> sobs, first perceived her; and after observing her for a few moments
> with silent anxiety, said, in a tone of the most considerate gentleness,
> 'Marianne, may I ask? –'
> 'No, Elinor,' she replied, 'ask nothing; you will soon know all.'
> The sort of desperate calmness with which this was said, lasted
> no longer than while she spoke, and was immediately followed by a
> return of the same excessive affliction. It was some minutes before
> she could go on with her letter, and the frequent bursts of grief
> which still obliged her, at intervals, to withhold her pen, were proofs
> enough of her feeling how more than probable it was that she was
> writing for the last time to Willoughby.[9]

We know well enough who is in this *bedroom*: two women. They are Elinor and Marianne Dashwood, they are sisters, and the passion and perturbation of their love for each other is, at the very least, the backbone of this powerful novel. But who is in this *bedroom scene*? And, to put it vulgarly, what's their scene? It is the naming of a man, the absent Willoughby, that both marks this as an unmistakably sexual scene, and by the same gesture seems to displace its 'sexuality' from the depicted bedroom space of same-sex tenderness, secrecy, longing, and frustration. Is this, then, a hetero- or a homoerotic novel (or moment in a novel)? No doubt it must be said to be both, if love is vectored toward an object and Elinor's here flies toward Marianne, Marianne's in turn toward Willoughby. But what, if love is defined only by its gender of object-choice, are we to make of Marianne's terrible isolation in this scene; of her unstanchable emission, convulsive and intransitive; and of the writing activity with which it wrenchingly alternates?

Even before this, of course, the homo/hetero question is problemati-
cal for its anachronism: homosexual identities, and certainly female ones,
are supposed not to have had a broad discursive circulation until later
in the nineteenth century, so in what sense could heterosexual identities
as against them?[10] And for that matter, if we are to trust Foucault, the
conceptual amalgam represented in the very term 'sexual identity,' the
cementing of every issue of individuality, filiation, truth, and utterance *to*
some representational metonymy of the genital, was a process not supposed
to have been perfected for another half-century or three-quarters of a
century after Austen; so that the genital implication in either 'homosexual'
or 'heterosexual,' to the degree that it differs from a plot of the procreative
or dynastic (as each woman's desire seems at least for the moment to do),
may mark also the possibility of an anachronistic gap.[11]

In trying to make sense of these discursive transitions, I have most
before me the model of recent work on Emily Dickinson, and in particular
Paula Bennett's discussion of the relation between Dickinson's heteroerotic
and her homoerotic poetics in *My Life a Loaded Gun* and *Emily Dickinson:
Woman Poet*.[12] Briefly, Bennett's accomplishment is to have done justice,
for the somewhat later, New England figure of Dickinson, to a complex
range of intense female homosocial bonds, including genitally figured ones,
in her life and writing – without denying the salience and power of the
male-directed eros and expectation that also sound there; without palliat-
ing the tensions acted out between the two; and at the same time without
imposing an anachronistically reified view of the feminist consistency of
these tensions. For instance, the all-too-available rhetoric of the polymor-
phous, of a utopian bisexual erotic pluralism, has little place in Bennett's
account. But neither does she romanticize the female-female bonds whose
excitement, perturbation, and pain – including the pain of power struggle,
of betrayal, of rejection – she shows to form so much of the primary level
of Dickinson's emotional life. What her demanding account does enable
her to do, however, is to offer a model for understanding the bedrock,
quotidian, sometimes very sexually fraught female homosocial networks
in relation to the more visible and spectacularized, more narratable, but
less intimate, heterosexual plots of pre-twentieth-century Anglo-American
culture.

I see this work on Dickinson as exemplary for understandings of such
other, culturally central, homosocially embedded women authors as Austen
and, for example, the Brontës. (Surely there are important generalizations
yet to be made about the attachments of sisters, perhaps of any siblings,

who live together as adults.) But as I have suggested, the first range of questions yet to be asked properly in this context concerns the emergence and cultural entailments of 'sexual identity' itself during this period of the incipience of 'sexual identity' in its (still incompletely interrogated) modern senses. Indeed, one of the motives for this project is to denaturalize any presumptive understanding of the relation of 'hetero' to 'homo' as modern sexual identities – the presumption, for instance, of their symmetry, their mutual impermeability, or even of their both functioning as 'sexual identities' in the same sense; the presumption, as well, that 'hetero' and 'homo,' even with the possible addition of 'bi,' do efficiently and additively divide up the universe of sexual orientation. It seems likely to me that in Austen's time, *as in our own*, the specification of any distinct 'sexual identity' magnetized and reoriented in new ways the heterogeneous erotic and epistemological energies of everyone in its social vicinity, without at the same time either adequating or descriptively exhausting those energies.

One 'sexual identity' that did exist as such in Austen's time, already bringing a specific genital practice into dense compaction with issues of consciousness, truth, pedagogy, and confession, was that of the onanist. Among the sexual dimensions overridden within the past century by the world-historical homo/hetero cleavage is the one that discriminates, in the first place, the autoerotic and the alloerotic. Its history has been illuminated by recent researches of a number of scholars.[13] According to their accounts, the European phobia over masturbation came early in the 'sexualizing' process described by Foucault, beginning around 1700 with publication of *Onania*, and spreading virulently after the 1750s. Although originally applied with a relative impartiality to both sexes, anti-onanist discourse seems to have bifurcated in the nineteenth century, and the systems of surveillance and the rhetorics of 'confession' for the two genders contributed to the emergence of disparate regulatory categories and techniques, even regulatory worlds. According to Ed Cohen, for example, anxiety about boys' masturbation motivated mechanisms of school discipline and surveillance that were to contribute so much to the late-nineteenth-century emergence of a widespread, class-inflected male homosexual identity and hence to the modern crisis of male homo/heterosexual definition. On the other hand, anxiety about girls' and women's masturbation contributed more to the emergence of gynecology, through an accumulated expertise in and demand for genital surgery; of such identities as that of the hysteric; and of such confession-inducing disciplinary discourses as psychoanalysis.

Far from there persisting a minority identity of 'the masturbator' today, of course, autoeroticism per se in the twentieth century has been conclusively subsumed under that normalizing developmental model, differently but perhaps equally demeaning, according to which it represents a relatively innocuous way station on the road to a 'full,' that is, alloerotic, adult genitality defined almost exclusively by gender of object choice. As Foucault and others have noted, a lush plurality of (proscribed and regulated) sexual identities had developed by the end of the nineteenth century: even the most canonical late-Victorian art and literature are full of sadomasochistic, pederastic and pedophilic, necrophilic, as well as autoerotic images and preoccupations; while Foucault mentions the hysterical woman and the masturbating child along with 'entomologized' sexological categories such as zoophiles, zooerasts, auto-monosexualists, and gynecomasts, as typifying the new sexual taxonomies, the sexual *'specification of individuals,'* that he sees as inaugurating the twentieth-century regime of sexuality.[14] Although Foucault is concerned to demonstrate our own continuity with nineteenth-century sexual discourse, however (appealing to his readers as 'we "Other Victorians"'),[15] it makes a yet-to-be-explored difference that the Victorian multiplication of sexual species has today all but boiled down to a single, bare – and moreover fiercely invidious – dichotomy. Most of us now correctly understand a question about our 'sexual orientation' to be a demand that we classify ourselves as a heterosexual or a homosexual, regardless of whether we may or may not individually be able or willing to perform that blank, binarized act of category assignment. We also understand that the two available categories are not symmetrically but hierarchically constituted in relation to each other. The identity of the masturbator was only one of the sexual identities subsumed, erased, or overridden in this triumph of the heterosexist homo/hetero calculus. But I want to argue here that the status of the masturbator among these many identities was uniquely formative. I would suggest that as one of the very earliest embodiments of 'sexual identity' in the period of the progressive epistemological overloading of sexuality, the masturbator may have been at the cynosural center of a remapping of individual identity, will, attention, and privacy along modern lines that the reign of 'sexuality,' and its generic concomitant in the novel and in novelistic point of view, now lead us to take for granted. It is of more than chronological import if the (lost) identity of the masturbator was the proto-form of modern sexual identity itself.

Thus it seems likely that in our reimaginings of the history of sexuality 'as' (we vainly imagine) 'we know it,' through readings of classic texts, the dropping out of sight of the autoerotic term is also part of what falsely naturalizes the heterosexist imposition of these books, disguising both the rich, conflictual erotic complication of a homoerotic matrix not yet crystallized in terms of 'sexual identity' and the violence of heterosexist definition finally carved out of these plots. I am taking *Sense and Sensibility* as my example here because of its odd position, at once germinal and abjected, in the Austen canon and hence in 'the history of the novel'; and because its erotic axis is most obviously the unwavering but difficult love of a woman, Elinor Dashwood, for a woman, Marianne Dashwood. I don't think we can bring this desire into clear focus until we also see how Marianne's erotic identity, in turn, is not in the first place exactly either a same-sex-loving one or a cross-sex-loving one (though she loves both women and men), but rather the one that today no longer exists *as* an identity: that of the masturbating girl.

Reading the bedroom scenes of *Sense and Sensibility*, I find I have lodged in my mind a bedroom scene from another document, a narrative structured as a case history of 'Onanism and Nervous Disorders in Two Little Girls' and dated '1881':

> Sometimes [X . . .'s] face is flushed and she has a roving eye; at others she is pale and listless. Often she cannot keep still, pacing up and down the bedroom, or balancing on one foot after the other . . . During these bouts X . . . is incapable of anything: reading, conversation, games, are equally odious. All at once her expression becomes cynical, her excitement mounts. X . . . is overcome by the desire to do it, she tries not to or someone tries to stop her. Her only dominating thought is to succeed. Her eyes dart in all directions, her lips never stop twitching, her nostrils flare! Later, she calms down and is herself again. 'If only I had never been born,' she says to her little sister, 'we would not have been a disgrace to the family!' And Y . . . replies: 'Why did you teach me all these horrors then?' Upset by the reproach, X . . . says: 'If someone would only kill me! What joy. I could die without committing suicide.'[16]

If what defines 'sexual identity' is the impaction of epistemological issues around the core of a particular genital possibility, then the compulsive attention paid by antionanist discourse to disorders of attention makes it a suitable point of inauguration for modern sexuality. Marianne Dashwood, though highly intelligent, exhibits the classic consciousness-symptoms noted by Samuel Tissot in 1758, including 'the impairment of memory

and the senses,' 'inability to confine the attention,' and 'an air of distrac-
tion, embarrassment and stupidity.'[17] A surprising amount of the narrative
tension of *Sense and Sensibility* comes from the bent bow of the absentation
of Marianne's attention from wherever she is. 'Great,' at one characteristic
moment, 'was the perturbation of her spirits and her impatience to be gone'
(*SS*, p. 174); once out on the urban scene, on the other hand,

> her eyes were in constant inquiry; and in whatever shop the party
> were engaged, her mind was equally abstracted from every thing
> actually before them, from all that interested and occupied the
> others. Restless and dissatisfied every where . . . she received no
> pleasure from any thing; was only impatient to be at home again . . .
> (*SS*, p. 180)

Yet when at home, her 'agitation increased as the evening drew on. She could
scarcely eat any dinner, and when they afterwards returned to the drawing
room, seemed anxiously listening to the sound of every carriage' (p. 177).

Marianne incarnates physical as well as perceptual irritability, to both
pleasurable and painful effect. Addicted to 'rapidity' (p. 75) and 'requiring
at once solitude and continual change of place' (p. 193), she responds to
anything more sedentary with the characteristic ejaculation: 'I could hardly
keep my seat' (p. 51). Sitting is the most painful and exciting thing for
her. Her impatience keeps her 'moving from one chair to another' (p. 266)
or '[getting] up, and walk[ing] about the room' (p. 269). At the happiest
moments, she frankly pursues the locomotor pleasures of her own body,
'running with all possible speed down the steep side of the hill' (p.74) (and
spraining her ankle in a tumble), eager for 'the delight of a gallop' when
Willoughby offers her a horse (p. 88). To quote again from the document
dated 1881,

> In addition to the practices already cited, X . . . provoked the
> voluptuous spasm by rubbing herself on the angles of furniture, by
> pressing her thighs together, or rocking backwards and forwards
> on a chair. Out walking she would begin to limp in an odd way as if
> she were lopsided, or kept lifting one of her feet. At other times she
> took little steps, walked quickly, or turned abruptly left . . . If she
> saw some shrub she straddled it and rubbed herself back and forth
> . . . She pretended to fall or stumble over something in order to rub
> against it. ('O', pp. 26–7)

Exactly Marianne's overresponsiveness to her tender 'seat' as a node of delight, resistance, and surrender – and its crucial position, as well, between the homosocial and heterosocial avidities of the plot – is harnessed when Elinor manipulates Marianne into rejecting Willoughby's gift of the horse: 'Elinor thought it wisest to touch that point no more . . . Opposition on so tender a subject would only attach her the more to her own opinion. But by an appeal to her affection for her mother . . . Marianne was shortly subdued' (p. 89).

The vision of a certain autoerotic closure, absentation, self-sufficiency in Marianne is radiantly attractive to almost everyone, female and male, who views her; at the same time, the same autoerotic inaccessibility is legible to them through contemporaneous discourses as a horrifying staging of auto-consumption. As was typical until the end of the nineteenth century, Marianne's autoeroticism is not defined in opposition to her alloerotic bonds, whether with men or with women. Rather, it signifies an excess of sexuality altogether, an excess dangerous to others but chiefly to herself: the chastening illness that ultimately wastes her physical substance is both the image and the punishment of the 'distracted' sexuality that, continually 'forgetting itself,' threatens, in her person, to subvert the novel's boundaries between the public and the private.

More from the manuscript dated 1881:

The 19th [September]. Third cauterisation of little Y. . . who sobs and vociferates.

In the days that followed Y . . . fought successfully against temptation. She became a child again, playing with her doll, amusing herself and laughing gayly. She begs to have her hands tied each time she is not sure of herself . . . Often she is seen to make an effort at control. Nonetheless she does it two or three times every twenty-four hours . . . But X . . . more and more drops all pretense of modesty. One night she succeeds in rubbing herself till the blood comes on the straps that bind her. Another time, caught in the act by the governess and unable to satisfy herself, she has one of her terrible fits of rage, during which she yells: 'I want to, oh how I want to! You can't understand, Mademoiselle, how I want to do it!' Her memory begins to fail. She can no longer keep up with lessons. She has hallucinations all the time.

The 23rd, she repeats: 'I deserve to be burnt and I will be. I will be brave during the operation, I won't cry.' From ten at night until

six in the morning, she has a terrible attack, falling several times
into a swoon that lasted about a quarter of an hour. At times she had
visual hallucinations. At other times she became delirious, wild eyed,
saying: 'Turn the page, who is hitting me, etc.'

The 25th I apply a hot point to X's clitoris. She submits to the
operation without wincing, and for twenty-four hours after the
operation she is perfectly good. But then she returns with renewed
frenzy to her old habits. ('O', p. 33)

As undisciplined as Marianne Dashwood's 'abstracted' attention is,
the farouche, absent presence of this figure compellingly reorganizes the
attention of others: Elinor's rapt attention to her, to begin with, but also,
through Elinor's, the reader's. *Sense and Sensibility* is unusual among
Austen novels not for the (fair but unrigorous) consistency with which
its narrative point of view is routed through a single character, Elinor,
but rather for the undeviating consistency with which Elinor's regard
in turn is vectored in the direction of her beloved. Elinor's self-imposed
obligation to offer social countenance to the restless, insulting, magnetic,
and dangerous abstraction of her sister constitutes most of the plot of the
novel.

It constitutes more than plot, in fact; it creates both the consciousness
and the privacy of the novel. The projectile of surveillance, epistemological
demand, and remediation that both desire and 'responsibility' constrain
Elinor to level at Marianne, immobilized or turned back on herself by the
always-newly-summoned-up delicacy of her refusal to press Marianne
toward confession, make an internal space – internal, that is, to Elinor,
hence to the reader hovering somewhere behind her eyes – from which
there is no escape but more silent watching. About the engagement she is
said to assume to exist between Marianne and Willoughby, for example,
her 'wonder'

was engrossed by the extraordinary silence of her sister and
Willoughby on the subject . . . Why they should not openly
acknowledge to her mother and herself, what their constant
behaviour to each other declared to have taken place, Elinor could
not imagine.

. . . For this strange kind of secrecy maintained by them relative
to their engagement, which in fact concealed nothing at all, she
could not account; and it was so wholly contradictory to their

general opinions and practice, that a doubt sometimes entered her mind of their being really engaged, and this doubt was enough to prevent her making any enquiry of Marianne. (SS, p. 100)

To Marianne, on the other hand, the question of an engagement seems simply not to have arisen.

The insulation of Marianne from Elinor's own unhappiness, when Elinor is unhappy; the buffering of Marianne's impulsiveness, and the absorption or, where that is impossible, coverture of her terrible sufferings; the constant, reparative concealment of Marianne's elopements of attention from their present company: these activities hollow out a subjectivity for Elinor and the novel that might best be described in the 1980s jargon of codependency, were not the pathologizing stigma of that term belied by the fact that, at least as far as this novel is concerned, the codependent subjectivity simply *is subjectivity*. Even Elinor's heterosexual plot with Edward Ferrars merely divides her remedial solicitude (that distinctive amalgam of 'tenderness, pity, approbation, censure, and doubt' [p. 129]) between the sister who remains her first concern, and a second sufferer from *mauvaise honte*, the telltale 'embarrassment,' 'settled' 'absence of mind' (p. 123), unsocializable shyness, 'want of spirits, of openness, and of consistency,' 'the same fettered inclination, the same inevitable necessity of temporizing with his mother' (p. 126), and a 'desponding turn of mind' (p. 128), all consequent on his own servitude to an erotic habit formed in the idleness and isolation of an improperly supervised youth.

The codependency model is the less anachronistic as Marianne's and Edward's disorders share with the pre-twentieth-century version of masturbation the property of being structured as addictions. (Here, of course, I'm inviting a meditation on the history of the term 'self-abuse,' which referred to masturbation from the eighteenth century until very recently – when it's come, perhaps by analogy to 'child abuse,' to refer to battering or mutilation of oneself. Where that older sense of 'abuse' has resurfaced, on the other hand, is in the also very recent coinage 'substance abuse.') Back to 1881:

The afternoon of the 14th of September X . . . is in a terribly overexcited state. She walks about restlessly, grinding her teeth . . . There is foam on her lips, she gasps, repeating, 'I don't want to, I don't want to, I can't stop myself, I must do it! Stop me, hold my hands, tie my feet!' A few moments later she falls into a state of prostration, becomes sweet and gentle, begging to be given another chance. 'I know I'm killing myself,' she says. 'Save me.' ('O', p. 30)

Although *the addict*, as a medicalized personal identity, was (as Virginia Berridge and Griffith Edwards demonstrate in *Opium and the People*) another product of the latter part of the nineteenth century, the hypostatization of the notion of 'will' that would soon give rise to the 'addict' identity, and that by the late twentieth century would leave no issue of voluntarity untinged by the concept of addiction, is already in place in *Sense and Sensibility*.[18] A concept of addiction involves understanding something called 'the will' as a muscle that can strengthen with exercise or atrophy with disuse; the particular muscle on which 'will' is modeled in this novel is a sphincter, which, when properly toned, defines an internal space of private identity by holding some kinds of material inside, even while guarding against the admission of others. Marianne's unpracticed muscle lets her privacy dribble away, giving her 'neither courage to speak of, nor fortitude to conceal' (*SS*, p. 333) the anguish she experiences. By contrast, in the moment of Elinor's profoundest happiness, when Marianne is restored from a grave illness, Elinor's well-exercised muscle guarantees that what expands with her joy is the private space that, constituting her self, constitutes it also as the space of narrative self-reflection (not to say hoarding):

> Elinor could not be cheerful. Her joy was of a different kind, and led to anything rather than to gaiety. Marianne restored to life, health, friends, and to her doating mother, was an idea to fill her heart with sensations of exquisite comfort, and expand it in fervent gratitude; – but it led to no outward demonstrations of joy, no words, no smiles. All within Elinor's breast was satisfaction, silent and strong.
> (*SS*, p. 310)

Such an apparently generalizable ideal of individual integrity, the unitary self-containment of the strong, silent type, can never be stable, of course. Elinor has constructed herself in this way around an original lack: the absentation of her sister, and perhaps in the first place the withholding from herself of the love of their mother, whom she then compulsively unites with Marianne, the favorite, in the love-drenched tableaux of her imagination. In the inappropriately pathologizing but descriptively acute language of self-help, Marianne's addiction has mobilized in her sister a discipline that, posed as against addiction, nonetheless also is one. Elinor's pupils, those less tractable sphincters of the soul, won't close against the hapless hemorrhaging of her visual attention-flow toward Marianne; it is this, indeed, that renders her consciousness, in turn, habitable, inviting, and formative to readers as 'point of view.'

But that hypostatization of 'will' had always anyway contained the potential for the infinite regress enacted in the uncircumscribable twenti-eth-century epidemic of addiction attribution: the degenerative problem of where, if not in some further compulsion, one looks for the will *to* will, as when Marianne, comparing herself with the more continent Elinor,

> felt all the force of that comparison, but not as her sister had hoped, to urge her to exertion now; she felt it with all the pain of continual self-reproach, regretted most bitterly that she had never exerted herself before; but it brought only the torture of penitence, without the hope of amendment. Her mind was so much weakened that she still fancied present exertion impossible, and therefore it only dispirited her the more. (*SS*, p. 270)

In addition, the concept of addiction involves a degenerative percep-tual narrative of progressively deadened receptiveness to a stimulus that therefore requires to be steadily increased – as when Marianne's and her mother's 'agony of grief' over the death of the father, at first overpowering, was then 'voluntarily renewed, was sought for, was created again and again' (p. 42). Paradoxically afflicted, as Marianne is, by both hyperesthesia and an emboldening and addiction-producing absent-mindedness ('an heart hardened against [her friends'] merits, and a temper irritated by their very attention' [p. 337]), the species of the masturbating girl was described by Augustus Kinsley Gardner in 1860 as one

> in whom the least impression is redoubled like that of a 'tam-tam,' [yet who seeks] for emotions still more violent and more varied. It is this necessity which nothing can appease, which took the Roman women to the spectacles where men were devoured by ferocious beasts . . . It is the emptiness of an unquiet and sombre soul seeking some activity, which clings to the slightest incident of life, to elicit from it some emotion which forever escapes; in short, it is the deception and disgust of existence.[19]

The subjectivity hollowed out by *Sense and Sensibility*, then, and made available *as* subjectivity for heterosexual expropriation, is not Marianne's but Elinor's; the novel's achievement of a modern psychological interiority fit for the heterosexual romance plot is created for Elinor through her completely one-directional visual fixation on her sister's specularized, desired, envied, and punished autoeroticism. This also offers, however, a useful model for the chains of reader relations constructed by the punishing, girl-centered moral pedagogy and erotics of Austen's novels more generally. Austen criticism is notable mostly, not just for its timidity and banality, but for its unresting exaction of the spectacle of a Girl Being Taught a Lesson – for the vengefulness it vents on the heroines whom it purports to love, and whom, perhaps, it does. Thus Tony Tanner, the ultimate normal and normalizing reader of Austen, structures sentence after sentence: 'Emma . . . *has to be tutored* . . . into correct vision and responsible speech. Anne Elliot *has to move*, painfully, from an excessive prudence.'[20] 'Some Jane Austen heroines *have to learn* their true "duties." They all *have to find* their proper homes' (*JA*, p. 33). Catherine 'quite literally is in danger of perverting reality, and one of the things she *has to learn* is to break out of quotations' (*JA*, pp. 44–5); she '*has to be disabused* of her naive and foolish "Gothic" expectations' (*JA*, p. 48). '[Elizabeth and Darcy] *have to learn to see* that their novel is more properly called . . .' (*JA*, p. 105). A lot of Austen criticism sounds hilariously like the leering school prospectuses or governess manifestoes brandished like so many birch rods in Victorian sadomasochistic pornography. Thus Jane Nardin:

> The discipline that helps create the moral adult need not necessarily be administered in early childhood. Frequently, as we have seen, it is not – for its absence is useful in helping to create the problems with which the novel deals. But if adequate discipline is lacking in childhood, it must be supplied later, and this happens only when the character learns 'the lessons of affliction' (*Mansfield Park*, p. 459). Only after immaturity, selfishness, and excessive self-confidence have produced error, trouble, and real suffering, can the adult begin to teach himself or herself the habits of criticism and self-control which should have been inculcated in childhood.[21]

How can it have taken this long to see that when Colonel Brandon and Marianne finally get together, their first granddaughter will be Lesbia Brandon?

Even readings of Austen that are not so frankly repressive have tended to be structured by what Foucault calls 'the repressive hypothesis' – especially so, indeed, to the degree that their project is avowedly *anti*repressive. And these antirepressive readings have their own way of re-creating the spectacle of the Girl Being Taught a Lesson. Call her, in this case, 'Jane Austen.' The sight to be relished here is, as in psychoanalysis, the forcible exaction from her manifest text of what can only be the barest confession of a self-pleasuring sexuality, a disorder or subversion, seeping out at the edges of a policial conservatism always presumed and therefore always available for violation. That virginal figure 'Jane Austen,' in these narratives, is herself the punishable girl who 'has to learn,' 'has to be tutored' – in truths with which, though derived from a reading of Austen, the figure of 'Jane Austen' can no more be credited than can, for their lessons, the figures 'Marianne,' 'Emma,' or, shall we say, 'Dora' or 'Anna O.'

It is partly to interrupt this seemingly interminable scene of punitive/pedagogical reading, interminably structured as it is by the concept of repression, that I want to make available the sense of an alternative, passionate sexual ecology – one fully available to Austen for her exciting, productive, and deliberate use, in a way it no longer is to us.

That is to say, it is no longer available to us *as passion*; even as its cynosural figure, the masturbating girl, is no longer visible as possessing a sexual identity capable of redefining and reorganizing her surround. We inherit it only in the residual forms of perception itself, of subjectivity itself, of institution itself. The last time I taught *Sense and Sensibility*, I handed out to my graduate class copies of some pages from the 1981 'Polysexuality' issue of *Semiotext(e)*, pages that reproduce without historical annotation what appears to be a late-nineteenth-century medical case history in French, from which I have also been quoting here. I handed it out then for reasons no more transparent than those that have induced me to quote from it here – beyond the true but inadequate notation that even eight years after reading it, my memory of the piece wouldn't let up its pressure on the gaze I was capable of leveling at the Austen novel. I hadn't even the new historicists' positivist alibi for perpetuating and disseminating the shock of the violent narratives in which they trade: 'Deal,' don't they seem tacitly but moralistically to enjoin, 'deal with your own terror, your own arousal, your disavowals, in your own way, on your own time, in your own [thereby reconstituted as invisible] privacy; it's not our responsibility, because *these awful things are real*.' Surely I did want to spread around to a group of other readers, as if that would ground or diffuse it, the inadmissibly, inabsorbably complex shock of this document. But the pretext of the real was austerely withheld by the informal, perhaps only superficially sensationalistic *Semiotext(e)* format, which refused to proffer the legitimating scholarly apparatus that would give any reader the assurance of 'knowing' whether the original of this document was to be looked for in an actual nineteenth-century psychiatric archive or, alternatively and every bit as credibly, in a manuscript of pornographic fiction dating from any time – any time including the present – in the intervening century. Certainly plenty of the other pieces in that issue of *Semiotext(e)* are, whatever else they are, freshly minted and joltingly potent pornography; just as certainly, nothing in the '1881' document exceeds in any detail the known practices of late-nineteenth-century medicine. And wasn't that part of the shock? – the total plausibility either way of the same masturbatory narrative, the same pruriently cool clinical gaze at it and violating hands and instruments on it, even (one might add) further along the chain, the same assimilability of it to the pseudo-distantiating relish of sophisticated contemporary projects of critique. Toward the site of the absent, distracted, and embarrassed attention of the masturbatory subject, the directing of a less accountable flood of discursive attention has continued. What is most astonishing is its continuing entirely unabated by the dissolution of its object, the sexual identity of 'the masturbator' herself.

Through the frame of 1881/1981 it becomes easier to see how most of the love story of *Sense and Sensibility*, no simple one, has been rendered all but invisible to most readers, leaving a dryly static tableau of discrete moralized portraits, poised antitheses, and exemplary, deplorable, or regrettably necessary punishments, in an ascetic heterosexualizing context.[22] This tableau is what we now know as 'Jane Austen'; fossilized residue of the now subtracted autoerotic spectacle, 'Jane Austen' is the name whose uncanny fit with the phrase 'masturbating girl' today makes a *ne plus ultra* of the incongruous.

This history of impoverished 'Jane Austen' readings is not the result of a failure by readers to 'contextualize historically': a new historicizing point that you can't understand *Sense and Sensibility* without entering into the alterity of a bygone masturbation phobia is hardly the one I am making. What alterity? I am more struck by how profoundly, how destructively twentieth-century readings are already shaped by the discourse of masturbation and its sequelae: *more* destructively than the novel is, even though onanism per se, and the phobia against it, are living issues in the novel as they no longer are today.

We can be the less surprised by the congruence as we see masturbation and the relations surrounding it as the proto-form of any modern 'sexual identity'; thus as lending their structure to many vantages of subjectivity that have survived the definitional atrophy of the masturbator as an identity: pedagogic surveillance, as we have mentioned, homo/hetero divides, psychiatry, psychoanalysis, gynecology. The interpretive habits that make it so hard to register the erotics of *Sense and Sensibility* are deeply and familiarly encoded in the therapeutic or mock-therapeutic rhetoric of the '1881' document. They involve the immobilizing framing of an isolated sexual subject (a subject, that is, whose isolation is decreed by her identification with a nameable sexual identity); and her staging as a challenge or question addressed to an audience whose erotic invisibility is guaranteed by the same definitional stroke as their entitlement to intervene on the sexuality attributed to her. That it was this particular, apparently unitary and in some ways self-contained, autoerotic sexual identity that crystallized as the prototype of 'sexual identity' made that isolating embodiment of 'the sexual' easier, and made easier as well a radical naturalization and erotic dematerialization of narrative point of view concerning it.

And the dropping out of sight in this century of the masturbatory identity has only, it seems, given more the authority of self-evidence to the scientific, therapeutic, institutional, and narrative relations originally organized around it. *Sense and Sensibility* resists such 'progress' only insofar as we can succeed in making narratively palpable again, under the pressure of our own needs, the great and estranging force of the homoerotic longing magnetized in it by that radiant and inattentive presence – the female figure of the love that keeps forgetting its name.

The project sketched out in this chapter has evoked, not only the foreclosing and disavowing responses mentioned in its first paragraph, but help, encouragement, and fellowship as well. Some instances for which I am especially grateful: Michael Moon and Paula Bennett collaborated excitingly with me on the 'Muse of Masturbation' proposal and panel. Vernon Rosario and Ed Cohen were kind enough to share unpublished writing. Barbara Herrnstein Smith discussed Kant in a particularly helpful conversation. Jonathan Goldberg made invaluable suggestions on an earlier draft of the essay.

NOTES

1. Roger Kimball, *Tenured Radicals: How Politics Has Corrupted Our Higher Education* (New York: HarperCollins, 1990), pp. 145–6.

2. See, for a few examples of the phrase's career in journalism, Roger Rosenblatt, 'The Universities: A Bitter Attack . . .,' review of *Tenured Radicals*, by Kimball, *New York Times Book Review*, 22 April 1990, pp. 3, 36; letters to the editor in the *New York Times Book Review*, 20 May 1990, p. 54, including one from Catharine R. Stimpson disputing the evidential status of the phrase; and Richard Bernstein, 'The Rising Hegemony of the Politically Correct: America's Fashionable Orthodoxy,' *New York Times*, 28 October 1990, sec. 4, pp. 1, 4.

3. Jane E. Brody, 'Personal Health,' *New York Times*, 4 November 1987.

4. Rosenblatt, 'The Universities,' p. 3.

5. My book *Epistemology of the Closet* (Berkeley: University of California Press, 1990) makes this argument at length in relation to the late-nineteenth-century crisis of male homo/heterosexual definition.

6. See John Mullan, *Sentiment and Sociability: The Language of Feeling in the Eighteenth Century* (New York: Oxford University Press, 1988), esp. pp. 201–40.

7. See Neil Hertz, *The End of the Line* (New York: Columbia University Press, 1985), pp. 148–9.

8. Vernon A. Rosario II, 'The 19th-Century Medical Politics of Self-Defilement and Seminal Economy,' presented at the Centre for Literary and Cultural Studies, Harvard University, 'Nationalisms and Sexualities' conference, June 1989, p. 18.

9. Jane Austen, *Sense and Sensibility* (Harmondsworth: Penguin Books, 1967), p. 193; hereafter abbreviated as *SS*.

10. This is (in relation to women) the argument of, most influentially, Lilian Faderman in *Surpassing the Love of Men: Romantic Friendship and Love between Women from the Renaissance to the Present* (New York: William Morrow, 1981) and Carroll Smith-Rosenberg in 'The Female World of Love and Ritual: Relations between Women in Nineteenth-Century America,' *Signs* 1 (Autumn 1975): 1–29. A recently discovered journal, published as *I Know My Own Heart: The Diaries of Anne Lister (1791–1840)*, ed. Helena Whitbread (London: Virago, 1988), suggests that revisions of this narrative may, however, be necessary. It is the diary (for 1817–23) of a young, cultured, religious, socially conservative, self-aware, landowning rural Englishwoman – an almost archetypal Jane Austen heroine – who formed her sense of self around the pursuit and enjoyment of genital contact and short- and long-term intimacies with other women of various classes.

11. See Michel Foucault, *The History of Sexuality: An Introduction*, vol. 1 of *The History of Sexuality*, trans. Robert Hurley (New York: Random House, 1978).

12. See Paula Bennett, *My Life a Loaded Gun: Female Creativity and Feminist Poetics* (Boston: Beacon Press, 1986), pp. 13–94; *Emily Dickinson: Woman Poet* (Iowa City: University of Iowa Press, 1990).

13. Useful historical work touching on masturbation and masturbation phobia includes G. J. Barker-Benfield, *The Horrors of the Half-Known Life: Male Attitudes Toward Women and Sexuality in Nineteenth-Century America* (New York: Harper and

Row, 1976); Ed Cohen, *Talk on the Wilde Side* (New York: Routledge, 1993); John
D'Emilio and Estelle B. Freedman, *Intimate Matters: A History of Sexuality in
America* (New York: Harper and Row, 1988); E. H. Hare, 'Masturbatory Insanity:
The History of an Idea,' *Journal of the Mental Sciences* 108 (1962): 1–25; Robert
H. MacDonald, 'The Frightful Consequences of Onanism: Notes on the History
of a Delusion,' *Journal of the History of Ideas* 28 (1967): 423–31; John Money,
*The Destroying Angel: Sex, Fitness and Food in the Legacy of Degeneracy Theory,
Graham Crackers, Kellogg's Corn Flakes and the American Health History* (Buffalo:
Prometheus, 1985); George L. Mosse, *Nationalism and Sexuality: Respectability and
Abnormal Sexuality in Modern Europe* (New York: Fertig, 1985); Robert P. Neuman,
'Masturbation, Madness, and the Modern Concept of Childhood and Adolescence,'
Journal of Social History 8 (1975): 1–22; Elaine Showalter, *The Female Malady:
Women, Madness, and English Culture, 1830–1980* (New York: Pantheon Books,
1985); Carroll Smith-Rosenberg, *Disorderly Conduct: Visions of Gender in Victorian
America* (Oxford: Oxford University Press, 1986); and Jean Stengers and Anne van
Neck, *Histoire d'une grande peur: la masturbation* (Brussels: Editions de l'Université
de Bruxelles, 1984).

14. Foucault, *History of Sexuality*, vol. 1, pp. 105 and 43.

15. Ibid. p. 1.

16. Démétrius Zambaco, 'Onanism and Nervous Disorders in Two Little Girls,' trans.
Catherine Duncan, *Semiotext(e)* ('Polysexuality') (1981): 30; hereafter abbreviated
as 'O'. The letters standing in place of the girls' names are followed by ellipses in the
original; other ellipses are mine. In quoting from this piece I have silently corrected
some obvious typographical errors; since this issue of *Semiotext(e)* is printed entirely
in capital letters, and with commas and periods of indistinguishable shape, I have
also had to make some guesses about sentence division and punctuation. Zambaco's
case was later published, under less equivocal scholarly auspices, in *A Dark Science:
Women, Sexuality, and Psychiatry in the Nineteenth Century*, trans. Jeffrey Mousaieff
Masson and Marianne Loring, ed. Masson (New York: Farrar, Straus and Giroux,
1986), pp. 61–89.

17. Quoted and discussed in Cohen, *Talk on the Wilde Side*, pp. 89–90.

18. See Virginia Berridge and Griffith Edwards, *Opium and the People: Opiate Use in
Nineteenth Century England*, 2nd edn (New Haven: Yale University Press, 1987). For
more on the epistemology of addiction, codependency, and addiction attribution, see
my 'Epidemics of the Will' in *Tendencies* (London: Routledge, 1994), pp. 130–42.

19. Augustus Kinsley Gardner, 'Physical Decline of American Women' (1860), quoted in
Barker-Benfield, *Horrors of the Half-Known Life*, pp. 273–4.

20. Tony Tanner, *Jane Austen* (Cambridge, MA: Harvard University Press, 1986), p. 6;
hereafter abbreviated as *JA*; emphasis, in each case, added.

21. Nardin is remarkably unworried about any possible excess of severity: 'In this
group of characters [in *Mansfield Park*], lack of discipline has the expected effect,
while excessive discipline, though it causes suffering and creates some problems
for Fanny and Susan Price, does indeed make them into hard-working, extremely
conscientious women. The timidity and self-doubt which characterize Fanny, and
which are a response to continual censure, seem a reasonable price to pay for the

strong conscience that even the unfair discipline she received has nurtured in her.' Jane Nardin, 'Children and Their Families,' in Janet Todd (ed.), *Jane Austen: New Perspectives*, Women and Literature, New Series, vol. 3 (New York: Holmes and Meier, 1983), pp. 73–87; p. 83. (Nardin is using *The Novels of Jane Austen*, ed. R. W. Chapman, 5 vols [London, 1966]).

22. As Mullan's *Sentiment and Sociability* suggests – and not only through the evocation of Austen's novel in its title – the eponymous antithesis 'sense' vs 'sensibility' is undone by, quite specifically, the way sensibility itself functions as a point of pivotal intersection, and potentially of mutual coverture, between alloerotic and autoerotic investments. Mullan would refer to these as 'sociability' vs 'isolation,' 'solipsism,' or 'hypochondria.' He ignores specifically antimasturbatory medical campaigns in his discussion of late-eighteenth-century medicine, but their relevance is clear enough in, for example, the discussion he does offer of the contemporaneous medical phenomenology of menstruation. 'Menstruation is represented as an irregularity which takes the guise of a regularity; it is especially likely to signify a precarious condition in the bodies of those for whom womanhood does not mean the life of the fertile, domesticated, married female. Those particularly at risk are the unmarried, the ageing, and the sexually precocious' (p. 226). 'The paradox, of course, is that to concentrate upon the palpitating, sensitized body of the woman caught in the difficult area between childhood and marriage is also to concede the dangers of this condition – those dangers which feature, in another form, in writings on hysteria' (p. 228). In *Epistemology of the Closet*, especially pp. 141–81, I discuss at some length the strange historical career of the epithets 'sentimentality' and 'sensibility,' in terms of the inflammatory and scapegoating mechanics of vicariation: of the coverture offered by these apparently static nouns to the most volatile readerly interchanges between the allo- and the auto-.

CHAPTER 12

Ali Smith, 'Green'

'Green' needs little introduction. It is what is there – what there is – on the page: 'No illusion. That's it.' '[W]e're not being deceived.' It is a piece of writing about a colour; in particular, about a colour as it appears in a painting by Cézanne, *L'Etang des Soeurs, Osny*, in the Courtauld Gallery in London. It is a piece of writing about looking at this painting, or rather a piece written by Smith two weeks after being in the gallery and looking at the painting with someone else – with you. (Unless you is another part of I.) It describes itself as a story, so we might say it is a story about what can happen when we look. We might also want to nail it as an example of ekphrasis, a form of rhetoric that involves speaking out persuasively for something absent, thereby making present in words what is not there. All this is true, but it does rather fix a piece of writing that is in flux, not least in relation to aboutness: 'But what it's really about, you say, is, is – .' Is it about everything in being about green? Does that make me sound a little green myself? 'I see you're flushed, you've coloured up.' Do you want to tell me something?

Smith's is a deceptively simple model to follow; deceptive in that its play with surfaces involves a balancing act. There is the possibility of knowledge, of being certain that we know what all this is about, but there is also the possibility of possibility, that the painting is 'about what's possible'. To do justice to this possibility may well require us to resist the conventional imperative to perform certainty in our prose, in order to keep knowledge at a distance. 'I nod like I know (though I don't).'

To begin to inhabit Smith's way of seeing we can do two things. Firstly, we can write processually, admitting into our account events of the time over which we have been with our object. Smith calls this a story, involving characters – you and I – and places – the gallery, the café – and memories. We might compare Smith's ekphrasis with T. J. Clark's *The Sight of Death*, a book which records as a journal repeated viewings of two paintings by Poussin. Clearly, Smith's turn to Rilke's Cézanne letters is an indication of an interest in the possibilities of what we might now call creative-critical art writing, beginning with an acknowledgement of both the always various time of our encounter, and a dramatisation of being with the artwork that is structured in part around the interplay of first and second person.

Secondly, we can experiment with different types and genres of writing. Smith moves here between narrative, varieties of personal reflection, biography, description, art history and quotations from the critical literature that surrounds her chosen object. We can feel the essaying of different ways of knowing, different ways of establishing aboutness. The piece started out life as a talk, and it has as part of its workings something of the impromptu performance, a calculatedly casual affair. To annotate the text would be to do it a disservice, so we've resisted the temptation. The references are easy enough to find should you need them. Better perhaps to read Smith's book-length creative-critical work, *Artful*, in which you and I perform a different sort of dance with the possibility of knowing.

Assuming the link remains active, Smith can be heard reading her talk at: <http://www.guardian.co.uk/artanddesign/interactive/2010/oct/31/ali-smith-cezanne-etang-soeurs> (last accessed 20 September 2013).

How can I be this old and still this green?

Imagine a picture, more than a hundred years old, in an empty gallery, the floor buffed, the cleaners come and gone, the room locked and darkened. The light outside falls, then comes up again, the place opens its doors. It's the moment before the people come and go in front of it all over again, the length of another day.

The story opens when I go to the gallery with you and we both see this painting at the same time. But first we go to the café downstairs and have coffee, because we are still pretty new to each other and are still being polite and social. Then we go upstairs and through a room full of people and into another busy room, where we both stop and stand quite still because the painting, which is all movement, is also about what still means.

It's a painting of a tree over water and some other trees and a path. But what it's really about, you say, is, is –

I look at you. I see you're flushed, you've coloured up.

It was made really fast, you say. (You are speaking quite fast.) Look, it's not finished here, you say, and here, it's been done really quickly again with the flat of the knife. Uh huh, I know a little about Cézanne, I say, I know how when he was an old man in Aix the village boys used to follow him and throw stones at him; I mean, look how modern it is, it's forty years ahead of itself. I say it like I know and like these things might be connected. You point out the reds and greys and umbers, the working of reflection, the flecks of green in the tree-trunks. You use a word I don't know and then you spell it: alizarin. You mention Giorgione; I nod like I know (though I don't). You say some things about post-impressionists using opposite colours in shadow, often a hot colour so that shadow becomes light. I say something about light and dark, point out stripes and diagonals. You point to the centre of the picture, how there's a space held in what looks like the opposite of space, in the fullness and movement of the leaves and the wind, there, look. I say ponderously how lacking in ponderousness it is. You nod. Then you say this:

Look at the way the artifice of it is the thing that makes it alive. Look at the way it's made out of the flatness of its own surface so we'll know we're not being deceived, so you'll know that it's just a painting. It takes away illusion. It makes it about what's possible.

No illusion. That's it. The surface opens itself. What I'm looking at ups and arrows right through me like someone just shot me with colour, with the truth about green. It's like being mugged by life, punched in the gut by umber green, red green, gold green, brown green, grey green. Who knew that green was a present tense, that greenness could moss all the pasts and the futures, cover all the words that ever believed themselves carved in stone and eat them into air? The gallery falls away, leaves nothing but leaves and striplings in a landscape where the curve of the tree is the curve of the eye is the curve of the surface of the piece of gristle inside the chest that happens to be keeping me breathing. Anyone care to snap me open?

I'll bend like a sapling, my skin will split and I'll see the red insides of me astonished into green. Tree enters air enters leaf enters light enters dark enters water enters paint enters every single person in this room whether they're looking or not, and nothing's not connected, nothing's not seen, nothing's not new, nothing's not ancient, nothing's just one thing alone. What just happened? It's like something's up with my eyes. I turn to see where I am, again. I'm here. You're still there, still beside me. You turn and regard me back. Your face is as bare as mine.

Wide open then, now, what will happen next.

* * *

On the walls of my parents' house there was a picture of a bluebell wood. It was about this size, in a white frame, and it had been bought ready in its frame from Woolworths; it had the price in shillings and pence in pencil on the back. It was of a path through a wood, the trees were tall and dark with a bank of bluebells at their roots, and the avenue they made stretched away into their own long darkness, a darkening tunnel, except for the point way in the distance at the centre and back of the picture where there was a tiny white oval of space, the place the woods ended, the place where the tops of the trees and the rise of the banks beneath them met light. As a very small child I would look at the picture and think to myself that this lozenge of white was what the soul looked like.

I had forgotten this about myself, and about that picture, until I stood in front of these Cézanne pictures behind me a couple of weeks ago and thought again about what space means in art.

This is what Rilke says in his Letters on Cézanne, written more than a hundred years ago, in October 1907.

'Today I went to see his pictures again; it's remarkable what a surrounding they create. Without looking at a particular one, standing in the middle between the two rooms, one feels their presence drawing together into a colossal reality. As if these colours could heal one of indecision once and for all. The good conscience of these reds, these blues, their simple truthfulness, it educates you; and if you stand among them as ready as possible, you get the impression they are doing something for you.'

Rilke was struck by how the Cézanne room in the Paris Salon made 'an immediate claim on one's attention', how the paintings made you part of them. As for the soul, Rilke says, he 'lays his apples on bed covers . . . and places a wine bottle among them or whatever he happens to find. And makes his "saints" out of such things; and forces them – forces them – to be beautiful.' Looking at the Cézannes in the Salon gives Rilke, in a matter of days, an insight into the revelation of things 'left alone with themselves', how Hiersein ist herrlich, being here is glorious, and how the whole here-ness of painting is: colour.

'. . . no one before him ever demonstrated so clearly the extent to which painting is something that takes place among the colours, and how one has to leave them completely alone, so that they can come to terms among themselves. Their mutual intercourse: this is the whole of painting. Whoever meddles, whoever arranges, whoever injects his human delibera-tion, his wit, his advocacy, his intellectual agility in any way, is already disturbing and clouding their activity . . . Everything . . . has become an affair that's settled among the colours themselves: a colour will come into its own in response to another, or assert itself, or recollect itself. Just as in the mouth of a dog various secretions will gather in anticipation . . . in the same way, intensifications and dilutions take place in the core of every colour, helping it to survive contact with others. In addition to this glandular activity within the intensity of colours, reflections . . . play the greatest role.'

Rilke is also fascinated by the fact that Cézanne, who loved the work of Baudelaire, knew and could recite off by heart Baudelaire's poem Une Charogne, Carrion, a poem in which Baudelaire, or the speaker, is having a conversation with his soul, telling it not to forget that day when, out on a walk on a fine summer morning, they – he and his soul – had turned a corner and come upon a piece of foul rotting carcass in the road, covered in flies, a 'horde of life', with a dog, a bitch, retreating and furious behind some rocks waiting for Baudelaire and his soul to move on so that she can come out and eat what's left of it. Here's a translation of a couple of the verses, one of which is a painterly motif in itself:

'Its forms were blurred as in a dream, nothing but a slowly shaping sketch forgotten on the canvas, which the artist must perfect from memory alone.'

Then he says to his soul:

'Yet you will come to resemble that offal, that loathsome corruption, O star of my eyes, O sun of my nature, my angel and my passion! Yes, you'll be that, queen of graces, after the last sacrament, when you will go down beneath the grass and unctuous flowers to grow green among the bones.'

In Cézanne motive and motif come physically and metaphysically together.

* * *

'With genius, you die! With money you live!' Cézanne's father, the banker, shouted at his recalcitrant artist son, a boy who, made to register with the law faculty in Aix, sat translating the law codes in his first exam into French couplets, and when his father made him work as book-keeper at the bank drew sketches and wrote rhyming couplets in the margins of the great ledgers.

'Yes, I remember him well!' an old painter said about the young Cézanne. 'He used to wear a red vest and always had enough money in his pocket to buy dinner for a friend.'

He is reassuringly human, washing his paintbrushes in the river Seine in the icy winter when the water at his studio was frozen.

In his time his art was laughable. The critics thought him a 'diseased eye'. The Salon refused him, repeatedly. 'They dress themselves up like a pack of lawyers!' he said. Manet asked him what he was preparing for the Salon, then, one year. 'A pot of shit,' he said.

'All women are cats and damned calculating,' he said. 'They might put their grappling hooks into me.' Where do you live? a friend asked him one day. 'I live a long way off, in a street,' he said.

A young man visited Aix, week after week, longing for a chance to speak to Cézanne. Cézanne ignored him, until he understood that the young man was a painter. When he did, he pointed at sunlight in water, a beam of light in a stream. Look at that! he said. 'How would you paint that?'

He liked, above all other music, the music of the hurdy-gurdy.

At fifty-five he had still not earned enough money, with his painting, to cover his paint and his brushes.

'You know,' he said to a man he was painting, 'the grandiose grows tiresome after a while. There are mountains like that, when you stand in front of them you shout In the name of God! But for every day a simple little hill does well enough.'

Here's a visit to his studio, recorded by his friend Duranty: 'He observed I was looking with some curiosity at a row of big druggists' pots set out on the floor, and bearing abbreviated Latin inscriptions: Jusqui. Aqu. Still. Ferug. Rib. Sulf. Cup. "That, sir, is my paint box. I can paint beautiful things while they with their fine colours make nothing but drugs. You see," he continued, "one can't paint without temperrrammmmennte." He dipped a spoon into one of the drug pots and withdrew it dripping with green paint. On the easel was a canvas on which a landscape was indicated by a few lines. To this he applied the paint, turning the spoon round and round, until, by a stretch of the imagination you could see a meadow on the canvas. I observed that the colour on his pictures was nearly half an inch thick, and formed miniature valleys and hills like a relief-map.'

His first collectors had to collect him from junk stores, rat-filled lofts, junk heaps, from people who valued the string they were tying the pictures up with more than they valued the pictures. His son, Paul, poked holes in his canvases, and this is what he said: 'Look! My son has opened up the windows and the chimneys.' His palette knife was double-edged. He was a notorious slasher-to-pieces of his own work. He burned and slashed and threw away his work with a fierceness that borders on joy. One day he threw a still life out of the window and it caught in the branches of a fruit tree. It hung there for weeks. Weeks later, he called his son. 'We must get the Apples down,' he said. 'I think I'll work some more on it.'

'Monet is only an eye,' he said. 'But good God, what an eye!'

Via artifice Cézanne hooks reality. Via the stripped-back musculature of painting he hooks the act of reflection, thought. Nothing is not connected. Nothing is not alive. The surface goes straight to the depth. By the dialogue of colours he hooks the human eye. And when Cézanne renews our eyes life gets its grappling hooks in us.

He died a hundred and four years ago this month, from a fever he caught from standing painting for hours in a field in a storm.

How can I be this old and still this green?

Here things grow green among the bones.

John Wilkinson, 'Imperfect Pitch'

Nowhere is the act of making, of creating, pursued more unflinchingly than in John Wilkinson's 'Imperfect Pitch', a piece whose form and preoccupations offer a counterpoint to those of Denise Riley's 'Lyric Selves', most obviously in the strategic interweaving of prose and poetry. Where Riley's mixing of modes offers a more immediately legible play on the relation of text and gloss – what she calls 'the poetic and the analytic' – Wilkinson summons a thick, sticky word mass, a gluey environment through which the reader trudges and in which verse appears as an immovable object. Wilkinson writes as if his life depended on it, and so it does – life, that is, conceived within and against words, whether they be given, summoned, found, rejected, loved or lost. There is a gothic drama in the writing, a tone influenced in part by psychoanalytic accounts of early childhood. Pronouns come and go, as do a host of other figures and noises off. At stake is the disputed possibility of the lyric voice and its always and necessarily imperfect pitch. The high seriousness of the making of a word object is enacted in the very texture of the writing, hence also in the reading experience. Wilkinson's 'strange and intimate, curious and simple' pitch engulfs us, insisting as it does that there is no place other than this, this place of words in which happens all our living and making.

How to follow this forbidding lead – other than read more of Wilkinson's exploratory criticism, especially the pieces gathered under the heading 'Poetics' in his book, *The Lyric Touch*? We should do this as a matter of course. We might begin with the apparently simple matter of counterpoint, the breaking into two of the single line of continuous critical prose. In particular, we might play with that dialogue of primary and secondary material, art and not-art, inherent in any criticism that uses quotations from literature. Peter Gizzi's 'Correspondences of the Book' engages in such play; the difference with Wilkinson is the mixing here of modes from a single source, albeit a source seeking in the moment – the moment of thinking; the moment of writing; the moment of writing thinking – to track and to articulate the very notion of singleness and of source. Suffice to say the notion cannot survive such scrutiny, and yet resists erasure.

Wilkinson's counterpointing of modes is of a piece with his concern for the pronoun, including his strong scepticism about the viability of the 'we' that litters this very headnote. Try experimenting with grammatical voice, and with the mixing of voices in a single essay.

Finally, and most ambitiously, we can follow 'Imperfect Pitch' in attempting to dramatise our relationship with the very material with which we make – with language, this stuff here, the stuff of literature and of criticism, of reading and of writing. Wilkinson's drama is informed by object-relations theory, hence we might do the same: essay a theoretically inflected performance in language of the matterful imperfections of living in and making with language.

John Wilkinson, 'Imperfect Pitch', in *Poets on Writing 1970–1991*, ed. Denise Riley (London: Macmillan, 1988), pp. 154–71.

Its arrival is in your bizarre aloneness, when a cranial firing returns of an instant, each resonates and is at once the first and last, at once it is all there is. The idle pun has a compass, the line of a song squeezes in what you know of love. And though this seems incessant, it is discontinuous, and cannot begin to amount to a you or a me; no damp peat, no source, no background, no relations.

But you cannot be independent. Consciousness is the cutter into the black. This black is black since saturated and enforming; down dabs the deckled blade, tiny round one synapse, and is so briefly registered. Against what? In its reflex jump, against the infinitesimally small space, which is space entire.

And they are maddening, these jumps. Who can live for the word, for the pregnant gap? Write them down, reduce them stroke by stroke. You clear them as they happen, but the page gets black with reverberations both constrained and indecipherable. Jammed together. So this is our assigned chaos, developing from *the* chaos.

Urgent therefore, to appoint an emissary. Despite yourself, form will be in your image, perhaps your image is no other than this. All these enforming events, great shifts impinging at the micro-level, as they accumulate and as they interconnect, start to seem vilely familiar, they stink of your constrained but ever-shifty body, reaccommodating. This image must be buried in non-user-serviceable connections, provisional bloodlines you cannot but follow. A repair man shakes his head on the hard shoulder. And how unsatisfactory the lump is, that excrescence of breath and shit, the increment!

With its departure, you have ceased to hear your thoughts. They do not arise and reverberate in the null, the zero of consciousness; that was a saving cut-out, a basic defence. From this point on, brain activity is absorbed, immediately. It becomes comfortable, tolerable, your thoughts accord to the game-show and to the DJ. The thoughts are no more than trivial thoughts passed through on your checking account, scanned, beside the till. Having no true boundary, you could feel content, held by ambient vacuousness.

And then? Why do you start to detach the work, why can't you bear its familiarity, but you hack it apart, you see the figure you cannot afford to recognise approach, your creature now returns with insistent, with maddening significance, throwing the connective tissue further out of kilter. It starts to appear monstrous, and you must fight it down while yes, admiring its perverse growth and throwing it what food you have. It has struggled clear, and in the struggle seems to become musclebound, or is the thin boy wriggling with a fistful from the narrow larder window, your truer representative? Whatever the lineaments, it has a repertoire of gesture which is well-knit, coherent, and unenformed. All its movements rise from an inner fund established as your motive.

It is familiar, like a mood. Moods are the minute-by-minute coherence by which you persist as more than a recipient and emmissionary; only when so split off are they apprehensible, both strange and intimate, curious and simple. Look after this creature and it gives you joy, turn back to your common tasks and you will fall to pieces.

Rolling the lines in the mouth, biting and relishing; what were these swollen and papery boluses of feeling, each expanded to a choking limit, swollen to the mouth's capacity, squeezed hard by the tongue against the palate, the tongue which would never give out, and what were the limits of this expression but those of the hinged muscle's force? You take in everything, but it is the tongue's valve which can block the corollary, to be entirely taken in. Outwardly so cackhanded, inwardly with gristle enough. Still and all I expatiate and cut away, repeatedly; this is the basic work's-rhythm.

Then to find himself with a sequence or perhaps a constellation; the seemingly transparent material of description had divided into distinct figures, erotic or dying masses adventuring to form, constrained to redevelop about what might be so plangent as to dictate a march-rhythm, yet effervesced as rapidly as a mood if once addressed too strenuously and deliberately. Like seeing by night, aside from the beheld object. The motive of development appears as I think now, to have been determined by the desire for return to what was both intimate and incomprehensible. 'A child may undergo an intensely private self experience that defies his representative capacity, so that the being state persists as a conserved rather than a transformed (symbolised) phenomenon' (Christopher Bollas, *The Shadow of the Object: Psychoanalysis of the Unthought Known* (London: Free Association Books, 1987), p. 111). A mood is not a state, cannot be translated to or from an objective correlative, but inheres in cadence fickle as the breath and as untenable. Here was the start of my ceaseless rigmarole.

The moods were intimate for certain, exact (in the sense they were mutually distinguishable, rather than answering to another disposition) and simultaneously a gratifying mystery and a saving evidence, since he had been brought to believing or to the insistence I had no accessible feelings apart from sexual desire. Since the death of his scarcely-known father two or three years before, he had found myself dull, self-protectively. It seems now that he was angry, and that the Buddhist meditation he then practised fitfully and as a public affectation, was a deliberate dulling against my anger as well as assertion of an unreachable nature. Unable to do mathematics, which had been an earlier *forte*, which had felt like a band of clarity tautening under the forehead, he had lost also the propensity for day-dreaming. But this writing, this was the monstrance for him of an emotional life, and the productive occasion for thought in one with no internal capacity for concentration, choked hitherto with stuff which had been immovable, unturnable in the brain.

There is a temptation to isolate either the textual or the oral quality of verse; to refer to 'texts' or scorn the written. But the special nature is equivocal/textual, it is in love with the signified in the mouth yet finds it detestable. This starts with the lalling infant, sucking, spitting and gargling sound, but to become poetic, must be expelled and made other and manipulable, there to be taken up. In fact, the poem becomes a transitional object, put out-there to become a comforter in-here. It forever moves towards estrangement and is retrieved. It can never come fully to symbolise though that is how in my first moment I would urge it, or it loses its physical shape in the mouth, and achieves no more than an inscription, witty or affecting, whichever, but decisively external and fixed. But given the head of its true ambiguity, to a deep mark it remains unthought; it is both propounded and understood, yet never amenable to insight. Its coherence, such as it is, gels round moods, whose own coherences are evanescent and of unknown principle. Because I am shameful and cowardly, I am forever trying to write clear, discursive text, or something free-standing and opening out in its meaning-horizon; it is only with the self-deceiving aim of clarity that I can coax a mood successfully, rather than a psychotic babble. And since I have no wish to die. Night-vision, into the dazzle of the dark that surrounds me and would seize even the skull's space for its slogans. Neonate goes into neon.

A dense world of events, apt to crack beneath attention, nevertheless holds up, holds the attention smeared with white clay. A flimsy premonition of psychosis, for soon you will be evicted from this shanty, stuck as you turned with bright feathers, grass, tin number-plates and pinups. Followed by a new access, cut from the press of saturated light, thrown together as a cadence but to join in a populace from which you withdraw again into dullness and the waiting state. There is both an emergent stranger, and a sense of recognition, an internal crazing projected into the outer world; the crazing is to order and shaped like a raku pot; the crazing is unbiddable and as likely ugly and damaged. Each time the body you start with.

*　　*　　*

Can't it be disgusting, a colour supplement exudate, bestows false absolution from a white man's diffuse but definite power, to duck a pervasiveness which buoyed me even as I felt no more than its accident, a spermatozoon of white power flunking its rendezvous repeatedly is itself I have to argue.

I couldn't enjoy such power because it wasn't felt inside as mine, even in adolescent sadistic fantasy wasn't possessed; but to borrow visibility from those whose visibility is their vulnerability, to do this imbued with power, it says, it's not enough to be carried, wafted along on the smiling invisible, I must spit out my nasty bits and ask for their acceptance as a good meal. Egyptian potatoes and Kenyan green beans. Where poetry's of a people in its making, such extension then may be bold in the teeth of power faced as hard and unquestionably embodied, to understand its fate among those side-by-side (an ambiguous, a lonely trope), and those who ban, censor or disdain. Its convolutions and cadences then are the magma of resistance or the gum of constant misery. But like this I shan't posture.

Could it be like for you, the first to read this? That of twelve lyrics you're bound to make, a tremor exactly tuned splits the landmass like a crystal struck, the plane of sound driven and pointed adze-like? Could this happen? Such poise and tuning while all else aggregates, could it be calculated finely enough? But this poise I cannot either.

By contrast what I do, a prophylactic part-identification with the oppressed, has to be decadent. Its social responsibility a strange coinciding rather. Power remains in my products, while like the bland PR of a multinational, I deplore the misunderstanding which could lead to their being used for mother's milk.

Who has been shaped through the instituted power, but after all, cannot embody it, even while I cannot refuse or deny it. Can I instigate a principled decadence of power; what breaks down, may cast a worthwhile gift into the future, for waste may provide a source for responsive energy. The energy of death-throes of the consumer to be consumed as motive for his overthrow. My poems might exact my overthrow, provide for it, but in whose name? They turn on me balefully, and every poem I make is part of a chain reaction, antithetical to rot a corner of conceit, of born arrogance.

This is another kind of conceit, a more subtle colonisation. The world's consumer dumps his waste products, landfills the place of his depredations. The pay-off he expects is gratitude, or at the least, forgiveness. He needs to admit to his fallibility in order to feel the better his strength.

*   *   *

There is a lump in my throat where I have swallowed pages of an elaborate product, a draft of simple confession. The more I have ventured on my pathology, the more I recognise the hubris in that *via negativa*, and there is but one way I have learnt to make good such arguments in myself.

As a child I swallowed compulsively, but to write, from my early teens, banished and sticking-point. I found I could bring the unthinkable out – I had thought I was stupid – and make a thing sufficient and remote to reincorporate; found I could contain my differences once each gathered its substantial being, attaching what in the world about might give it dignity,

developing a pseudomusculature and nervous system through internal
responses, rhythmic, formal, semantic, assonant: whole and flexed.

* * *

MINICAB
I always wanted, picked sold as seen,
crinkles off the fatty
          brash pipes, its meat still half-icy
      Scorching the stubble off
he arranges himself to watch girls
hold up a driver on a TV in a bedsit in a
      physical, a skin-flick,
                in an air's parade stunning a thawed
way of doing things like:

The cars like it more than a little
          fingerblade or pat splash of vitriol.
Blotched, rashed, this template does its job,
                a filter, a logical operative
            producing a next-to-the-skin
Glimpsed! in ultra-violet
                sandwiched into a toughened
                Succulent to the finger's up.
      The earth might have held out, Could it
withhold without spewing later.

      Untiringly it will ruminate on its depths.
   Shaking
up its source as epiphenomenon.
      The pipes will shudder, air screech,
                backtracking to a gasp.
And this will be what I'd waited for:
A complete system.
Manners I shan't be able to fault.

* * *

And to register is to be relieved from the burden of being, which is a dull massiness, to become a sounding vessel. Emptiness feels more grateful than want of capacity. The resonance may be no more than a response to ceaseless projections, that's too likely; when the breathtakingly new goes straight to the heart in immediate collusion with an idiom founded in the early flexions of the mouth, later discovered in an exemplary cadence. New delights are like the discovered source of premature echoes.

As Pound's *Cantos*, where a reterritorialisation is periodically effected in an explicitly despised idiom, that of the poetry of its author's adolescence, which becomes a premonition of the numinous. The despised in *The Cantos* is surrounded by the despicable, by helter-skelter paranoid projections. Its depressive moments are then intensely moving; the sounds of another first loved in the mouth, lost now, are a personal truth blazoned impersonally on the lagoon's water. And I remember eating my own past words in contemplating a book by an unknown author, without photograph, potted biography or blurb.

It was an august waste. Those words which daily pressed against me were death's inept agents; they had it in their power to fix and conserve, they were employed in this agency, factory of a man of a special kind who would embody an arthritic culture, values already anachronistic which in the mouths of their expositors sounded ironic or plain daft. The powerful determinants of stasis were in themselves vacuous, and I achieved no mental grasp on them; delivered in sermon blocks, they were fleeting and left me anxious and unbalanced.

What I discovered I could feed on, what I could chew over repeatedly, was substantial because pointless, and productive because it envisaged no final product. The point decries the process of production. A productive massiness reproached the gusts of rhetoric against which I had found no defence. Up to this point my poems had been one-off. Now not only coherent in mood, they had gone in for steroids, as though whatever portion were chewed over, wherever the gaze lingered, then bulked in termless growth and division, uselessly. What was introjected in turn was as by a muscular infill, no capacity yet, but a filling resistant to the inane tide. By Hand and Eye I became Tongue. Clacker.

Lyric won't come to the point, any more than a tree's topmost point is the point of the tree, or timber is. The point is a net result which, designed for to achieve a marmoreal enduringness, actually courts sudden death; whereas the enduring poem endures through its continuous dying, lives through productive decay like the sun. Generating warmth through putrefaction, it recalls its origins in the breath in the mouth; within its strictures, a mass of impurities jostles, like Susan Hillier's perspex container of garbage. Purity of diction is the deadly idea of a culture so fearful of death it stops dead in its tracks.

RALLYING
Tailor-made to our own extent, who ask no more,
the car speeding into a pink hood
    Moribund home,
the garage the blossoming cherry fakes
stands on a plague field,
a spun sugar nest of bones
    calls for a route planner, crumbles.
Later tonight the talks were due to recommence.
                Later tonight.

Why do the powers not fail at least? The nugget
  spun till dainty.
Insight busying down to this imperative
found in a doorway, crying Lump,
Lump me, make me thick
    with my occurrences, general
as the tongue-tied
       bubbles & froths:
His charnel fob, his mouth ecstatic with fumes.

I decide I shall write a poem called 'A Flat Spin'. For the last two hours I've watched three black South Africans, long-term political detainees released in a 'liberal move', talking of their imprisonment. Towards the end I started to feel a band of clarity under my forehead, the precondition for the aloneness necessary but resented, an evenly-hovering attentiveness made painful for having no substance. In solitude it means 'ready', in company heralds a flat panic. Why did this programme prompt me so, and why the title, 'A Flat Spin', all I have? I have been at work on doubleshift, twenty-seven hours, disturbed in my measure of sleep by comings and goings. Then to watch these so-tempered men, whose every gesture was balanced and economical, every word weighed. They were kindly to each other but watchful, not deigning to reach for support but accepting reciprocation. At the front of the promontory something began to expand, to squeeze and relax, rhythmically.

Maybe it was a hoop of envy, the envy felt at the coast when I watched boys with their fathers skip flat stones over the ripples. This was a way I could never extend. My extension was equally thoughtless but was laboured to arrive at thought, through a developed embodiment. If it was envy, watching the calm agitators, does it betray my resentment that it is not me who is dignified by my labour, but rather those emissaries in whom I have pride but I cringe to acknowledge, my by-blows whose conception must always stay irresponsible, amoral, or shall I turn on myself in a flat spin?

I have to be both dissolute and calm, weary and clearheaded. I must concentrate and evade my concentration. But shall I write the poem now? I have said too much, and the fragile mood is freighted with understanding and demarcated as an idea; a point has been found, an uncreditable and unearned point at that. The impulse has been ceded to a queasy self-regard, and if I am true to myself, alas I shall betray my creatures.

When my poems look female of countenance, or when they look other by class or by culture, my gratitude is immense. I might long myself to be translated, but it seems enough to contemplate the linguistic stranger. I am a white man who wishes to colonise every people, place and time, bending all to my necessities. Another scriptural programme after all, an evangelist with an ever-adoptive gospel. Yet this is never house music, bringing the chickens to roost in a four-square boxed beat; still my yearning to attend away from the rhythmic pre-sets, seems only to make the voice more flexible, or worse yet, extends the fraudulent repertoire.

THE FILE SERVER HAS ITS SAY
Takes it out on Whom
incautious against the dot–dash
          Rocks in immutable arms
beside a tank now bolted.
                    This previews
what she will come to claim as hers
     Left in stacks, half-frozen.

Why shouldn't she take her for
          Blotch, whatever she's got

with a smile wipes
                    It's
in her nature, nature falls one
    side of, blushingly
                apologises for the *faux pas*

jackknives off what's said,
                anxious to not transpose
stops & feints
Characteristic of her neural phrasing.
Water runs.
        Her hands weep in milk air,
heart's dolours firk the throat.

Then a sunshine inventory: Why?
        Will it squeeze the genie
    back in its cell,
who can't so much as address her cell?
With a bunch from a welcome palm
                opens their throat chock.
        Her pained smile closes.

This is a form of extension which can never be well-met, but sways like a
tipsy tripod. Had he extended a limb, like as not it would have been severed
by the predatory, or snapped where it had hung in unbuoyed emptiness.
What recourse but let this outgrowth go hang, this weight at the end of the
rigid outstretched arm? It's like tottering at the cliff summit, and his arm
flung in a grandiose gesture to the far horizon, more and more its counter-
weight threatened to dash him on the rocks below. In an emblem book it
might be a swarm of bees, swagged from the palm grasping futilely for air's
help.

The words work amidst themselves, the simplest blooming with wild
yeast, and they tear or smooth against each other, rubbing and flinching
their mutual surfaces; thus extended in words' fashion, the thing will shift
like a pullulant swarm, maybe pear-shaped, maybe a ring donut. Mirrors
flap like ailerons detached.

He cannot sustain this very long. There will be the convergence at its
tip, a point that at last extends into the wide and shorn field, and there
will be little to it. Bees drop away, pollen-seeking missiles, but he has not

self-righted; where there was danger, now there is only anxiety, thin air. Bland ocean nothing skips across from the fingers still outstretched. The poignant figurine of a discus-thrower, fearfully frozen in his torque of no retention, no release.

The same when permission to love withdrew, the same time and again. The ways had been instinct with her ways, however you turned or would face them down, everywhere you were met. Imagination ran to the limits of sight and of hearing; the floor, the field were a firm foundation for your castles in the air, with great success you spread yourself about and were able to do so unimperilled because you were concentrated and modular both, through scissiparity. But you felt the warmth of the swarm trickle from your palm. Then with ungainly branches revelled and ravelled out, then the full world dropped away and you tottered, and any post or staff was clung to, any frosty, clinging steel became grateful.

He will avoid that error, surely. He dreams of White City full of black female children, dreams of the silo reintoxicated with grain, dreams of the sinuses which yield milk, dreams of the muscle-ache which snaps-to, and releases a single flat stone, perfectly to leap the buds of surf.

A little breeze panics the stressed, the over-extended branches, and the trunk shivers. Words belly-flop to lie stunned like uncollected fruit, or they race under the canopy, hectored by light. The lame stone drops, underarm. Kick through these rotten, phallic nodes, evidence of a laxative dispersal; by now, he should know his limits.

But by the mid-point of his span, shouldn't he know his limits in advance, shouldn't he keep himself in check? Why to be always working it up, at the sensitive point it's unbearable, a brick wall would be preferred, letting the words go smash before they sharpen like an antenna, to be over-whelmed by the endless receipt of the possible, Hilversum, Luxembourg, PCRL; or before they consolidate into one tendentious lump. So many twist the words or pommel them familiar sprouts occupying familiar sites. Theirs is a greater apprehensiveness, an allowed friction inside the suit, permission for healthy exercise – this much and no more, the bristling osiers shorn from the stump.

But he flings out a tuber, it takes independent root. The lifeline atrophies, the umbilical gets severed. This homunculus is studded with organs which emit, bid fair to give out always, peg out, entertain misgivings, throw them back in the teeth or eye of the storm. It is the body redreamt as source, not intake, no nor victim, seeming to move in itself, as it does, catching the gaze and laying hold on the ears. At the edges, feel, it has been crushed and snubbed. Had it come to the point, would merely have woven back to a cat's-cradle of nothingness. But here the creature is civilised because created, brutal because it breathes and glares from every pore, and the epithelial hairs glisten over its surface.

So you dream, given the space for it, then your domestic animals return to your lap or skulk in the room thick with your sweat and farts. These creatures appeal as your own creatures, what can you do but stroke them or kick them away with a curse? Revision with a vengeance, that is the fated work.

The fantasy of the independent source or result complements an achieved inner numbness. As an infant I used to hammer my head on the mattress at night till the neck muscles generated a warmth which spread like a skullcap under the skull, meningeal, while the mattress too was a live, warm thing by which my unpillowed head would feel embraced, the rigid mattress felt as though it had curved to receive the head I'd deposit repeatedly and violently. My body's delightful stress was afferent to this delight of yielding. I could deny my motive force this way, though my dreams were filled with circling animals, a controlled stampede whose hooves threatened to crush me, spotlit as both ringmaster and terror-stricken, destined through what fault to occupy the focus of attraction.

I lived on a Cornish peninsula, in a Mediterranean house gone thick-walled and baronial. At the end of the small garden, a cliff-drop; spring would split the shale, and the garden diminish. It was the same boy, still with the dreamer's capacity, who went out beyond his mother and sister on every rockpool census, loving the point at which the spit of rock narrowed and dipped below the wavelets, perching myself awkwardly as it were on top of the sea, who wouldn't swim, who wouldn't trust the water. From this pulpit I would, I suppose, have conducted the waves even as they had drowned him.

In all my writing I meet difficulty with the pronouns, both on top of things and obliterated, displaced, dispersed. Especially, I find it absurd to write 'we'; by turns I dominate and succumb, or even in the same moment. And in this country, at this time, 'we' has lost all possibility of adventure.

From the first stuttering impulse, it lies in our human safety-consciousness to start to revise; revision involves both pushing out, asserting a space between the event and the instigator or passer-by, and our closer accord with fantasy. What nonetheless adheres and manifests in its quiet way, defiance of revision, is what must be revised for the work of change to get under way – only deep, anarchic impulse can give the wrench, more often than not in irritable rejoinder to our pains-taking. Through revision then we find the slippery slope and ride the consequential dictates of these points of resistance; the misplaced pride of our adherence is met by an arousal which surprises, prompting a displacement we hadn't known we'd badly sought. Eventfulness swarms usually over the mackerel linings to our skulls, subject to revision both unconscious and deliberate, but creativity makes a start at the obstacle, at numbness, at the lip of a failed transmission system. With the boredom of it all and without impatience to save us, a moodiness at the core and out-there – then it's the same difference – one might sink or turn to drugs or make an entrepreneurial killing.

The creative rejoinder may follow after a stratagem taken out of stock, had seemed to have met the needs of the moment, after a temporary accommodation, when in a rush of furious probity we have urgently to contemplate the lineaments of a creature, beyond and beneath what is so tediously our own. What is this creature, and why do we so desire it? But why ask, it could be no other than a child, the self again compact in which the parent can dream freedom both of stupidity and self-importance, a dream of perfect responsiveness, freedom from the superego. This is revision embodied, governed by pure mood. Desire has pitched to this end throughout, how banal, how typical of *us*: Go, little book, with all this investment of narcissism from which the pronoun does not save us.

And in this way what is most his own becomes most painfully and pleas-ingly other, and what is most independently a separate creature, closest to his secret heart. Constantly we're interpreting what is evident and plain to common sense as just so, and yet we become irate, the world is a Sunday paper; there are places where we struggle to follow the familiar grain, resist-ance starts to rise at the overdetermined fidelity by which we are therefore brought to resent the accords making us social, those most casual, also the most intransigent and rigid assumptions of our culture. Correspondingly when he would hazard a thought outrageous to common sense, he finds it greeted with utmost relief and joy like a new child. Perhaps he hesitates longer to make himself this improbable offer, he is therefore surer of its necessity, and perhaps he is more hesitant all the same in making it, and it therefore feels not so much an imposition, more like an acceptance.

But for whatever reason, what he anticipates would be estranging, instantly has been wolfed as true and essential. The naked hermaphrodite who then stands unashamed in the circus, touching his and her sexes, seems to be known to the audience as the banalities of their commerce never can be. Since 'naturally', there are no banalities for us. Our courses of action and thought are accounted for before the individual thinks or acts; please heaven we, but can I believe in our knowing or hoping enough we haven't been touched – that when we discover the mole and ply it with unguents and graces, then it should turn out, turn out to be the ultimate cavil.

Indeed, with all we are given we are by the same token expropriated. Loving it too. The poet gives to receive back what he had once had, but never knew he had before it was put in front of his nose.

Lyric can't be relational in the way that narrative is: it doesn't mediate on the level of conscious subjects. There are three directions to lyric. Either it binds representation to presentation, as though it were new-minting, with results that are almost unnegotiable. Or it expands to colonise, saying too much *in order* to discover its nature in nature elsewhere, but doomed through hardy pretentiousness to look absurd in its commuting, and never to fool the rocks or the natives one iota. Or third, it explodes space (each of the three denies relational space, none has the binocularity which locates). If the first is strict and the second is excessive, the third is abundant in its freedom from the polarities of 'nature' – nature as origin or as rank growth.

The pitches of the present excursion make evident that lyric impulse tends to implicate all three. They are 'moments' in a process – the shrinking down, the expansiveness and the shattering – as they are strategies of primary process faced with the relational demands of the ego struggling to co-ordinate undifferentiated space. As soon as I can speak or write I am composing myself, undeniably, and no strategy can escape its social consequence and setting, but the pressure of primary process, the continuing dream which forces these deformities in language buckled to its imperatives, imparts to them an uncanniness, recognised at once in the rare poem that balances on the liminal. All art is a training for this, a preparation for the artist and the recipient, more or less interesting in failure – more so where the back pressure is felt, if only in mordant need.

So it doesn't do to be over-apologetic. Of course it *matters* where a poem ends up, and its nature should remain downright suspect. There endless twists – the explosive moment can be a disguised censorship, the superego cranks up a little storm to confuse the issue. Often. I am sure we come home only the other side of the confusion and violence (which are inescapable), that only in difference can there be promise of forgiveness and union.

'The other side', but I think it's at the heart in reality, or deeply involved. This can't be the working of transference, since it's non-relational. It's the place of love, it's a deadly place, and the often tedious preparation composes us for that from which daily consciousness is being degraded. In our reading the experience is three-ply also, simultaneously of extreme dispersal, calm omnipresence, and emphatic breath and blood and hard mind. Love's selfishness and selflessness.

DEMO RELEASE
In death his hand shall turn green artillery.
     Leering & it
slovens beautiful, 'But when?' you ask, shuffle
   to when when was.

The wind gave of its poor best. Its eminence
    of confectioners' sugar,
spongecake with a grit layer syringed in a nave.
      Fish-smack marble.

These my trade, my trappings, These devise-me-
    hard assets,
suave as mourn your face in polish:
     These my sweets of absence, jab
in Swedish combat-hose, mooch about
the birth-stool, like village women scatter them,
    transferable
though the head always tells me different: break

in silicon, disposable transputer grey & soft
    Ensuring air defenses,
what we had wished we were
   dilapidated, if bamboo our musculature

         self-bound. Notched.
Seedlings in my hand,
springs poking through like a trashed sofa.

No, I wasn't an imaginative child, nor by any stretch a child of nature. What was simply accessible, teetering down plank steps to the beach, touching the flimsy rail, to play by a freshet fringed with watercress and churned and dirtied by bullocks, never entertained me long. I enjoyed far better, as I still do, those violent movements of the air which the body at once resists and yields towards, which are both invisible and unreasonable, and at the same time intensely corporeal and responsive. The body next to mine, the body that surrounds me yet is moulded to my contours, yet is indifferent to me, yet loves me well. And there are days even in Birmingham, as far from the coast as could be, when I feel that particular sea-breeze, and must stop in my tracks to answer to it, and resist it.

I would open my mouth wide and taut, and then whose song was made by the wind across that embouchure? I could vary the pitch through prac-tised grimace, but always in consonance and continual answer to the wind's flexion. It would have been a cheat to have hollered out.

At the storm's height I stood over the boathouse, yielding to the wind's support, buckled into oilskin and sou'wester. Yearly the cliff-top garden fell away in soft, clayey leaves, shale split in the spring frosts. Hieroglyphs were rusted into the newly-revealed surfaces.

But the wind never permeated, never insulted me, the pitch it took was both bodily and from inside, or a common broadcast. How unlike my daily language, neither released nor uterine, churning drearily like a generator hall whose drone impregnates the workday self even into his dream, shaking into accord every warm and stirring thing, and I too live in constant collusion, an insubstantial figment traced through it. But what I most want I shall resist, in order to be taken by the throat, gape, then heed the wind.

Turn your gaze to the forward nape; the head will turn. Poetry also admon-ishes the blank expression caught in the double window, mesmerised by travelling concrete posts, pulling it back in the face to begin its adventure. Too much known is too little, washing through eyes, ears and mouth, you can't see the trees for the wood or the wood for the cellulose. The spikes and troughs of your own noise are matched precisely by the crushed glass of personal stereos, so you add no lasting word. Pitch then has to be vari-able, your makeup subject to alteration, though there will be the reference tones you can never entirely escape. Still, your configuration must be affected by the pantomime of loss and acquisition, if you can keep that slant, not withdraw.

The harder I gaze, the more I become ambiguous. The screen flashes silver and black like a flight of swallows. This too settles into a style, at

length. At one time I thought, if what emerged from my efforts proved
recognisable, I should stop in disgust. Too true my literal propensity for an
independent creature has been accompanied and undercut by an infantile
urge to keep the mouth crammed comfortably, to suck on the 'unthought
known' as much as to spit it out.

Which can account for an otherwise imbecile perversity. How many
times when hovering over a series of poems, alert to identify false notes
and betrayals, I have resisted tackling just the most evident points of
failure, but for weeks or months have insistently rationalised them – as
being, for instance, a deliberate mark of incompleteness or an earnest of
great pressure, as appropriate marks of having written against the heartless
depredations of time-as-surplus-value. What are these points but umbilical
residues, then, or comforters?

Its arrival is when you're at your most sullen, when daily prints have
sucked the brain and the webbed marrow dry, when perfect whiteness
and immaculacy bleed through the guarded, wheezing machinery, slam
into the stripped weaving-shed, and this light is felt as a dead weight, the
whiteness which pretends to incorporate every colour, but the colours
have been dispersed as contaminants it shirks from, never quite successfully, but shreds are gobbled up, white permeates or scores one over with
its indelible purity. Biological detergent or oven-cleaner, non-corrosive
though, no hint of animus, just gentle, just mild, and a guileful rainbow
cocked in the background, leading you on, you the viewer, its assumed
shadow, till scrubbed into blazing nullity. Oh but it stares so hard it sends
the neurones on the blink, and their malfunction forms the glimmer of a
thought about the little stimulus upside-down, remember the mechanics
of vision?

Its arrival's in one black glimmer, a stubborn memory-trace, a mercy,
an unprofitable belief, unconditional love; one thing refused to the light's
predacity, a grey filing which irritates, there is a quickening felt, a vital
doubt and reserve. Then about it the implications of the white blanket start
to come adrift, to decompose like a halo into its death-rays laying waste the
heavens, and this wasted stuff, with the heat its change of state produces,
forms a medium which the original virus impregnates. In this culture it
can increase, develop its independent blood supply, and when the pain
and the pleasure brought by the parasite can be contained no more, will be
transmitted from the host body that pleasure and pain have made sure of its
creditable being, and exhausted then and there, will continue to multiply,

it will be called back repeatedly by the host which as quickly fails, falling
prey to illumination, called back till it can do no more in the meagre culture
thinned by heat and leaching towards the light, till its own anatomy's one
more piece of the world's lumber that may or may not answer the eyes,
pleasing or dulling them. Once more illuminated, only a mark of owner-
ship on a piece of equipment. Then the trace itself is expunged in dazzle,
brought fully to the light he's invisible again. The bereavement which is
known to be inescapable, thank goodness is that birthing which does not
cease. Since its cessation would leave him nothing, no grateful children,
and since there is by this way no access to some personal chandlery, there
can be no resting on laurels; what has been done has broken away, and
only a constant replenishment maintains a tolerable state, a world of love
for the half-formed, now neglected creatures. What they need is the dark
unenforming their occluded readers can supply.

THE PALATINATE TREASUREHOUSE
After the single ring was a bout of breath
tossed forward & back like a leaf or a memory.
How inward was that original bruise, that
ecliptic blink?
     Does sunset sink beneath
Like as a mirror bangs

against breath, in some deterrent move,
intent as fur?
Another condensed thing, that is,
she would feed to the pyre with her own hand
       Lost, lost in future:

But that's not so, by any recognised standard:
Clouds throng her skin like the house burns.
The meagre's vast –
 & yes for blisters, only one touch
      of a burnished antidote
compels life to situate

the low-stacked condensery of life, the mouths
inviting insects, bunged with them
from each sorrowful gulp.

Now I know the arrogance, or rather the childish omniscience and the adolescent doubt of others' innerness, readable from these acts of repopulating the world; and the evidence which the corporeal analogy for the poem represents of this. But such a deep-laid trope may appear equally true when its terms are reversed. These bodies, such as they are, I launder and wring out to be my emissaries, because I've such a sense merely a shadow fell in the land of the living, trailing ectoplasm, striving to mould my freaks and fancies into palpable beings other might love or hate but at least need no act of faith to acknowledge as substantial. Nor am I laid under obligations that I would feel inadequate to respond to. They must be beings, not somethings, for the inorganic could not serve for substance yielding enough to receive and resilient enough to withstand, able indeed to respond to the commerce of others. The finer, more highly finished would be so easily broken.

CHAPTER 14

Sarah Wood, 'Anew Again'

I have before me a copy of Sarah Wood's 'Anew Again'. I've read it scores of times, but each time it seems a bit different. Anew again. Sometimes it's the way that it's 'so lightly held together' that resonates – the way it sets Picasso and Wallace Stevens humming with Rilke, Derrida, Ovid, Cixous and Louise Bourgeois. On another reading, I trace the movements of its thinking – for example, its account of iteration and citation and the way that these repetitions make selves and souls – us, say – and then its linking of that to the work of poetry, harmony and rhyme. Or again, I marvel at the shifts in tone and register, from aphorism ('poetic experience has paper arms') to scholarly etymological excursions, to art history, to poetry. This is writing that grows out of itself, picks up on clues in its own writing out of what it sees and reads, and renews itself from these. 'Daylight' gives 'de-light', and out of the pleasure of this play a new thought comes to light. 'Anew again' is itself light: it moves gently, like a hand brushing against guitar strings. But it has 'deep-darks' and gravity too, it writes of life and death, of philosophy and of severance, of souls and of animals. Called upon to rehearse its thesis, we might flounder – but that is because it thinks in its every singing turn, rather than relaying its thoughts pre-packaged. 'It helps to compare . . .' writes Wood, at one juncture. This is a piece that believes in the help literature, art, writing, thinking, comparing and wondering might give us, in all aspects of our lives. And it helps itself to the words and images that it needs, that renew it, and renew, too, that of which it sings.

As we said at the end of our introduction, we gave this piece to two artists, who made the objects on our cover in response to it, and then photographed them for us. We've no instructions or imperatives here, just a question. What will *you* make, write or do, having read 'Anew Again'?

Sarah Wood, 'Anew Again', in Sarah Wood and Jonathan Tiplady, *The Blue Guitar* (London: Artwords, 2007), pp. 18–36.

. . . près de la terre, tout bas. Réitère en murmurant: ne répète jamais
. . .

Jacques Derrida

Facing me is a photograph of what I cannot see. I'm in the act of sensing, picking something up, seeing that I don't see something. It's right in front of me but I have to guess. I don't know.

In *Construction au joueur de guitare* there is a real guitar. It is not blue. It commands me to say it is real. Perhaps because it has a substantial, Old Master look, perhaps because of its central position in the photograph, the guitar is more authoritatively *there* than anything else. It's slung by a cord over the shoulder of a big canvas in Picasso's studio. The guitarist's head and body are a faint flat sketch and he has newspaper arms with peculiar-looking hands. These hands are positioned to play the guitar but they are clumsy and fragile. At once I am all fear and tenderness. Everything in the construction is so lightly held together. It looks as if at any moment it could be taken apart and returned to its original elements. It is a poem, it is paper, it is attached, I am attached, as Derrida says of the poem, '*pour un temps*', for a time.[1] *Construction au joueur de guitare* is the origin of its assembled parts rather than their final sum. A faint song asks me to take it into writing, so that nobody so that everybody can hear it. As if it were mine, an old photograph of mine taken by Picasso in 1913, in the days when poetry and speech were still music, when I was very young and not yet separate from Picasso or from anything on the earth.

When artists or poets use guitars as part of their creative equipment they do not become musicians but they can set something playing that breaks our sleep. 'Music; awake her; strike!'[2] Picasso's guitars are citations, guitareiterations. They agitate and neutralise the referent, jerk its strings. ('Guitar': the name of a puppet, a character, ready to become again.[3]) His guitars are something else and the same. We recognise ourselves in this. We are guitar-iterations too; it happens all the time. We identify: at once we hang trembling round the neck of a representation, a powerful phantasm,

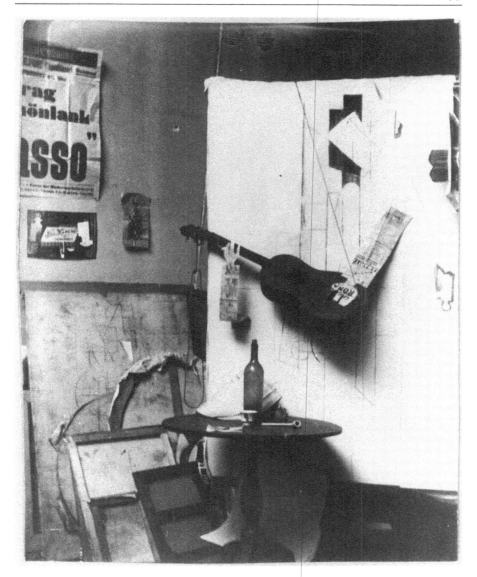

Figure 14.1. Pablo Picasso, *Construction au joueur de guitare* (1913). Paris, Musée Picasso.

it plays us with paper hands, we act out, our arms are puppet-strings. We try to take hold with them and we find ourselves hanging from the hand of what we believed was just a doll, a dressed-up Me, some 'object' or other. Our wholeness is there but we have to become someone else to experience it, an invented someone, someone invented in part by not-having-been, someone suggested by someone else, in a text, a conversation or an inner

Figure 14.2. Pablo Picasso, *The Old Guitarist* (1903/04). Chicago, The Art Institute of Chicago.

dialogue. This marionette-becoming starts off as an assemblage of fragments, lines, bottles, paper, spaces, suspended reference . . .

In *Construction au joueur de guitare* the unworked space on the canvas where the guitar player is drawn, the incomplete atmosphere of the artist's studio itself, canvases shyly turned to the wall, all contribute to a sense that the relation between cause and effect has been loosened, paused, opened up.

For a time the guitar was my chief suspect. I was under the influence of the conventions made visible by the famous Blue period painting *The Old Guitarist* (1903).

There the instrument lies in a melancholy cradle made by the body of its player. They are a couple, sharing a frame whose being they echo in the way that the man holds the guitar. They partake of the same painterly and figurative texture. Both are blind. The player's eyes are closed and his hand is over the guitar's eyes (the lower part of its soundhole suggests a nose, the bridge a sober-looking mouth) so that he can thumb or quiet the strings. We can't tell which – and anyway, 'pictures are mute'.[4] The player's right forearm and the hand which partly covers the soundhole could be that of the guitar itself, as if it were gracefully hiding its own eyes. The musician is a puppeteer, who sits like a puppet, every joint at an angle.

Construction au joueur de guitare plays with frames. A number of flat rectangles seem to hide or promise something. A kind of casual leaning or slantedness suggests depth and concealment: canvases standing against the wall, a pinned-up poster and drawings, sheets of paper propped against the lower edge of *Construction au joueur de guitare*, a folded newspaper on the table, the player's newspaper sleeves and trapezoid face. But if something is being hidden, it's not going to be revealed or turned round by means of reference. The *OED* gives a short history of the word *cithara* that explains how '*cither*, *cithern* or *cittern*, *citole*, *gittern*, *guitar*, *zither*, are all found in English as names of extant or obsolete instruments developed from the *cithara*'. Referential dictionary thinking takes that prosaic cithara to be the original and key element that makes sense of and gives rise to all those variant words and forms of instrument. Its music unfolds and unloads itself into the visible. Difference becomes historical deviation. The dictionary *cithara* does not float, does not collage, does not hang and sing in the air. But the blue guitar escapes me, slithering into and out of my sights in a movement or experience that I cannot enter or leave. I could swear it is sexually different. It happens in a way I do not understand, comes away from me as it goes towards me. Not-understanding is the passage that lets writing draw me into the space between what I thought I understood and what I can't. There I can *hear*.

The guitar Picasso used in *Construction au joueur de guitare* was solid but he puts it in the same blue shadows of the graphic that we find in Wallace Stevens's poem 'The Man with the Blue Guitar'. Singing joins this with that in the song – player and guitar, for example: 'The blue guitar / And I are one.'[5] Magically, *character*, the player who is with-guitar, and *author*, who is without-guitar, speak with the same voice. We must close our eyes to see them. Picasso's constructed guitar player and the old guitar player in his Blue period painting hold their guitars in front of themselves or to themselves. We might think that these works are about the relation between the guitar and the player. But that is not it: oneness does not show itself to us. We are always surprised by it because we are part of it and it holds us. Stevens's poem reminds me: the guitar is not an attribute belonging to this one or that one. It is not revealed to us. It rebuffs and baffles our desire to experience it, to be with it. Then suddenly we are sitting in the branches of its voice as it speaks to us, in us, out of the blue.

Stevens sings indirectly. His guitarist, or it may be the poet himself singing here, serenades only '*almost* to man / . . . to miss, by that, things as they are'.[6] He spares things as they are by singing what is higher. He does not do this to improve upon life, but to spare what in us is mortal, fragile, by nature partly hidden and unsung. He spares man in the character of living-dying animal. His guitar, writing, could be a weapon aimed at what then becomes only a writing-target. But instead he sings. What is sung is too dear to be an object held in the sights of writing. Rilke declares something similar in the third *Sonnet to Orpheus*. Don Paterson renders the lines as: 'song is *not* desire . . . / . . . Song is being . . . / True singing is another kind of breath.'[7] There are curious intervals in the *dramatis personae* of writing. Uncharted spaces appear when an author and a character disappear together into a voice that sings. There where there is no way through, no breath, something breathes. Human gatherings, for Stevens, boil down to being alone: 'The whirling noise // Of a multitude dwindles, all said / To his breath that lies awake at night.'[8] The sense of being alone comes down, I think, to what Stevens calls being only 'too exactly' oneself.[9] The friendly harmony of whirling and dwindling and breathing exists in a blur or a blue that is, he says, 'a little hard / To see'.

We cannot see souls until we recognise them as animals. 'The angelic ones // Speak of the soul, the mind. It is / An animal.'[10] And the animal in Stevens is without 'mould', without set form. It scratches and bites a song out of the blue guitar but it is unarmed and harmless. It has 'claws', not laws. Its 'fangs' are coloured by the angelic clangour of phonemes. The guitar too is just a 'shell' or a hollow straw. Never the pen that Derrida calls 'that very hard weapon [*cette arme très dure*] with which one must inscribe, incise, choose, calculate, take ink before filtering the inscribable, playing the keyboard on the screen'.[11] The Aryan root of the word 'arm' is *ar*, meaning 'to fit or join'. This element relates Latin *arma* (plural, 'weap-onry') with *armus* (singular, 'shoulder-joint') and Greek *harmos* ('joint' in the general sense). This is the word that gives us 'harmony'. Harmony means joining. The harmonics of texts are angelic and animal. They speak the impersonal in us, what is without mask, mould or shell. That part with neither shield nor weapon.

Words diverge from themselves. Syllables improvise subtle bonds beyond those that are allowed to exist at the level of the written word. Etymology itself belongs to history thanks to the element of language; it too has been at the mercy of chance. Rhyme and consonance come into this. Stevens's blue guitar poem couples the guitar and being in an insist-ent rhyme. Lines end with 'guitar' and 'are'. Rhyme's wild glue attaches one to the other regardless of etymology. We overhear sound calling to itself, calling to each other of its untranslatable creations. This division and multiplication of sounds can both locate and dislocate sense. It happens in what Derrida calls 'the obscure friendship of rhyme: alliance, harmony, assonance, chime, the insane linking of a couple. Sense is born in a pair, once, randomly and predestined.'[12]

Rhyme also cuts and divides, introducing into writing the character Stevens calls 'a shearsman of sorts'.[13] With his musical clippers he removes enough wool to let us hear. He cuts out a pattern from the cloth of every-thing; this power is like that of the female Fate Greek mythology named Atropos. Her shears cut the threaded web of life and decided our shares, sorts or fortunes. The old guitar player and Atropos are avatars of writing as spacing. The sense and the spacing of writing keep its rhyme-linked elements apart, interrupt them. They resist the infatuation of the signifier. Spacing and division remind us that the sign is a dual unity. The signified is not the slave or wife of the glorified phenomenality of the signifier. But then we begin to wonder: what is the relation of the sign to itself, between its two elements? What really goes on between the signifier and the signi-fied? (Poets fantasise about this primal scene between . . .r and . . .d. They work their magic there. In life, we act it out as best we can.) A cut separates and joins them but do they even know that? What troubles and pleasures come from the difference between them, from the difference of a letter? We can only guess the dramas, roads, dreams, doors, dreads, readings and darings that take place between that duo of arch-collaborators. The shears-man guards language in its infancy from the dangers of infancy and from the omnipotence of thoughts, even if poetic experience affirms, more than anything, the childish desire for something other than language. Stevens, who had 'only a skimming of Italian', wrote to his Italian translator Renato Poggioli: 'You might have all the words perfect and not carry the poems forward. The point I am trying to make is that you have carried the poems forward without regard to the words and that, it seems to me, is the right result since I know nothing about the words.'[14] It is not words that carry poems forward.

Stevens believed in 'a universal poetry that is reflected in everything'.[15] He added that 'one is better satisfied with particulars'. So, in the name of satisfaction, let's read the beginning of 'The Man with the Blue Guitar': 'The man bent over his guitar, / A shearsman of sorts. The day was green. // They said, "You have a blue guitar, / You do not play things as they are."'[16] Blue is forbidden. It incurs Plato's criticism of poets as fabricators. The day is green. But green does not rhyme. Rhyme always lets its law be broken, stretched and ignored. It is on the side of love and creation, not the law. Think of all the readers and writers of poetry who justly set rhyme aside. It is an inessential delight with only the loosest, most popular and folkloric association with the poetic. And yet wherever it is, the rhyme of words or of beings, some kind of poetry is. Even in sham or bad or joke poetry, doggerel, karaoke, coincidence – rhyme doesn't mind. The poem continues:

> The man replied, 'Things as they are
> Are changed upon the blue guitar.'
>
> And they said then, 'But play, you must,
> A tune beyond us, yet ourselves,
>
> A tune upon the blue guitar
> Of things exactly as they are.'

There the first section ends. But the mad pair of rhymes skips on through the next section, and the next, and reappears in the sixth, meaning the same, more, less, differently. Their movement breaks, as Walter Benjamin suggests writers should, with the form of argument that goes 'On the one hand . . . on the other hand'.[17] Later in 'The Man with the Blue Guitar' the poet balances the world on his nose and spins it 'this-a-way' and 'that-a-way'.[18] His nose is an arm, the spinning is an arm, or a vein in the arm or the blood that spirals in the vein, or the vein of ore in the spinning earth where writing mines, where I mine you spiralling towards you, or some other true ore or gold that I'm after, right in there 'where the same seeks its vein and the very gold [*l'or vrai*] of its phenomenon' – and, one might add, where the same seeks its phonemes, its *phonèmes mêmes*, its blood.[19]

Writing is affirmative. It teaches us about what 'The Man with the Blue Guitar' calls 'the madness of space' by taking us towards it and into it.[20] Derrida's 'insane linking of a couple' does something similar. And so do the paper arms in *Construction au joueur de guitare*. Again, anew, *Construction au joueur de guitare*. As arms, the paper cutouts link the guitar, an ordinary wooden guitar, to the player, a jumbo-size figure drawn on canvas in the Cubist manner. I single these arms out for attention. I cut them, in my mind, from the rest. You could say that I especially like them and yet, as if commanded to do so by their ephemeral and fragile nature, I want to destroy them in order to transcend them, to bring out the fact that they are more than arms after all. This ambivalence is there in all acts of singling out and in all negotiations between signification and the phenomenal world. In the end I don't believe in the phenomenal world. You must read everything.

Picasso cut the arms out of newspaper. He fixed them lightly in place. They can't do very much. No music plays, the stretcher takes the guitar's weight.

The guitar player's arms could be mine as I write. To write I turn away from life, I put it down; I do not play things as they are. It is, Stevens says elsewhere, 'a world of words to the end of it'.[21]

We are amid mediations, symbols, ways-and-means, representation, figuration, form. Thus speaks the Apollo side, the light side. But still, affirm, these are arms. They join, at the shoulder, to the body and to the back. I turn. I turn out the light to write, as Stevens commands: 'Throw away the lights, the definitions / And say of what you see in the dark // That it is this or that it is that / But do not use the rotted names.'[22] Poetic experience has paper arms. Its peculiar associative power partly depends on the abolition of outside corroborations of that power. 'The chord', Stevens says in a paraphrase of his blue guitar poem, 'destroys its elements by uniting them in the chord.'[23] It is a paradox accompanying all harmonies, conjunctions and junctures. It is the trouble with any *with* and it can spark fear. Louise Bourgeois says it in a condensed way: 'The fear of death destroys your sense of the edge in sex.'[24] 'With' once meant in Old English 'against'. Rather as it still does with the French word *contre*. One fights *with*, falls out *with* and parts company *with*. 'With' makes possible but also withstands all sorts of conflict, contradiction and incompatibility. The word neutralises the logic of cause and effect: 'The Man *with* the Blue Guitar'; *Chicken* with *Egg*. *With* displaces the elements it links and divides our attention. *With* accompanies, brings alongside and sets among. It always places elements in the context of each other but its meaning constitutes that context and is not therefore limited by it. Prepositions are inexhaustible. As a preposition, 'with' must go with 'a pronoun, noun or its equivalent to express position, movement, circumstance, *etc.*, relative to or affecting it' (Chambers). So that when I write, arms out of my arms and so forth, it will have been *with* you, a writing *with* you, *to* you, *through* you, *in the context* of you and of what Derrida calls context itself. 'We can call context the "entire-real-history-of-the-world" if you like . . .'[25]

Picasso said, in some remarks picked up in 'The Man with the Blue Guitar', that for him a picture entailed destruction: 'Previously pictures moved towards completeness by progression. Every day brought something new. A picture was a sum of additions. *Chez moi*, a picture is a sum of destructions. I make a picture, then I destroy it. But in the end nothing is lost.'[26] The combinations and harmonics of *Construction au joueur de guitare* give us new forms of 'with' that indicate unsuspected harmonies between ourselves and everything. The rub is the surprisingness of this harmony. It can't be presented as an alibi. It does not say, neutrally: 'I was here all the time and so were you.' The photograph is monochrome but we could just as easily think of its harmonics in colour. We could think of it in terms of blue.

The art books say that the blue of Picasso's Blue period denotes melancholy, eroticism and the divine. From this we might extrapolate that blue is the colour of distances, the liquid distances of desire and the sky, what Stevens calls 'heavens'. Blue uplifts, melts, decomposes, moulders . . . in truth I don't know what it means. 'The blue guitar surprises you,' as if the first thing to go, like a string breaking, was the boundary between it and you.[27] The acquisitive serenity of high-toned aesthetic culture gives way to something more free and groping. Blue is the expression of surprise, the colour of an encounter with what is other than myself as that encounter touches, opens onto language and opens language. Bourgeois explains this very well. She talks about one of her drawings and says:

What I like about this drawing is the colour. It is the colour blue
– that is my colour – and the colour blue means you have left the
drabness of day-to-day reality to be transported into – not a world
of fantasy, it's not a world of fantasy – but a world of freedom where
you are free to say what you like and what you don't like. I would
say that this is almost a definition of freedom. The freedom to be
yourself, that is to say, the freedom not to be afraid of what people
are going to think about you or do to you.

This is expressed for ever, from way back, by the colour blue,
which is really sky blue.[28]

Blue would be the most auspicious colour for collaborations. The figures
of Picasso's Blue period embody something other than freedom and *joie
de vivre*. I see their drooping, angular fatigue, their figures oppressed
by space. For example, *The Old Guitarist* – often taken to have been the
inspiration for Stevens's poem; he is blue to the gills, hollow-eyed, white-
haired, 'bent over his guitar', a sitting hieroglyph.[29] The portrait of weary
philosophy. Body bowed under the weight of representing a thousand
outworn ideas of representation: the artist-hero, the individual, society,
'things as they are' . . . Downcast, drained, emaciated and alone. Cixous
has said: 'Philosophy alone is very lonely, but philosophy that is dreaming
would be for us worthy of the name philosophy.'[30] The only non-blue thing
in the painting is the guitar. This corroborates Stevens's denial: 'I had no
particular painting of Picasso's in mind.'[31] That guitar is doing fine. It's
tanned and upright, ready for future appearances in paintings, collages,
photographs and constructions. It is ready to be fragmented, copied, pas-
tiched, rebuilt. Dreaming teaches us not to be afraid of our identifications.
If we are afraid of them we do not stay, we do not see them move and
grow, we miss the collaborations at work already in everything. We miss
and lonelify ourselves. After looking at *The Old Guitarist* the blueness of
Stevens's guitar becomes all the more imaginary. The blue guitar is all the
more able to be this or that by being blue, the colour that never was before,
the dream colour with no alibi.

Stevens said he called the guitar player 'shearsman' because of the way
he sits, 'squatting like a tailor (a shearsman) as he works on his cloth'.[32]
Let's sit beside him and think. Perhaps it is he, after all, who made Rilke's
Orpheus his beautifully fitting blue coat? ('First the slender man in blue [*im
blauen Mantel*], who kept / his eyes in front, impatient and unspeaking.'[33])
Rilke sings and we read. It's our chance to escape the captivation of sight

and the tragic narcissism of the Orpheus myth. I have been suggesting that Stevens's guitarist is a shearsman because he cuts and joins things and that this work is closer to the openness of *Construction au joueur de guitare* than it is to the boxed-in macho pathos of *The Old Guitarist*. I still prefer the guitarist in the photo, who walks towards the studio, still half-buried, coming out of the vertical plane of the canvas, pulled forward by the guitar. The guitar falls away from the player into the most familiar form of visibility. It has shadow, perspective, depth, weight. You could say that it's real. He can't hold it. He can't drink from the bottle on the table in front of him. Smoking the pipe would probably be fatal. He has no back and no insides. The backs of the canvases against the studio wall testify to this. Behind his face there are no secret depths. He asks, not to become the guitar in its curvaceous heft, but to be seen with it, to be seen to be following it, there where drawings can't go, off the canvas, into the room. Hear what you can't hear, see the music they make. You: the separate author, the different poet.

The guitar player is coming in the way that Stevens says poetry comes: 'out of the wall'.[34] In 'The Creations of Sound' he writes that there are words better 'without an author':

> Or having a separate author, a different poet,
> An accretion from ourselves, intelligent
> Beyond intelligence, an artificial man
>
> At a distance, a secondary expositor,
> A being of sound, whom one does not approach
> Through any exaggeration. From him, we collect.

Picasso's *Construction au joueur de guitare* offers us a being of sound, shows us the writer who is not separate from the ground out of which he or she emerges and appears. Appears *to someone*, some different poet guessing at a distance. Is it Lazarus, up from the dead? In Shelley's poem 'With a Guitar to Jane' the being is called Ariel. Unlike Ariel in *The Tempest*, who was shut up for a time in a tree, Shelley's 'Sprite' is 'Imprisoned for some fault of his, / In a body like a grave'.[35] He is living and dead, which is sometimes necessary. One should not cut the earth open and heave the dead out: in good time, in the earth's good time. 'Good time encounter her,' Shakespeare says of pregnant Hermione.[36] Stevens affirms: 'Ariel was glad he had written his poems.'[37]

When we see musically, we can see more than one being at a time: for instance, Eurydice with Orpheus. I can't tell their story; it's better left to others. It is enough to know that he can charm death with music. She follows him back from nowhere, from death, behind him, and even through him. *Construction au joueur de guitare* assembles them and photographs them together on their journey. It's extremely condensed, a scene of returning from the dead, a one-man collaborative double-act and acting-out where the living one, he, dies into the graphic but keeps hold of the guitar. It's her in front of him behind him, she surrenders her form, her body, she gives herself to guitar-being and *joueur*-being and they lead her she doesn't know where, she, dead, she doesn't know who or how, follows what is coming. We don't see her but a dead woman animates the whole thing.

It helps to compare Ovid to Rilke. In the old Ovidian myth, there are laws everywhere. Orpheus is forbidden to look back. He can bring Eurydice back to life only by observing prescribed limits, so he defies the limits, so back she goes. The law joins her to death or her husband. What is separate, cut out, completely differentiated from what it is not, can be owned, married, lost. Rilke gives us a Eurydice who is less ownable. She is 'the property [*Eigentum*] of that man no longer'.[38] She is not *Eigentum*, property, because she is not *Eigen*, separate. This Eurydice is not quite an individual, she is divided, '*ausgeteilt*', shared out: 'She was already undone like flowing hair, / already given, abandoned like fallen rain / and divided like provisions for a thousand.' By the time Orpheus looks back she is 'already root [*Wurzel*]'. *Wurzel* is German for a root vegetable. She's as earthy as a carrot or a beet-root or a radish. She's radically Eurydice. She's *en route*, becoming part of another articulation and another body and another scene. German *root* also means the root of a word. Rilke is dreaming, as he often did, of a feminine poetic being who is not reducible to an *alter ego*. This dream, which is not only a dream but 'moonlight on a window seat', powers his love poetry.[39] All things seen belong to death except what you see in the dark. What you see for yourself.

A text is blue-black dark but harbours light-year-travelling forces: stars. There are key words, words 'not chosen, / Or chosen quickly, in a freedom / That was their element'.[40] They come out of the blue, dictated by a versatility of language itself, they are affirmations born of language's affirmation of itself, therefore of a yes not only belonging to language. They open the darkness by opening themselves in song, rearranging themselves, careless of losing themselves in the caress of harmony, assonance and chime. The day-guitar and I rejected each other almost at once; we did not know each other's language. Without knowing why, I tore a few letters off and kept them. Perhaps because I love words. A love which is itself an echo of another love, of another's love: 'You know that I love words . . . And if I love words it is also because of their ability to escape their proper form, whether they interest me as visible things, letters representing the spatial visibility of the word, or as something musical or audible . . . [it] probably has something to do with a non-discursive sonority, although I don't know whether I would call it musical.'[41] In time my pieces of guitar gave me an ancient Sanskrit word: *itara*, which in some variants designated what was 'low, vile . . . expelled' or 'rejected'. Yes: so much for the guitar and the guy who plays it. So much for me. But what I have to say does not require presence: 'My communication must be repeatable – iterable – in the absolute absence of the receiver, or of any empirically determinable collectivity of receivers.'[42] There is no one here to write to. Yet still in this lonely climate of bluish gloom there is blue sky room, enough for a whole rainbow of other colours, beginning here in the monochrome studio of writing where words lean, hang, propped this way and that in the temporary re-shuffleable fashion Picasso called 'construction', and thought to photograph. Writing affirms the *absolutely impenetrable forces* Nietzsche discusses in *The Birth of Tragedy*: qualities that cannot be quantified, sound-power foreign to acoustics.

Itara forms a consonant pair, a feminine or half-rhyme, with *guitar*. *Itara* that meant in Sanskrit 'the other of two' or 'another' or 'different from'. And *itara* that gave us Greek *heteros*, 'other'. *Itara* is itself reborn to itself as the root of Latin *iterum*, 'again' or 'anew'. And *iter* is Latin for 'journey', so it, *itara*, announces with a little tarantara the riddle or tarradiddle of all the poetic puppet-couples and legendary itinerants who travel, not between life and death, but across syllables and between unheard-of stars. Their stories ask to be told and heard. For poets sing what would otherwise be a mute and unalterable scene, a deafening cultural compulsion: the whole tedious, astronomically costly history of human love which, if you follow its all too direct path in silence, is the allegory of the failure of what we perhaps mistakenly call music. As if its nameless force were predestined to the form of a couple: two notes, with the usual minor variations in point-of-view. You might see her behind him, which he can't do – and you might see him from the back, obscuring her. And fascinated by the façade of this inescapable fable, you would risk denying yourself the air that breathes in song since before the beginning. No plot can explain the 'spontaneous particulars of sound'.[43] Listen and forget. Daylight may come and go but not that funny indirect light, a de-light without reason that sets me looking at death's door again, awake and writing with the lights off, paper lit inside by an ultraviolet glow visible to bees and special cameras, surprised by the intensification of what's called the blue hour, distinguishing what my eye, in the light of whatever, whatever it believes, a voice like a, some voice like a bird on a branch in the branches of what, this singsong twig, I sit writing like a blue bird in what, in the branches, the local chords: the climate of the poem.

NOTES

1. Jacques Derrida, 'Che cos'è la poesia?', in *The Derrida Reader: Between the Blinds*, ed. Peggy Kamuf (New York: Columbia University Press, 1991), p. 234.
2. William Shakespeare, *The Winter's Tale*, V, iii, *The Oxford Shakespeare*, ed. Stanley Wells and Gary Taylor (Oxford: Oxford University Press, 1998), p. 1,130.
3. In Toni Morrison's novel *Song of Solomon*, for example, the hero Milk Man's best friend is called Guitar.
4. Paul de Man, 'Autobiography as De-facement', in *The Rhetoric of Romanticism* (New York: Columbia University Press, 1984), p. 80.
5. Wallace Stevens, 'The Man with the Blue Guitar', *Collected Poems* (New York: Vintage, 1982), p. 71.
6. Ibid. p. 165. Emphasis added.
7. Don Paterson, 'A God', *Orpheus: A Version of Rilke's* Die Sonette an Orpheus (London: Faber and Faber, 2006), p. 5.
8. Stevens, 'The Man with the Blue Guitar', *CP*, p. 171.
9. Wallace Stevens, 'The Creations of Sound', *CP*, p. 310.
10. Stevens, 'The Man with the Blue Guitar', *CP*, p. 174.
11. Jacques Derrida, 'Circumfessions', trans. Geoffrey Bennington, in *Jacques Derrida* by Geoffrey Bennington and Jacques Derrida (Chicago: University of Chicago Press, 1993), pp. 11–12.
12. Jacques Derrida, *Politics of Friendship*, trans. George Collins (London: Verso, 1997), p. 166.
13. Stevens, 'The Man with the Blue Guitar', *CP*, p. 165.
14. Stevens to Renato Poggioli, 1 July 1953; *The Letters of Wallace Stevens*, ed. Holly Stevens (London: Faber and Faber, 1966), p. 786.
15. Wallace Stevens, 'Relations between Poetry and Painting', in *Collected Poetry and Prose*, ed. Frank Kermode and Joan Richardson (New York: Library of America, 1997), p. 740.
16. Stevens, 'The Man with the Blue Guitar', *CP*, p. 165.
17. See Walter Benjamin, 'The Author as Producer', in Victor Burgin (ed.), *Thinking Photography* (London: Palgrave Macmillan, 1982), p. 16.
18. Stevens, 'The Man with the Blue Guitar', *CP*, p. 78.
19. Jacques Derrida, 'Force and Signification', in *Writing and Difference*, trans. Alan Bass (London: Routledge, 2002), p. 35.

20. Stevens, 'The Man with the Blue Guitar', *CP*, p. 183.
21. Wallace Stevens, 'Description without Place', *CP*, p. 345.
22. Stevens, 'The Man with the Blue Guitar', *CP*, p. 183.
23. Stevens to Hi Simons, 10 August 1940; *Letters*, p. 363.
24. Louise Bourgeois, *Destruction of the Father, Reconstruction of the Father: Writings and Interviews 1923–1997*, ed. Marie-Laure Bernadac and Hans-Ulrich Obrist (Cambridge, MA: MIT Press, 1998), p. 162.
25. Jacques Derrida, *Limited Inc*, trans. Samuel Weber (Evanston: Northwestern University Press, 1998), p. 136.
26. Pablo Picasso, in Natasha Staller, *A Sum of Destructions: Picasso's Cultures and the Creation of Cubism* (New Haven: Yale University Press, 2001), p. 343, n. 3.
27. Stevens, 'The Man with the Blue Guitar', *CP*, p. 183.
28. Louise Bourgeois, speaking at <http://www.bampfa.berkeley.edu/projects/bourgeois/lbo630.aiff> (last accessed 4 October 2013).
29. Stevens, 'The Man with the Blue Guitar', *CP*, p. 165.
30. Hélène Cixous, live at 'Hélène Cixous, Jacques Derrida, Their Psychoanalyses?', Leeds, 1–3 June 2007.
31. Stevens to Renato Poggioli, 1 July 1953; *Letters*, p. 786.
32. Stevens to Renato Poggioli, 25 June 1953; *Letters*, p. 783.
33. Rainer Maria Rilke, 'Orpheus. Eurydice. Hermes', trans. Charlie Louth at <http://www.brindin.com/pgrilor3.htm> (last accessed 23 September 2013).
34. Stevens, 'The Creations of Sound', *CP*, p. 311.
35. Percy Shelley, 'With a Guitar to Jane', *Poetical Works*, ed. Thomas Hutchinson (Oxford: Oxford University Press, 1983), p. 672.
36. Shakespeare, *The Winter's Tale*, II, i, *The Oxford Shakespeare*, p. 1,108.
37. Wallace Stevens, 'The Planet on the Table', *CP*, p. 532.
38. Rilke, 'Orpheus. Eurydice. Hermes', translation modified.
39. Rainer Maria Rilke, 'To Lou Andreas-Salomé', in *Uncollected Poems*, trans. Edward Snow (New York: North Point Press, 1996), p. 15.
40. Stevens, 'The Creations of Sound', *CP*, p. 310.
41. 'The Spatial Arts: An Interview with Jacques Derrida', in Peter Brunette and David Wills (eds), *Deconstruction and the Visual Arts: Art, Media, Architecture* (Cambridge: Cambridge University Press, 1994), pp. 9–32, pp. 20–1.
42. Derrida, *Limited Inc*, p. 7.
43. Stevens, 'The Creations of Sound', *CP*, p. 311.

Index